Thomas Reid and the Defence of Duty

Edinburgh Studies in Scottish Philosophy

Series Editor: James A. Harris, University of St Andrews

Scottish Philosophy Through the Ages

This new series will cover the full range of Scottish philosophy over five centuries – from the medieval period through the Reformation and Enlightenment periods, to the nineteenth and early twentieth centuries.

The series will publish innovative studies on major figures and themes. It also aims to stimulate new work in less intensively studied areas, by a new generation of philosophers and intellectual historians. The books will combine historical sensitivity and philosophical substance which will serve to cast new light on the rich intellectual inheritance of Scottish philosophy.

Editorial Advisory Board

Angela Coventry, University of Portland, Oregon
Fonna Forman, University of California, San Diego
Alison McIntyre, Wellesley College
Alexander Broadie, University of Glasgow
Remy Debes, University of Memphis
John Haldane, University of St Andrews and Baylor University, Texas

Books available

Adam Smith and Rousseau: Ethics, Politics, Economics, edited by Maria Pia Paganelli, Dennis C. Rasmussen and Craig Smith
Thomas Reid and the Problem of Secondary Qualities, Christopher A. Shrock
Hume's Sceptical Enlightenment, Ryu Susato
Imagination in Hume's Philosophy: The Canvas of the Mind, Timothy M. Costelloe
Essays on Hume, Smith and the Scottish Enlightenment, Christopher J. Berry
Adam Ferguson and the Idea of Civil Society: Moral Science in the Scottish Enlightenment, Craig Smith
Hume's Scepticism: Pyrrhonian and Academic, Peter S. Fosl
Scottish Philosophy After the Enlightenment, Gordon Graham
Adam Ferguson's Later Writings: New Letters and an Essay on the French Revolution, Ian Stewart and Max Skjönsberg
Eighteenth-Century Scottish Aesthetics: Not Just a Matter of Taste, Rachel Zuckert
Thomas Reid and the Defence of Duty, James J. S. Foster

Books forthcoming

The Sociological Heritage of the Scottish Enlightenment, Tamas Demeter

edinburghuniversitypress.com/series/essp

Thomas Reid and the Defence of Duty

James J. S. Foster

EDINBURGH
University Press

Edinburgh University Press is one of the leading university presses in the UK. We publish academic books and journals in our selected subject areas across the humanities and social sciences, combining cutting-edge scholarship with high editorial and production values to produce academic works of lasting importance. For more information visit our website: edinburghuniversitypress.com

Edinburgh University Press Ltd
13 Infirmary Street
Edinburgh EH1 1LT

Typeset in 11/13 Adobe Sabon by
IDSUK (DataConnection) Ltd, and
printed and bound in Great Britain

A CIP record for this book is available from the British Library

ISBN 978 1 4744 5534 3 (hardback)
ISBN 978 1 4744 5537 4 (webready PDF)
ISBN 978 1 4744 5536 7 (epub)

Contents

Series Editor's Introduction

Philosophy has been taught and written in Scotland since the fifteenth century. The purpose of this series is to publish new scholarly work on any and every aspect of the history of Scottish philosophising, from John Mair to John Macmurray. Scotland's most celebrated philosophical achievements remain those produced by Hume, Smith, Reid and their contemporaries in the eighteenth century. It is, however, no longer possible to believe that the Scottish Enlightenment had no indigenous roots. Nor is it possible to believe that there was no significant philosophy produced in Scotland once the Enlightenment was over.

There is no single set of intellectual concerns distinctive of and unique to philosophy as it has been taught and written in Scotland. Historical study of Scottish philosophy must be, to a significant extent, study of the changing nature of philosophy itself. It should be open to the idea that the preoccupations and methods of philosophers today may not be those of philosophers in the past. It should also concern itself with philosophical connections and intellectual affinities between Scotland, England, Ireland and the rest of Europe, and, where appropriate, between Scotland and America.

James Harris

Preface

Are there certain actions which are just wrong, or is every obligation and prohibition reducible to our preferences? Or, to give examples, are murder, theft and promise-breaking wrong because they are wrong *per se*, or are they wrong because we do not like them or their consequences? To ask these questions is to ask whether the apparent rightness and wrongness of actions is ever a fact independent of our sentiments, to ask whether the part of human life that we often call 'moral' is based on something objective or subjective.

These are questions with which I often begin my undergraduate philosophy classes. And, over the years, I have been surprised by the answers. Despite teaching at a small, religiously affiliated, liberal arts college, most of my students take the latter option. They typically agree that actions like murder, theft and promise-breaking are wrong, and would like to say some actions – like infant torture – are objectively horrific, but they do not believe that they can justify the stance that anything is wrong *per se*. There could be, my students tell me, some societies which, or some people who, consider actions like murder, theft and promise-breaking to be either good or indifferent. And so those actions would not be wrong for them.

It is difficult to say exactly what makes moral subjectivism so popular with my students. No doubt the modern emphasis on tolerance and a bias for treating only mathematics and the natural sciences as objective play some role. But it seems to me that my students' dissatisfaction with the standard philosophical accounts of moral objectivity is also a factor. Platonism, for instance, has its attractions, but even students who are predisposed to defend an objective conception of morality find its metaphysical account of abstract goodness implausible. Similarly, despite Kant's genius and philosophical rigour, many students complain that the categorical imperative is too abstract, and thus there is no clear way to use it as a reliable guide to the granular decisions of common life. Some students appreciate the simplicity of divine command theory – things are good or evil because God wills it to be so – but even here most would like to say that some things are wrong even if, *per impossible*, God commanded them. Moral subjectivism, by contrast, seems simpler, more concrete and better able to account for their experience.

This aim of this book is to make the case that Thomas Reid provides a compelling account of moral objectivism which is both metaphysically modest and chimes with lived experience. Naturally, I hope that it will therefore be interesting to those who already have an interest in Reid or Scottish Enlightenment philosophy. But I also hope that it will be of interest to those who, like my students, are interested in moral objectivism but do not find the usual options compelling. As I see it, what makes Reid interesting is that he offers to us an option not typically found in the ethics textbooks of college classrooms. He is not a naturalist, a utilitarian, an egoist, a hedonist, a Platonist or a Kantian. Rather, he is, for lack of a better phrase, a rationalist intuitionist, who believes that some actions are wrong because they violate objective moral relationships, and that human beings have the capacity to immediately perceive and be motivated by these relations on account of an innate and rational moral sense. Further, he justifies this stance not by appeal to metaphysics or pure practical reason, but by carefully observing what human beings actually think, say and do.

So far, interest in Reid's moral philosophy has been rather limited, especially compared to interest in his epistemology. Still, there are already several good books worth reading on the topic, including William L. Rowe's *Thomas Reid on Freedom and Morality*, Terence Cuneo's *Thomas Reid on the Ethical Life* and William C. Davis' *Thomas Reid's Ethics*. There are also several collections, parts of collections and journal articles which give Reid's ethics pride of place, including, most notably, Sabine Roeser's *Reid's Ethics* and Rebecca Copenhaver's and Todd Buras' *Thomas Reid on Mind, Knowledge, and Value*. In this present work, I hope to contribute to the nascent but ongoing conversation about, distinguish my approach towards and spur further interest in Reid's moral philosophy in chiefly three ways.

First, unlike Rowe, Cuneo and Davis – who discuss Reid's moral philosophy in the context of his account of freedom, the ethical life and judgement, respectively – this book is chiefly concerned with

Reid's explanation and defence of the concept of 'duty'. My hope is that, by means of this focus, I have produced a clearer and more enjoyable book than if I had attempted to address Reid's 'ethics', by which I mean his more general account of how human beings should live.[1] Yet there is a cost to this focus, and it is that I have not been able to address in any detail important topics such as Reid's defence of free will, his place in eighteenth-century debates about natural law, the close analogy he draws between moral and aesthetic perception, his robust conception of human teleology or the way in which his theology intersects with his philosophy. The first three of these topics are happily addressed at length in the books mentioned above.[2] The latter two deserve more attention than they have yet received.[3]

Second, in this book I have tried to take Reid at his word regarding his intellectual debt to Francis Bacon. Throughout his works, Reid persistently distinguishes himself from other philosophers – both ancient and contemporary – on account of his thoroughgoing Baconianism, which for him means sedulous attention to the regularities of nature and constant vigilance against our natural tendency to build intellectual systems through analogous reasoning. While other works on Reid often note Reid's appreciation for Bacon – aside from Paul Wood's pioneering work on Reid's intellectual history – they do not, I think, recognise how strongly Reid's frequent praise for Bacon and his disciple Newton is related to his methodology. And this, I believe, leads to a misunderstanding both of what Reid is trying to do and how he is trying to do it.

Finally, despite the above-mentioned attention to Reid's Baconianism, this book is not a work of intellectual history. Quite the contrary, my approach has been inspired by Nicholas Wolterstorff's ground-breaking work *Thomas Reid and the Story of Epistemology*. Without presuming any comparison, it therefore tries to offer what Wolterstorff calls 'an *interpretation* . . . [not] a full treatment . . . [but] a line of interpretation, a way of reading' Reid's moral philosophy.[4] Intellectual history is not, of course, foreign to this endeavour, but it is not my focus. Rather, my focus is to present, as clearly as possible, Reid's defence of the concept 'duty'.

In order to accomplish this task, this book proceeds in three parts, each containing three chapters. The first part sets the stage for a discussion of Reid's moral philosophy by looking at his philosophical method, his theory of perception and the reasons for his rejection of subjectivism. Although the first two chapters of this section do not directly address Reid's moral philosophy, they are necessary because Reid's philosophical method and his theory of perception are both atypical and have a significant bearing on this moral theory. The second part – consisting of chapters four, five and six – then examines the essential facets of Reid's moral theory: first his account of the abstract concept of duty, then his understanding of moral perception, and finally his account of moral motivation. In these chapters, I aim to emphasise not only what Reid says about duty, but also why he says it, paying particular attention to his Baconian method of investigation. Finally, the last third of the book presents and attempts to answer three challenges to Reid's account of duty: the argument from strangeness, the argument from relativity and the argument from interminability. The point of these final chapters is to see if Reid's account of duty can respond to common complaints against moral intuitionism and objectivism.

No book is ever composed alone, even during a pandemic, and this one is no exception. First and foremost, I am deeply indebted to Gordon Graham. I would never have started, let alone finished this project without his wise counsel and encouragement. I am also thankful for suggestions made by James Harris, several anonymous reviewers of both the proposal and the manuscript, and the team at EUP. Although mistakes are, as ever, my own, it is a better book on account of their efforts. Further, I am indebted to my family: to my mother, Gloria, for reading the manuscript and offering grammatical and syntactical advice, and to my wife, Robyn, and children, Rennie and Rory, for bearing with me through the long process of composition and revision. I will endeavour henceforth to be more present and less grumpy. Along similar lines, I would like to thank my friends and colleagues at the University of Sioux Falls for giving me the time and space necessary to undertake this project and for not rolling their eyes too much when I, once again, began to ramble on about Reid. Finally, I would like to thank my students, whose perceptive questions and surprising insights make the job of teaching philosophy a true joy. This book is dedicated to them.

Notes

1. See Cuneo, *Thomas Reid on the Ethical Life*, p. 1.
2. For Reid on free will see also Harris, *Of Liberty and Necessity*, pp. 179–202, and Yaffe, *Manifest Action*. For Reid's place in the

eighteenth-century debate about natural law see also Haakonssen 'Introduction', in *Thomas Reid on Practical Ethics*, Garrett and Heydt, 'Moral Philosophy: Practical and Speculative', and Heydt, *Moral Philosophy in Eighteenth-Century Britain*.

3. Although, see Kroeker, 'A Common Sense Response to Hume's Moral Atheism: Reid on Morality and Theism', and Buras, 'Revisiting Reid on Religion'.

4. Wolterstorff, *Thomas Reid and the Story of Epistemology*, p. xi. Emphasis original.

Part I

Reid's Rejection of Moral Subjectivism

I

Reid's Way of Philosophy

The central thesis of this book is that Thomas Reid's moral philosophy presents a defensible account of objective and rationally motivating moral relations. Accordingly, the great majority of the pages that follow directly address his understanding and defence of the concept 'duty'. Yet before we can productively discuss Reid's theory of morals, we need to set it in the context of his understanding of philosophical inquiry.

The necessity of discussing Reid's approach to philosophy is at least partly his fault, because the way Reid writes, and the terms he uses, can give the wrong impression. Take, for example, the following declaration from the introduction of his first book: 'I despise Philosophy, and renounce its guidance: let my soul dwell with Common Sense'.[1] In context, the mocking irony of this statement is clear. Yet Reid's apparent disavowal of philosophy, his penchant for defending the views of non-philosophers, and his frequent, approving use of the term 'common sense', can mislead. For example, during Reid's lifetime, the English philosopher Joseph Priestley wrote that although Reid 'may talk as a philosopher . . . I am confident he conceives and thinks as the vulgar do'.[2] Thus, Priestly counted Reid as one of a group of Scottish academics with 'little and contracted minds, who, instead of doing, or attempting to do [philosophy] themselves . . . are busily employed in watching the footsteps of others, and cavilling at every thing they do'.[3] Whatever one thinks about the accuracy of Reid's work, this is decidedly not so. Reid was, in fact, a devoted and careful philosopher, who sought not to undermine confidence in philosophical inquiry, but to strengthen it.

To understand Reid's approach to philosophy, and to counter the impression of Reid typified by Priestley's accusations, it is helpful to begin by examining two related themes in Reid's work. The first is Reid's appreciation for Francis Bacon's method of observation, experiment and induction. As Paul Wood has convincingly shown, Reid's outlook was not anti-philosophy, but pro-Baconian science. For example, in his engagement with Priestly, Reid's chief complaint was not that Priestley's strict materialism ran contrary to the ideas of the common person, but that it ran contrary to Newtonian science.[4]

A second and related issue critical to understanding Reid's philosophy is his rejection of what he variously calls the 'way of ideas', the 'theory of ideas' and the 'ideal theory'. As with Priestley's materialism, Reid believed that this theory – or class of theories – of perception was not overly philosophical, but unphilosophical. Yet, due to the genius and sophistication of its proponents, the way of ideas had not only become generally popular, but was wrongly believed to be compatible with Baconianism.

In this chapter, which is devoted to explaining Reid's way of philosophy, we therefore take up these topics in turn, with the object of showing how Reid approached philosophical questions, and why he rejected the dominant epistemology of his day. These topics may initially seem beside the point in a book devoted to moral philosophy. But, as we will see, Reid's approach to philosophical investigation and his understanding of perception are crucial components in his defence of duty.

Reid's Baconian Philosophy

When discussing Reid's relationship to Bacon, it is helpful to begin with a terminological clarification. Today, 'philosophy' chiefly indicates the fields of metaphysics, aesthetics, ethics and epistemology, but in the eighteenth century, the meaning of 'philosophy' was far broader. In that context, 'philosophy' indicated any 'knowledge natural or moral', including disciplines now commonly classified as science, such as biology, astronomy, physics and chemistry.[5] This older definition explains how Bacon, who is often credited with inventing the 'scientific method', could exert so thorough an influence on Reid's 'philosophy'. For it was according to a broad understanding of what it is to do philosophy that Reid understood himself to be a Baconian, an interpreter of nature and a philosopher.

The methodological influence of Bacon on Reid is apparent in all of Reid's writings. This influence is often explicit, as when Reid calls Bacon 'a man of wonderful genius' who 'is worthy to be called the initiator into the mysteries of nature'.[6] But it also is apparent in Reid's attitude towards Isaac Newton, whom Reid considered a model Baconian. According to Reid, Newton not only followed Bacon in his own work, but accurately summarised the Baconian method in the *regulae philosophandi*, or 'rules for philosophizing', given in Book III of the *Principia*.[7] This is not to say that Reid is entirely uncritical of either Bacon or Newton, or that he never adapted their investigative methodologies to suit his own purposes. Yet because Baconianism so influenced Reid's own philosophical investigations, it is useful here to summarise what Reid believed to be the heart of the Baconian method, and the important methodological lessons he took from it in his own philosophy.

Francis Bacon proposed his method of investigation in his *New Organon*, published in 1620, with the express intention of providing a new 'instrument of rational thinking'.[8] This new instrument was intended to supplant the old organon, as Aristotle's six works on logic – *Categories*, *On Interpretation*, *Prior Analytics*, *Posterior Analytics*, *Topics* and *Sophistical Refutations* – are collectively known. As Alan Wade Davenport notes, Reid's appropriation of Bacon's method has both a positive and a negative aspect.[9] The positive aspect describes the set of features essential to a properly Baconian investigation. The negative aspect, on the other hand, points out common intellectual errors which lead to mistaken accounts of natural phenomena.

The Positive Aspects of Baconianism

Let us begin with the former. According to Bacon, the essential features of his method can be summarised by noting three ways that his new organon 'differs altogether' from the old.[10] The first is the end to which it is directed. According to Bacon, investigations based on Aristotle's method are largely intended to be intellectual exercises, with little practical application. For Bacon, however, knowledge is to be sought not for itself, but for the practical power that it may confer. Though the well-worn phrase 'knowledge is power' is often attributed to Bacon, it does not appear in his extant writings. What he does write, and what is perhaps the source of the pseudo-quotation, is that the 'two goals of man, knowledge and power, are twins and chiefly come to the same thing'.[11] Thus, for Bacon, the 'true and legitimate goal of the sciences is to endow human life with new discoveries and resources', by revealing the principles of nature, which is to say, the general rules according to which its operations may be predicted, managed and manipulated.[12] The goal of the new organon, in other words, is to catalogue the regularities of nature, so that this knowledge may be used to improve human life.

The second way that Bacon perceives his new method to differ from the old is in its order of demonstration. The old method, according to Bacon, is syllogistic. Its main activity is the drawing of particular inferences from general principles, by means of logical deduction. This serves its too-intellectual end and, as a result, the old organon frequently ignores or explains away evidence contrary to accepted principles by means of clever rhetoric and illegitimate distinctions.[13] In this way, it bends nature to our understanding. The new logic of Bacon's organon, on the other hand, bends our understanding to nature. To do so, it largely works not from, but towards general principles, by induction from particular instances. According to Bacon, what we want from a general principle is a testable description of the regularities we find in data collected through experiment and observation.

It should be kept in mind that, while this distinction between moving from general to particular via syllogism, and from particular to general via induction, characterises the typical movement of the old and new organon, respectively, both methods move in both directions. They must, for if they did not, the old organon could not justify its general principles, nor the new apply and test its discovered laws. The difference is the primary direction of travel; and that, according to Bacon, is the result of a difference in the speed with which each method reaches general principles, and the relative certainty with which each method holds them. As he writes in the *New Organon*:

> The way the thing has normally been done [in the syllogistic system] is to leap immediately from sense and particulars to the most general propositions, as to fixed poles around which disputations may revolve, then to derive everything else from then by means of intermediate propositions. By contrast, by our method, axioms are gradually elicited step by step, so that we reach the most general axioms only at the very end.[14]

It is because of this difference that the order of demonstration in the old instrument is, according to Bacon, 'completely reversed' in the new.[15]

There are two further consequences of Bacon's gradualism for the principles arrived at through his method. First, since they are arrived at by induction, they are always open to revision. This may seem a weakness when compared to the certainty promised by the syllogistic system, but Bacon argues that because the 'subtlety of nature far surpasses the subtlety of the sense and intellect', the apparent certainty of the old organon is a mirage upon which 'nothing sound is built'.[16] 'The only true hope' for increasing our understanding of nature, he writes, 'is induction'.[17] Baconianism, in other words, promises less but delivers more. Second, since the most general axioms are arrived at last, we frequently find ourselves with abstract explanatory principles which are not themselves explained. Consider, for instance, the theory of universal gravitation, first proposed by Newton. Although modern physics has modified Newton's theory substantially, contemporary physics still holds that any particle of matter in the universe attracts any other with a force varying directly as the product of the masses and inversely as the square of the distances between them. Yet how this happens – by what exact mechanism the attraction occurs – is still disputed. That is not to say that such general principles are unsupported. It is, rather, that the nature of their support is from collected evidence, not from a more general proposition; at least until a yet-more-general proposition can be formed which accounts for the previously unexplained principle.

The third difference between Bacon's method and the syllogistic method is their starting point. Whereas, according to Bacon, the syllogistic system is 'happy with the immediate perception of the healthy senses', in his system 'not one of the first things which the intellect has accumulated by itself [i.e. through the senses] escapes . . . suspicion'.[18] The reason for this difference is twofold. First, the senses themselves may be deceptive, especially when the things they observe are rare, small, distant, swift or familiar. Second, even when our senses do not mislead us, we may misinterpret their deliverances.

Bacon's suspicion of our perceptions may seem to point towards scepticism, but Bacon asserts that we must largely credit our senses or go insane.[19] Moreover, while Bacon believes that our perceptions are fallible, he does not think this fallibility justifies a general suspicion of all perception. Rather, his stance is that, while individual perceptions may be misleading, we can check them by means of careful experiment and observation, aided, where possible and necessary, by scientific instruments. Bacon's attitude towards sense perception may therefore be summarised by the old Russian proverb appropriated by former US president Ronald Reagan: Trust, but verify.

To summarise the positive aspects of Baconianism described above, the difference between the new organon and the old is that Bacon's method seeks to arrive at general axioms by induction from carefully collected and catalogued observations, while the syllogistic system hastily posits general axioms from cursory observations, and then attempts to justify them and the less-general principles deduced from them through logical and rhetorical subtlety. To be fair to his predecessors, the extent to which Bacon's new method differed from the old is disputed.[20] Yet even if Bacon overstates the distinction between the 'old' method and his own, the shift in emphasis from deduction to induction is significant and reflects careful attention to the nature of the human mind and its limits in the interpretation of nature.

The Negative Aspects of Baconianism

Bacon's careful attention to the limits of the human mind is similarly reflected in the negative aspects of Baconianism: the 'fallacies by which we misinterpret nature'.[21] Let us therefore turn to the negative aspects of Baconianism which were adopted by Reid in his philosophy. In the *Novum Organon* itself, Bacon describes these tendencies as four '*idola*' which may be variously translated as 'idols' or 'illusions'.[22] Although Reid believed the substance of Bacon's account was accurate, in his discussion of these tendencies Reid expressed ambivalence about Bacon's taxonomy, which he found a bit fanciful.[23] As Reid's account of moral error has some affinity to Bacon's four *idola*, we will have occasion to examine the negative aspects of Baconianism according to Bacon's suggested taxonomy in the final chapter. When discussing purely philosophical errors, however, I believe it is better to examine the negative aspects of Baconianism according to three categories of error discussed by Reid throughout his corpus: analogical reasoning, misleading terminology and unsupported hypothesis.[24]

The first category of error, analogical reasoning, is an impediment to proper Baconian thinking because it complicates induction. Unlike logical deduction, in which the truth of antecedent propositions is preserved in properly inferred conclusions, principles drawn from induction are creative attempts to explain a set of observations. It is therefore critical for Baconian science that we both collect accurate observations and propose general principles which account for those observations without exception. In both essential tasks, however, Bacon believes we are prone to be lazy. When collecting observations, we tend to notice those things which are already familiar to us, while ignoring those which are not. Similarly, when constructing explanations, we are prone to defend the opinions we already hold rather than to revise or to replace them when they entail outcomes contrary to observation. In both tasks, then, we reason analogously from what we already see or believe, rather than pay close attention to the phenomenon under observation.

The second cause of error, misleading terminology, is closely related to analogical reasoning, in that it also obscures what is truly before us. Bacon calls these errors 'the biggest nuisance of all', because our thinking relies on language, and misleading terminology imbeds errors in its very operations.[25] Although he does not make the connection explicitly, I think it is helpful to consider misleading terminology as reified analogical reasoning. Making this connection helps explain why these errors are such a nuisance; the faulty reasoning behind them is implicit and therefore difficult to recognise, let alone to correct. According to Bacon, ambiguous terminology deceives us in two ways: either by giving names to things which do not actually exist, or by giving names to things which do exist, but defining them so poorly that the names deceive us. Among the former, Bacon lists 'fortune, the first mover, the orbs of the planets, and the element of fire'.[26] Misleading terms such as these, he says, are relatively easy to overcome once we recognise them, because we only need to reject their use. They do not really refer to anything, so nothing is lost in their exclusion. The second kind of terms, however, are more difficult because they are words which have ambiguous definitions. Bacon himself uses the word 'wet' as an example, but since this word had, in Bacon's time, meanings which are not common today, we may more usefully consider the word 'cause'.

Depending on context, 'cause' could plausibly mean any number of things. Consider the question, 'What was the cause of the fire?'. The cause sought could be an agent, in which case we are looking for the name of a person (or, in the parlance of insurance adjusters, we could attribute it to an 'act of God'). Alternatively, it could be a physical event, like a lightning strike, or a clogged

dryer vent. It could even refer to something as abstract as a political movement, if we want to know whether the fire was motivated
by personal animus or ideology. Examples may be further multiplied. The point is that the ambiguity of the word 'cause' may
create problems if we apply it without care for context and intent.
'The observed reaction was caused by Jeremy' may be an accurate
description of events from one point of view, but is not likely to
earn you full marks on a chemistry exam.

The third error we are prone to in our reasoning, according
to Bacon, is the tendency to accept certain propositions as true
without sufficient evidence. As an example, Bacon gives the false
belief 'that *in the heavens all things move in perfect circles*', a Ptol-
emaic theory which Copernicus had retained, but which had been
disproven in Bacon's lifetime by Johannes Kepler.[27] Bacon thinks
there are multiple reasons why we are prone to accept such pet
theories despite a lack evidence, or even in the face of contrary
evidence. Sometimes we hold on to false ideas for personal reasons, on account of our particular history or constitution. Other
times we accept a mistaken theory because it is held by members of
our social circle. In the end, they all boil down to the same thing.
These ideas give us a narrative about how the world is and, once
accepted, it is difficult to dislodge that narrative from our minds.
Like ambiguous terminology, we may think of these false-but-
accepted ideas as formalised analogical reasoning, the difference
being that here the thinking is manifested in propositions instead
of concepts.

As Newton famously wrote '*hypotheses non fingo*' – 'I do
not feign hypotheses' – Reid calls these unproven suppositions
'hypotheses'.[28] Today, calling a proposition a 'hypothesis' typically indicates a lack of evidence; it means that a given proposition
might be true, but is not yet proven and should be held lightly until
it is confirmed. Reid means something more. He means not only
that a given proposition lacks compelling evidence, but also that
it is being treated as if it were supported by evidence. To maintain
terminological connection with Reid, but hopefully avoid confusion, in what follows I therefore adapt Reid's usage and call such
propositions 'unsupported hypotheses' to make clear that they
lack enough evidence to be taken as true.

According to Bacon, when we fall prey to these three errors they
produce faulty understandings of the world, which he calls 'antici-
pations of nature'.[29] What we want instead, according to Bacon,

are 'interpretations of nature'.[30] The former are so called because they are a 'risky, hasty business', leaping to conclusions ahead of evidence, but still presenting a plausible enough account to be believed.[31] The latter, on the other hand, are accurate accounts of nature's regularities, and can only be arrived at through the careful process of experiment, observation and induction.

Reid's Appropriation of Bacon

That Reid thought of himself as a Baconian is apparent through-out his corpus. A full accounting of the ways in which Reid was influenced by and modified Baconian and Newtonian methodol-ogy is worthy of its own book. Yet the following two quotations give a useful first impression.

> [O]ne may observe that there are two ways by which a human mind advances from the known to the unknown. One is a descent by which a move is made from universal propositions to particular propositions subordinate to them. The other, its contrary, is an ascent from par-ticulars to universals. The first way is straightforward and easy and in using it the mind does not much require the help of an art; but to take the reverse step is the task, the work of the philosopher. For in the nature of things particulars are known first by the senses, by experi-ment, by testimony, and by other means too. To ascend legitimately from particulars to laws of nature and general axioms is in truth to philosophise properly and worthily. But in this upward journey the syllogistic art is wholly out of place.
>
> And since it was plain that Aristotle's *Organum* was not up to this task, Francis Bacon, a man of wonderful genius and suited by nature to the work not just of improving but of restoring natural philosophy anew, was emboldened to work at his *Novum organon scientiarum*.[32]

> I am humbly of the opinion that, of all followers of Bacon, Newton has most closely followed his rules, without deviating to the right hand or to the left. The two first books of the 'Principia', are properly called 'Mathematical principles of natural philosophy' . . . The rules of philosophizing laid down in the beginning of the third book, are, I think, as good a comp<e>nd, as can be given, in so few words, of the *Novum Organum*. The phenomena are facts, and the proposi-tions are deduced from those facts, by reasoning according to the rules laid down.[33]

These quotations are from Reid's graduation oration of 1753 and from private correspondence in 1791, respectively. As Reid began his academic career at King's College in Aberdeen in 1752, and died in 1796, these quotations serve as near-bookends to his extant writings and are representative of the deep respect Reid pays Bacon and Newton in all his works. Yet beyond his explicit avowals of Baconianism, we also find Lord Verulam's influence on Reid's life. Reid is largely known for his epistemology today, but his academic interests were legion. Granted, his pursuits of these varied interests also varied in their success: he was considered a mathematical prodigy and a competent observational astronomer, but was partially and permanently blinded in one eye while trying to observe the transit of Venus in 1761.[34] Still, as his unpublished and minor papers reveal, even beyond his duties in the classroom, Reid seriously pursued studies and conducted experiments in a wide range of natural sciences including astronomy, agriculture, biology and chemistry.[35]

Beyond these admiring quotations and scientific endeavours, we can also see the influence of Bacon on Reid in the way he writes philosophy. When Reid criticises others' philosophical positions, he typically accuses them of one or more of the three errors – analogical reasoning, ambiguous terminology and unsupported hypotheses – which Bacon emphasises in the *Novum Organon*. And when Reid advances his own position, he typically does so in a Baconian manner, starting with an organised set of definitions, and proposing general principles by making inductive arguments based on observation and (sometimes) experiment.

This is not to say that, for Reid, Baconianism is a universal solvent. As he writes in a paper replying to Priestley:

> There are many important branches of human knowledge, to which Sir Isaac Newton's rules of Philosophizing have no relation, and to which they can with no propriety be applied. Such are Morals, Jurisprudence, Natural Theology, and the abstract Sciences of Mathematicks and Metaphysicks; because in none of those Sciences do we investigate the physical laws of Nature.[36]

To this list, Reid also adds the study of 'voluntary action'.[37] These branches of knowledge are excluded from Baconian investigation because they are not attempts to catalogue the observable regularities of nature. Rather, they either (like mathematics) deal with necessary relations, or (like natural theology) deal with voluntary actions of free agents.

As Reid believes voluntary actions, morals and jurisprudence are not appropriate objects of Baconian investigation, it may at first glance seem that a long discussion of Reid's Baconianism is out of place in a book on Reid's defence of duty. But this discussion is necessary because of the close connection between these subjects and the study of the human mind. As the working of the mind is a natural and observable phenomenon, Reid believed that Newton's laws of philosophising ought to be applied to this investigation, which in Reid's time was called 'pneumatology'. The crucial distinction here is that, in studying the human mind, we are not trying to predict the actions of voluntary agents or derive the laws of morals from the human constitution; we are studying the natural faculties common to all well-functioning human beings which enable us to recognise and act according to the moral law.

Even granting that the common capacities of human beings qualify as a natural phenomena, someone familiar with Reid's works might still reply that Reid does not, in fact, apply a properly Baconian method to this subject. In Reid's published philosophy we do not, for example, find anything like the mathematical elegance of Newton's *Principia*, or the sequential experiments of the *Opticks*. Nor does he strictly follow Bacon's suggestions regarding the observation of natural phenomenon, according to which investigation begins by the careful and laborious collection of data. Reid acknowledges these differences but claims that he cannot follow Bacon's and Newton's procedures in his pneumatology exactly, on account of the elusiveness of the human mind. As he writes in the *Inquiry* the 'anatomy [of the human mind] is much more difficult' than that of the body.[38] For, while the anatomist of the body

> may have access to examine with his own eyes, and with equal accuracy, bodies of all different ages, sexes, and conditions . . . the anatomist of the mind cannot have the same advantage. It is his own mind only that he can examine, with any degree of accuracy and distinctiveness. This is the only subject he can look into. He may, from outward signs, collect the operations of other minds; but these signs are for the most part ambiguous, and must be interpreted by what he perceives within himself.[39]

As indicated in the quotation above, the nature of the human mind and our mitigated access to it limit our avenues for, but do not entirely foreclose, investigation. According to Reid, there are chiefly three 'proper Means of knowing the Operations of the Mind': investigation of structure of language, investigation of typical human behaviour and careful reflection on the operations of our own mind.[40] All of these 'proper means', Reid concedes, have their problems. Language, as noted, can be deceiving, even when the speaker means to be truthful. Behaviour is similarly ambiguous, and even less precise. Finally, reflection upon the operations of our own minds is difficult on many counts: our thoughts are rapid, we are unaccustomed to reflection and prone to passion, and it is often difficult to distinguish one faculty from another on account of their slow development and overlapping activity. Further, the indeterminism of free agents means any observed regularity will be partial. We may, for instance, observe that parents generally care for and love their children; but, being free agents, they will not do so with the same invariability of a chemical reaction. Still, these means are the best that Reid had available and, despite advances in medical imaging and the statistical sophistication of the social sciences, perhaps the best we still have for uncovering the nature of the human mind.

Still, for all significant modifications necessitated by our limited access to the human mind, Reid's pneumatology is recognisably Baconian in that it is foundational – built upon a verified trust of our senses and reasoning faculties – and eschews metaphysics for a description of regularity. As Buras and Copenhaver put it, Reid, 'like Bacon and Newton', is 'searching not for causes but for laws'.[41] Further, although he is at a disadvantage when compared to those who study objects more regular and easily observable than the human mind, Reid employs two other Baconian concepts in his arguments: the linked concepts of heterogeneous instances and *experimentum crucis*.

Bacon uses the idea of a heterogenous instance when speaking of analogical reasoning. According to Bacon, we are prone to inappropriately extrapolate a general proposition from a few observations because our minds are 'very slow and ill adapted to make the long journey to those remote and heterogeneous instances which test axioms as in a fire'.[42] A heterogenous instance, therefore, is a situation in which a general proposition inferred from a small set of examples is shown to be incorrect or insufficient. The associated idea of an *experimentum crucis*, – a 'critical experiment' – which was used by later Baconians and popularised by Newton, is an experiment designed to reveal a heterogeneous instance.[43] Reid does not use the phrase 'heterogeneous instances' in his published work, and uses the phrase '*experimentum crucis*' only once, in the *Inquiry*.[44] But, as we will see, Reid effectively applies the concepts behind these terms when he engages with philosophical theories with which he disagrees.

The Way of Ideas

Of all the philosophical ideas with which Reid disagreed, none occupied his thoughts more than the epistemological theory he variously referred to as 'the way of ideas', 'the theory of ideas' and the 'ideal theory'. The central tenet of this theory of perception is that when we perceive the world, we do so through the mediation of mental objects. According to Reid, the idea that we indirectly perceive the world has exerted an enduring and unfortunate influence in philosophy. It is at least as old as Pythagoras, and was discussed at length by Plato.[45] More urgently, in Reid's time the ideal theory had become increasingly popular on account of the work of René Descartes and on account of John Locke's distinction between primary and secondary qualities.[46] According to this distinction, primary qualities are actual properties of the observed object – for Locke: solidity, extension, motion and figure – while secondary qualities are properties that depend upon subjective experience in an observer, e.g. colour, taste and smell.[47] In Reid's telling, it was only a short distance from this distinction, between those things that actually exist in the world and those that only exist in our minds, to the idealism of Bishop Berkeley, whose *esse est precipi* – 'to be is to be perceived' – made all qualities of external objects dependent on the observer and therefore, in effect, secondary.[48]

The consequence of Berkeley's idealism was to unmake the physical world. If all that is, is perceived, and all that is perceived exists in a mind, then everything is an idea. Bishop Berkeley, as his title suggests, drew a religious moral from this inference. For him, all that exists, exists in the mind of God. Yet as radical as this idea was, it was not Berkeley, according to Reid, but David Hume who took the way of ideas to its 'full length'.[49]

The opening lines of Hume's *Treatise of Human Nature* provide a succinct summary of his version of the ideal theory.

> All the perceptions of the human mind resolve themselves into two distinct kinds, which I shall call IMPRESSIONS and IDEAS. The difference betwixt these consists in the degrees of force and liveliness, with which they strike upon the mind, and make their way into our thought and consciousness. Those perceptions, which enter with most force and violence, we may name *impressions*; and under this name I comprehend all our sensations, passions and emotions, as they make their first appearance in the soul. By *ideas* I mean the faint images of these in thinking and reasoning . . .[50]

Impressions, therefore, are those perceptions which originate outside of the mind – either from the interaction of the world with our senses or from our own passions. Ideas, on the other hand, are copies of the former. Impressions, furthermore, are more 'bright' or 'lively', but require the at-present influence of something outside the mind; while ideas, though fainter, may be manipulated, combined or recalled at will. Thus, to take an example from the *Enquiry Concerning Human Understanding*, once we have copied impressions of '*gold*' and '*mountain*' into ideas, we may imaginatively combine them into a 'golden mountain', though such a thing has never been observed.[51] From the simple building blocks of impressions, ideas and their laws of association, Hume constructs a complex epistemology that attempts to account for every type of perception and thought.

According to Reid, the central insight of Hume's version of the ideal theory was to make both external perception and internal cognition acts of secondary sensation. This is a logical thing to do. If our at-present impressions are observations of mental objects, then why not also our internal ideas? Treating both external perception and internal cognition as acts of secondary sensation clearly has the benefit of consistency and explanatory simplicity. Yet this model of the mind has the same effect on the mental world as Berkeley's idealism had on the physical. According to Reid, if Hume is correct, then we have no assurance that there is either matter or mind in the universe, because all we perceive are ideas and impressions, which may or may not accurately depict the world within and without our mind.[52] Perhaps they do; perhaps the thoughts and feelings that seem to be ours really are, and really reflect how we, as a unified self, feel. But we have no more assurance of this fact than we do that the page at which we are presently looking exists. For if we perceive both the page and our mind only through the mediation of mental objects, we have no way of checking the accuracy, or even the fact, of those objects' resemblance to anything else.

Reid also agrees with Hume that a rigorous adherence to the stipulation, held by the way of ideas, that all ideas must be copies of impressions, undermines our concept of causality. For, even assuming there is an external world about which we have reliable impressions, we never receive an impression of causality. We do, of course, have impressions of temporal proximity and change – the room becomes bright when we flip the light switch – but although we have impressions of the room and impressions of the switch, we do not have an impression of the connection between the two. And if we have no impression of causality, we cannot have an idea of causality, since ideas are always copies of impressions. From whence, then, does this exceedingly common concept originate? Hume's answer is that our beliefs about cause and effect arise when we experience the 'customary conjunction' of two or more events.[53] In other words, when we observe one event (the room becomes bright) typically follows another (flipping the switch), we come to associate them together and expect the latter when the former occurs. But, although we do this habitually, naturally, even unavoidably, we do not do it rationally; for we obtain our beliefs about causality through natural habit, and not through 'reason or any other operation of the understanding'.[54]

Reid strongly disagreed with these sceptical conclusions, which is not to say that Reid thought Hume a poor philosopher. Quite the contrary, as Reid saw it, Hume, more than anyone else in the modern era, was the philosopher who

> saw very clearly the consequences of this theory, and adopted them in his speculative moments; but candidly acknowledges, that, in the common business of life, he found himself under a necessity of believing with the vulgar. His Treatise of Human Nature is the only system to which the theory of ideas leads; and in my apprehension is, in all its parts, the necessary consequence of that theory.[55]

Reid, in other words, found Hume to be the expositor *par excellence* of the theory of ideas. As far as the conclusions to be drawn from the tenet that 'nothing can ever be present to the mind but an image or perception', Reid is Hume's ardent admirer.[56] Yet, regarding Hume's devotion to this theory in the face of its apparently infelicitous consequences, Reid is nothing if not scornful. Indeed, with a nod to Bacon's *idola*, Reid compares Hume's devotion to the ideal system to religious zealotry, and his scepticism to a costly sacrifice to a false idol.[57]

That the doctrine of impressions and ideas led to a certain kind of scepticism, Hume did not deny. Indeed, in both the *Treatise* and the *Enquiry Concerning Human Understanding* Hume readily grants that his philosophy shows there is no rational foundation for our beliefs. Yet Hume did not consider himself a radical sceptic in practice. According to Hume, our natural human propensity to believe our external and internal perceptions makes practical scepticism impossible. Still, 'this universal and primary opinion [that we perceive the real properties of external objects] is soon destroyed by the slightest philosophy, which teaches us that nothing can ever be present to the mind but an image or perception'.[58] In other words, if Hume is a sceptic, he is, in his own parlance, a 'mitigated' one.[59] This mitigation comes at the cost of inconsistency. Hume acts as though he trusts his perceptions, lacking good reasons to do so. But this problem is admitted up front by Hume, who acknowledges his inconsistency not in the form of an excuse, but as a vista for further investigation.[60]

Why, then, is Reid so hostile to Hume's epistemology and indeed any version of the way of ideas? There are multiple reasons. For one thing, Reid did not consider the fact that Hume rejected scepticism in his daily life to be a point in his favour. According to Reid, if one's theory and practice are seriously out of alignment, that is a clear sign that something has gone wrong. That the error lay in theory seemed to Reid obvious. For he agreed with Hume – and Bacon – that to disbelieve our perceptions is a path to madness, writing:

> I resolve not to believe my senses. I break my nose against a post that comes in my way; I step into a dirty kennel; and, after twenty such wise and rational actions, I am taken up and clapt in a madhouse.[61]

Thus, when forced to choose between the ideal theory and sanity, Reid preferred the latter.

Further, Reid also could not accept the practical effects that Hume's epistemology had on the foundations of philosophy.

Whereas Reid's education had taught him that the way of ideas was compatible with, and even a product of, Baconian methodology, Hume decisively showed that they were incompatible. As Reid saw it, if Hume's sceptical conclusions were correct, then we could not trust the deliverances of our senses. And if we cannot trust our senses, then the foundation of Baconian science must crumble to dust. In short, if Hume is correct, then Newton is wrong, as is every other Baconian scientist, be they biologist, chemist, physicist or astronomer. As Reid writes in the *Active Powers*, 'The first principles of all sciences, must be the immediate dictates of our natural faculties; nor is it possible that we should have any other evidence of their truth'.[62] That Hume's scepticism also undermined the certainty of non-Baconian sciences like mathematics and geometry only made matters worse.[63]

Thus, Reid undertook the task of replying to Hume's epistemology not simply because it overturned common, everyday beliefs – although it did that too – but because it struck at the roots of all knowledge natural and moral, that is, at all philosophy. Reid's response to Hume was accordingly not to defend the common notions of the unlearned, but to shore up the foundation of sense perception and reason upon which philosophy was built. And his first task was to show that the ideal theory was incorrect.

Reid's Arguments against the Theory of Ideas

According to Reid, there is a rich irony to the sceptical conclusions which Hume drew from the way of ideas, because the initial impulse behind the formation of the theory of ideas was the desire to explain how our perceptions of the external world occur and why they are reliable.[64] Hume, according to Reid, blasted the second half of this motivation to pieces by pointing out that we have no way of knowing whether or not our impressions actually represent the external world, and no reason to trust our beliefs about cause and effect. In this judgement, Reid and Hume seem to agree, but take the moral of the story to be completely different. For Hume, there was no need to drop the premises of the way of ideas. If, for example, sound reasoning from the theory of ideas shows that there are no impressions of causation, then our belief in causes is rationally unjustified. Reid, on the other hand, felt that the unintuitive consequences which Hume ingeniously drew from the theory of ideas were reason to think again. And upon reconsideration, he found the ideal system wanting for chiefly two reasons.[65]

First, Reid believed that the ideal system failed its mandate. It simply didn't explain how perception occurs. To see this failure, one need only accept the central tenet of the way of ideas – nothing is perceived in the mind except ideas and impressions – and then ask whether we have gained any explanatory power concerning perception. At first glance it may seem that we have, since we can now say that the operation of the senses causes impressions, and impressions cause perception. Unfortunately, however, we now also need to explain how these internal impressions resemble the properties of the external objects that caused them, and how the mind itself perceives those impressions and copies them into ideas. The fact that we now need to explain all these processes in order to explain how perception functions shows not only that we have increased the number of things to be explained, but that we have also not explained what we set out to explain.[66] So far, all we have done is propose the existence of intervening entities which are at least as mysterious as external perception itself. To Reid, it seemed much better to cut out the middleman and admit the mysteriousness of external perception than to commit the fallacy of *ignotum per aeque ignotum* – explaining the unknown by the equally unknown.

Second, Reid believed that the way of ideas made a critical mistake regarding the operation of our senses. According to the ideal system, our ideas about properties of external objects are copies of sensory impressions. Thus, our idea of 'hardness' is a duplicate of the sensation of touching something hard. Hume, of course, showed that if this is the case, and all we perceive are the impressions and ideas in our mind, we can never know if they resemble an outside world. But Reid made note of a more fundamental error. Our sense perceptions simply do not resemble our sensations. Consider the quality of hardness. 'Hardness of bodies is a thing that we conceive as distinctly, and believe as firmly as any thing in nature,' Reid writes.[67] Yet, '[w]e have no way of coming at this conception and belief, but by means of a certain sensation of touch, to which hardness hath not the last similitude'.[68] We miss this fact, according to Reid, because we 'are so accustomed to use sensation as a sign' that we typically 'pass immediately to the hardness signified' without attending to it.[69] Should we turn our attention to the sensation itself, however, we will discover not only that the sensation

differs from the conception, but that there can be multiple sensations which give us the same perception of an external quality. To
use Reid's own example, when we touch a hard object lightly, we
experience the sensation of pressure. When we run against it vio-
lently, we feel pain. From these disparate and, in the former case,
often unnoticed sensations, however, we obtain a conception of
material cohesion.[70] Here, then, is a clear heterogeneous instance.
The ideal system tells us that our idea of hardness is a less-vivid
copy of the impression of hardness, which resembles the sensation
of hardness.[71] Yet the sensation of hardness is not itself hard.

Given these problems with the way of ideas, why was it so
influential among philosophers ancient and modern? Unsurpris-
ingly, we find in Reid's answer to this question all three of the
errors identified above as negative aspects of Baconianism. First,
according to Reid, we find the influence of analogical reasoning.

> Thought in the mind is conceived [by philosophers] to have some anal-
> ogy to motion in a body . . . In all the external senses, there must . . .
> be some impression made upon the organ of sense by the object, or by
> something coming from the object. And impression supposes contigu-
> ity. Hence we are led by analogy to conceive something similar in the
> operations of the mind.[72]

The analogy between mind and matter is common, but is also, as
analogies tend to be, potentially misleading.

Further, the errors caused by this analogy become even more
common and difficult to overcome once they are imbedded in
our vocabulary. In particular, Reid is concerned about the way
the ideal theory uses the words 'impressions and feelings', which
are 'manifestly borrowed from the sense of touch', and the word
'images', which is borrowed from the sense of sight.[73] As Reid
sees it, this analogous use of language, and the Newtonian dictum
that there is no action at a distance, led philosophers to postulate
the existence of physical entities which mediate between the external world and our minds.[74] Reid does not disagree with Newton's
laws of physical motion. But the application of this rule of physics
is inappropriate here, according to Reid, because an 'object, in
being perceived does not act at all' and there is 'little reason . . .
to believe, that in perception the mind acts upon the object'.[75]

Reid's point here is not that we must always speak literally,
or that we may never borrow words from one context to use in

another. It is that the way of ideas implicitly adopts a mechanical model of the mind, and draws conclusions from that assumption, without first offering evidence that ideas and impressions are physical objects. As Reid puckishly notes:

> We have not the least evidence that the image of any external object is formed in the brain. The brain has been dissected times innumerable by the nicest Anatomists; every part of it examined by the naked eye, and with the help of microscopes; but no vestige of an image of any external object was ever found.[76]

Absent this evidence, and in the face of the ideal theory's sceptical consequences, Reid suggests that our best move is to admit ignorance. Although 'we are conscious of perceiving objects', he writes, 'we are altogether ignorant how it is brought about'.[77]

Yet, being uncomfortable with our ignorance, philosophers tend to fall prey to the common 'avidity to know the causes of things'.[78] And this tendency, mixed with analogical reasoning and misleading terminology, leads them to accept an unsupported hypothesis. Indeed, the hypothesis behind the way of ideas is not just unsupported but untestable. For if the ideal theory is correct, we cannot check whether or not our impressions actually resemble the external world because we cannot access that world except through the mediation of impressions.

In sum, then, Reid rejects the ideal theory for violating both the positive and negative aspects of Baconianism. Specifically, in violation of the positive aspects, the ideal theory fails to make accurate observations regarding sensation and perception, and also fails to explain the phenomena under view by abandoning Newton's first law of philosophising, that '[n]o more causes of natural things should be admitted than are both true and sufficient to explain their phenomena'.[79] Further, the plausibility of the theory of ideas seems only to rely on the three negative aspects of Baconianism: analogous reasoning, misleading terminology and unsupported hypothesis. For these reasons, according to Reid, the way of ideas ought to be discarded.

Hume's own relationship with Bacon and Newton is complicated and contested, so the charge that his philosophy runs contrary to the inductive method may not have bothered him.[80] But one does not have to be a Baconian to find these criticisms compelling. Leaving scepticism aside, if Reid is correct that the ideal system fails to actually explain perception, proposes the existence of unobserved and unobservable entities, and misconstrues the relations between sensation and perception, it has little to recommend it. But here we find ourselves with a question. If the ideal theory is wrong, and we do not perceive the world through the medium of mental objects like impressions and ideas, how do we perceive it? In the next chapter, we take up that question by examining Reid's admittedly partial answer, which is founded on his understanding of 'common sense'.

Notes

1. Reid, *Inquiry into the Human Mind*, p. 18.
2. Priestley, *An Examination of Dr. Reid's Inquiry Into the Human Mind*, p. 45
3. Priestley, *An Examination of Dr. Reid's Inquiry Into the Human Mind*, p. 3.
4. See Wood, 'Introduction', in Reid, *Thomas Reid on Animate Creation*, p. 31.
5. Johnson, *A Dictionary of the English Language*, 'Philosophy'.
6. Reid, 'Oration I', in *Thomas Reid and the University*, pp. 56–57.
7. Although, see Todd, 'Introduction', in Reid, *The Philosophical Orations of Thomas Reid*, pp. 14–15.
8. Jardine and Silverthorne, 'Introduction', in Bacon, *New Organon*, p. xii.
9. Davenport, 'Reid's Indebtedness to Bacon', p. 499. See also Reid, *Inquiry*, p. 200. While indebted to Davenport's account, the following is my own reconstruction of the positive and negative aspects of Baconianism in Reid.
10. Bacon, *New Organon*, p. 15.
11. Bacon, *New Organon*, p. 24.
12. Bacon, *New Organon*, p. 66.
13. Bacon, *New Organon*, p. 97.
14. Bacon, *New Organon*, p. 16
15. Bacon, *New Organon*, p. 16.
16. Bacon, *New Organon*, pp. 34, 35.
17. Bacon, *New Organon*, p. 35.
18. Bacon, *New Organon*, p. 17.
19. Bacon, *New Organon*, p. 18.
20. See Rees, 'On Francis Bacon's Originality' and Todd, 'Introduction', in Reid, *The Philosophical Orations of Thomas Reid*, p. 16.

21. Reid, *Inquiry into the Human Mind*, p. 200. Quoted in Davenport, 'Reid's Indebtedness to Bacon', p. 497.

22. Bacon, *New Organon*, p. 18 n. 13.

23. See Reid, *Essays on the Intellectual Powers*, p. 527.

24. These categories roughly line up with Bacon's as follows: analogous reasoning / idols of the tribe, misleading terminology / idols of the marketplace, hypothesis / idols of the cave and idols of the theatre. For Reid's treatment see especially *Essays on the Intellectual Powers*, Essay I, Chapters 1 ('Explication of words'), 3 ('Of hypothesis'), and 4 ('Of analogy').

25. Bacon, *New Organon*, p. 48.

26. Bacon, *New Organon*, p. 49.

27. Bacon, *New Organon*, p. 42. Emphasis original.

28. Newton, *Principia*, p. 589. Quoted in Reid, *Essays on the Intellectual Powers*, p. 52.

29. Bacon, *New Organon*, p. 38.

30. Bacon, *New Organon*, p. 38. Reid's categories of '*the way of analogy*' and '*the way of reflection*' reflect this distinction. See Reid, *Inquiry into the Human Mind*, p. 203. Emphasis original.

31. Bacon, *New Organon*, p. 38.

32. Reid, 'Oration I', in *Thomas Reid and the University*, p. 55.

33. Reid, '117. To Edward Tatham', in *The Correspondence of Thomas Reid*, p. 225.

34. See Reid, *Inquiry into the Human Mind*, p. 131, and Wood, 'Introduction', in Reid, *Thomas Reid on Mathematics and Natural Philosophy*, pp. xxi, cxxi.

35. For Reid's interest and reading habits in natural science see Wood 'A Virtuoso Reader: Thomas Reid and the Practices of Reading in Eighteenth-Century Scotland'. For Reid's minor papers and notes see Reid, *Thomas Reid on Mathematics and Natural Philosophy* and Reid, *Thomas Reid on Animate Creation*.

36. Reid, 'Some Observations on the Modern System of Materialism', in *Thomas Reid on Animate Creation*, pp. 185–186.

37. Reid, 'Some Observations on the Modern System of Materialism', in *Thomas Reid on Animate Creation*, p. 185.

38. Reid, *Inquiry into the Human Mind*, p. 12.

39. Reid, *Inquiry into the Human Mind*, p. 13.

40. Reid, *Essays on the Intellectual Powers*, p. 56.

41. Copenhaver and Buras, 'Introduction', in *Thomas Reid on Mind, Knowledge, and Value*, p. 2. See also Reid, *Inquiry into the Human Mind*, pp. 125 and 132, *Essays on the Intellectual Powers*, p. 561, and *Essays on the Active Powers*, pp. 37, 211.

42. Bacon, *New Organon*, p. 43.
43. Lohne, '*Experimentum Crucis*', p. 179ff.
44. Reid, *Inquiry into the Human Mind*, p. 70.
45. Reid, *Essays on the Intellectual Powers*, 91. See e.g. Plato, *Theaetetus*, 191 d.
46. Reid, *Essays on the Active Powers*, p. 458. Reid is aware that the distinction between primary and secondary qualities is also ancient. See Reid, *Essays on the Intellectual Power*, p. 206.
47. Locke, *Essay Concerning Human Understanding*, p. 135.
48. Berkeley, 'A Treatise Concerning the Principles of Human Knowledge', p. 84.
49. Reid, *Inquiry into the Human Mind*, p. 20. Reid discusses the genealogy of the ideal theory several times in his published corpus, but the most detailed and lengthy treatment can be found in the *Essays on the Intellectual Powers*, pp. 104–200.
50. Hume, *Treatise on Human Nature*, p. 1. Formatting original.
51. Hume, *Enquiry Concerning Human Understanding*, p. 19. Emphasis original.
52. See Reid, *Essays on the Intellectual Powers*, p. 162 and Hume, *Treatise of Human Nature*, pp. 252–253.
53. Hume, *Enquiry Concerning Human Understanding*, p. 46.
54. Hume, *Enquiry Concerning Human Understanding*, p. 41.
55. Reid, *Essays on the Intellectual Powers*, p. 448. Formatting original.
56. Hume, *Enquiry Concerning Human Understanding*, p. 152.
57. Reid, *Essays on the Intellectual Powers*, p. 419.
58. Hume, *Enquiry Concerning Human Nature*, p. 152.
59. Hume, *Enquiry Concerning Human Nature*, pp. 161–162.
60. See, Hume, *Enquiry Concerning Human Nature*, p. 39.
61. Reid, *Inquiry into the Human Mind*, p 170.
62. Reid, *Essays on the Active Powers*, p. 178.
63. See Hume, *Treatise of Human Nature*, pp. 42–53. Hume seems to take a softer line toward geometry and mathematics in his later work. See Hume, *Enquiry Concerning Human Nature*, p. 48.
64. See Reid, *Essays on the Intellectual Powers*, p. 104.
65. See Wolterstorff, *Thomas Reid and the Story of Epistemology*, pp. 45–76.
66. See Wolterstorff, *Thomas Reid and the Story of Epistemology*, pp. 50–51.
67. Reid, *Inquiry into the Human Mind*, p. 57.
68. Reid, *Inquiry into the Human Mind*, p. 57.
69. Reid, *Inquiry into the Human Mind*, p. 56.
70. See Reid, *Inquiry into the Human Mind*, pp. 56–57.

71. As Wolterstorff notes, not all proponents of the way of ideas – e.g. Descartes – thought of impressions as sensations. See Wolterstorff, *Thomas Reid and The Story of Epistemology*, p. 77n.
72. Reid, *Essays on the Intellectual Powers*, pp. 177–178.
73. Reid, *Inquiry into the Human Mind*, p. 178.
74. See Reid, *Essays on the Intellectual Powers*, p. 177.
75. A modern reader may wish to quibble with this statement, on the basis of double slit experiment, which shows that quantum probability functions collapse under observation. To use words precisely, however, it is not the perception of an electromagnetic particle by a human being which collapses the wave function, but the act of detecting its place. Granted, the exact mechanism of this collapse is still somewhat mysterious, but to say that the wave function collapses under 'observation' is not the same as to say that it collapses under human perception.
76. Reid, *Essays on the Intellectual Powers*, p. 93.
77. Reid, *Essays on the Intellectual Powers*, p. 178
78. Reid, *Essays on the Intellectual Powers*, p. 101.
79. Newton, *Principia*, p. 440.
80. See, e.g. Penelhum, *Themes in Hume*, p. 43. Harris, *Hume*, pp. 84–85, and Demeter, *David Hume and the Culture of Scottish Newtonianism*.

2

Reid, Perception and Common Sense

In the previous chapter we saw that Reid was alerted to the problems inherent in the ideal theory by Hume, who demonstrated its incompatibility with Baconianism. So alerted, Reid undertook an investigation of the way of ideas and found it wanting in several respects: it fails to add to our understanding of perception, it misdescribes the relationship between sensation and perception, and its plausibility rests less upon evidence than analogy, misleading terminology and unsupported hypothesis. Yet in discarding the way of ideas, Reid did not also discard the questions which the ideal theory was originally proposed to answer: how do we have perceptions, and are we justified in trusting them? In this chapter, we therefore turn to Reid's account of perception, in order to see if he can supply better answers.

To spend another chapter on issues ancillary to moral philosophy in a book about duty may seem odd. Yet, although this chapter, like the last, does not directly address Reid's defence of duty, our discussion here will help us in two ways. First, by examining Reid's general account of perception, we will be prepared to investigate some of the more puzzling aspects of Reid's account of moral perception when we come to them in chapter five. Second, by showing the resiliency of Reid's epistemology to scepticism, we will bolster the plausibility of Reid's method of philosophical investigation and his account of duty when we subject them to criticism in the final third of this book.

To accomplish these two tasks, we begin with a short description of Reid's theory of perception, which, in its paradigmatic form, consists of two pieces: bare apprehension and immediate judgement. Secondly, we examine Reid's understanding of first principles and his (in)famous appeal to 'common sense', both of which are essential to his epistemology. Finally, having gained a good grip on the essential features of Reid's theory of perception, we test it against a classic sceptical argument, in order to see if Reid can provide rational justification for trusting our perceptions.

Reid's Theory of Perception: Apprehension and Judgement

In contrast to the theory of perception outlined in Hume's *Treatise* and *Enquiry Concerning Human Understanding*, and as a result of his views on Baconian method, Reid's account of perception is the product of observation and induction. To take just one remarkable example, consider Reid's discussion of single and double vision in his chapter 'Of Seeing' in the *Inquiry*. Here, the question that concerns Reid is why, if we have two eyes, we usually see one image. This question is important to Reid because, in the *Treatise*, Hume draws a sceptical conclusion from the fact that we may induce double vision by pressing our finger against the side of one of our eyes such that they do not point in the same direction.[1] According to Hume, because it is unlikely that this act produces the perception of two objects by producing two objects in the world, we ought to conclude that impressions stand between objects and our perceptions of them.

Although the details of the argument are beyond our purview here, Hume's reasoning in this matter is exactly the kind that Reid eschews.[2] In brief, Hume starts with the premises 1) we observe two objects and 2) objects alike in phenomenology must be ontologically similar, and from this infers 3) perception is always mediated by impressions. In Reid's counter-argument, by contrast, we find a very different method. In the first place, we find nothing resembling Hume's appeal to metaphysics in the second proposition above. Further, where Reid does advance theories, they are both testable and based on an extensive survey of contemporary medical literature. Reid even discloses that he has conducted experiments on 'above twenty persons that squinted' using an instrument of his own design.[3]

While it is amusing to note Reid's obvious delight in conducting these experiments – did he go about Aberdeen on constant lookout for lazy eyes? – we should not overlook their importance. For Reid, in contrast to the proponents of the ideal theory and a great deal of philosophical practice today, intellectual inquiry into topics that we now consider to be under the purview of philosophy – topics like epistemology and ethics – ought to be pursued using Baconian methodology.

Conception

Reid's theory of perception begins with an inversion of the ideal theory. Whereas Hume and the ideal theorists understand the mind to be passive in its reception of outside objects and qualities, Reid believes language, practice and introspection show it to be active. Perceptions do not happen to the mind. Instead, we say, the mind *perceives*. To see how this active concept of perception operates, consider Reid's brief discussion of perception in Book II, Chapter V of the *Intellectual Powers*. Here Reid notes two features of our perception of an external object. The first is that 'it is impossible to perceive an object without having some notion or conception of that which we perceive'.[4] The second is that the perception of external objects is typically accompanied by an immediate belief in the existence of an object having the observed properties.[5]

At first glance, it may seem odd that Reid says that the external senses give us a 'conception' of the thing perceived, as this may appear to align his theory of perception with the theory of ideas.[6] The confusion here is a result of the difference between the familiar, Kantian meaning of 'conception' and Reid's. Under the Kantian rubric, to have a conception of something requires that we have a concept to apply to the object. If we understand Reid's use in this way, then we will need to ask him all the same questions he asks of Hume. What kind of conception is invoked: a general conception about that type of object, in which case we run into the problem of universals, or a specific but no less mysterious conception of the object itself? And further, how is this conception related to the object of which it is a conception? As Nicholas Wolterstorff notes, though, this problem recedes once we pay close attention to what Reid means by 'bringing an object under conception'.[7]

When speaking of perception, what Reid usually means by 'conception' is what he also calls 'simple apprehension' or 'bare conception'.[8] This apprehension of an object is not the formation of an impression or an idea. It is, rather, merely the act of getting a 'mental grip' on an object 'without any judgement or belief about it'.[9] How exactly this happens, Reid is admittedly unable to say, but that is partly the point. He has no hypothesis concerning the method by which our senses allow us to bring external objects and properties under conception, only the observation that they do under certain conditions. To go further, as the way of ideas does, by postulating the existence of a mental impression, would violate his understanding of proper philosophical method.

Lest the statement that Reid must, on principle, stop here be misleading, note that Reid has quite a bit more to say about simple apprehension. Indeed, large sections of the *Inquiry* are devoted to describing various conditions under which we apprehend objects and properties through our five external senses. But in all these we find Reid proceeding in a Baconian manner: looking to describe regularities in perception, not proposing unobservable entities which facilitate it.

Judgement

While bare conception provides the first of Reid's two elements of perception, a second act of the mind gives us an immediate belief in the existence of the object brought under conception. This belief, although inextricably linked to the simple apprehension of a perceived object, is not strictly part of it. The crucial difference between them is that a belief 'can be expressed by a proposition only . . . but simple apprehension may be expressed by a word or words'.[10] In Reid's terminology, this means that the belief in the existence of those objects we perceive is a 'judgement'.

Of all the concepts necessary for understanding Reid's epistemology – and moral philosophy – judgement ranks at the very top. According to Reid, it is the common and mistaken conflation of reasoning and judgement, and the preference for the former, that has led to many philosophical errors. For him, the precise application of the word 'reasoning' refers only to the mental act of drawing a deductive conclusion from premises. Judgement, on the other hand, is 'that act of the mind, whereby one thing is affirmed or denied of another'.[11] To modify one of Reid's examples, we may see this difference by considering how we do our taxes – *reasoning* as best we can all the way through complex formulae – but, upon reaching an improbable figure at the end, *judging* that we made a mistake and starting again.[12] At first glance, this distinction may appear to be overly nice. In the common business of life, the words 'reasoning' and 'judgement' are used interchangeably. Reid grants that this is true, and does not fault the common usage, since a) both acts often occur together, and b) in everyday discussions, this conflation rarely causes confusion. His distinction between them should therefore be read as a technical distinction, made to draw the attention of the reader to an under-appreciated facet of human activity, and not as an attempt to correct general usage.

For Reid, the most important point that this distinction is intended to illuminate – and the one most crucially missed by his fellow philosophers – is that judgement may occur without reasoning, but reasoning always implies judgement. To make this point, Reid compares the 'immediate and intuitive judgement' that accompanies perception with the judgement that the two base angles of an isosceles triangle are equal.[13] Although he does not further describe the latter, it seems to be Reid's belief that if we consider our thought process regarding the relationship between isosceles triangles and the equality of their base angles, we will have to go through several steps. If the relationship of an isosceles triangle and the equality of its two base angles seems too obvious to require reasoning, however, then another, more difficult task, such as the tax example above, may be substituted. Regarding immediate, intuitive judgements, on the other hand, Reid writes that 'when I attend to colour, figure, weight, I cannot help judging these to be qualities which cannot exist without a subject; that is, something which is coloured, figured, heavy'.[14] Reid's point is that in judgements of this kind there is no reasoning, no step-by-step process of going from premises to conclusion. Rather, the judgement happens non-inferentially, immediately and intuitively.

Reid also describes this contrast by stating that while immediate, intuitive judgement draws conclusions about those things that are 'self-evident', reasoning draws conclusions about those things that are not self-evident from those that are.[15] In the latter we (ideally) reason from true propositions to further true propositions. So, for example, 'a=c' from the propositions 'a=b' and 'b=c'. With intuitive judgement, however, 'judgement follows apprehension . . . necessarily' with 'no searching for evidence, no weighing of arguments'.[16]

Because self-evidence is a contested term, it is critical to see what Reid does not say. He does not say that self-evident propositions are assented to without evidence, only that they are assented to without 'searching' for evidence. Of course, because these are not principles justified by prior propositions, this evidence must be non-propositional. Reid's position, therefore, is not that we assent to self-evident propositions without evidence, but that they give their own evidence; a self-evident proposition has, as Reid puts it, 'the light of truth in itself'.[17]

Yet this formulation prompts a question. How can our perceptual judgements give their own evidence? We might, for example, be willing to agree that analytic statements, like 'all maroon things are red', are self-evident. If you understand the words, you assent to the proposition. Such propositions are, as Reid puts it, 'no sooner understood than believed'.[18] But the mental action of recognising a definitionally true statement seems very different from the judgement that you have stepped on something sharp on account of a sensation of pain in your foot.

Clearly, if Reid is making any sense at all, he is using 'self-evident' in a non-standard way, but opinions differ as to what exactly he means.[19] To take just a sample: Wolterstorff thinks Reid's understanding is muddled and should be replaced with the related idea of 'adequate evidence', which is either non-propositional or contained in the proposition assented to itself.[20] James Van Cleve, largely agreeing with Wolterstorff, adds that one strand in Reid's thinking is that the self-evident is that which we cannot help but believe.[21] William C. Davis, on the other hand, believes Reid's account is perfectly clear and based upon Scottish legal doctrine. According to Davis, Reid's definition of self-evidence focuses on the nature of the agent who assents, not the nature of the proposition assented to. Self-evident propositions, under this rubric, are those propositions which are apparent to mature, unprejudiced minds when they have a clear and distinct conception of the matters at hand.[22]

For myself, I do not find in Reid any clear definition of self-evidence. Yet, as the above options demonstrate, even without one, Reid's general idea is apparent. Without attempting a final definition, let us therefore take Reid's use of 'self-evident' to indicate those propositions which we assent to immediately, once we clearly see the matters at hand, and without basing that assent on any other proposition or collecting evidence through, for example, scientific experiments.

First Principles and Common Sense

Reid's understanding of self-evidence is further illuminated by observing the role it plays in his epistemology. To see this, however, it is necessary to take a small detour away from our discussion of Reid's theory of perception and spend a little time discussing Reid's account of first principles, which he defines as propositions which are judged intuitively, and are typically self-evidently true.[23] These principles, as we just saw, play an important role in Reid's account of perception. Further, they are, for Reid, essential for all reasoning. Despite their importance though, Reid believes they are often neglected by philosophers, who rush past first principles without noting them. One consequence of this inattention is that these philosophers sometimes attempt to undermine first principles by means of principles which rationally rest upon them, a hopeless and self-defeating task. To combat this tendency, Reid therefore elucidates the nature of first principles by offering four propositions concerning them.

First, according to Reid, first principles are necessary for all reasoning. Reid's argument here is similar to the one found in the first paragraph of Wittgenstein's *Philosophical Investigations*: 'Explanations come to an end somewhere'.[24] Or, as Reid, borrowing from Aristotle and coming from the other direction, puts it: 'without first principles, analytical reasoning could have no beginning'.[25] Whichever way we travel, the truth is the same. For reasoning to function, we must either start with true propositions from which to build an argument, or, when analysing an argument, arrive at a foundation on which the explanation rests.

Reid's second proposition concerning first principles is that some first principles are necessary, while others are contingent. Reid gives us examples of each type. Propositions regarding definitions and logical and mathematical axioms are first principles of necessary truth. 'About most of' these, Reid falsely claims, 'there has been no dispute'.[26] This we must read as overstatement. For, while it is accurate to say that there has been less dispute in the cases of definitional, logical or mathematical axioms, Reid knew, for instance, that Hume questioned the truth of mathematical and geometrical axioms. Further, and more importantly for our purposes, Reid was acutely aware that there was an entire class of axioms which he believed to be necessary, whose nature and content were disputed: namely, moral axioms.

Saving that discussion for a later chapter, however, let us look at the second category of first principles: the first principles of contingent truth. Admitting to an incomplete list, Reid gives us twelve such principles.

1. The existence of every thing of which I am conscious.
2. The thoughts of which I am conscious, are the thoughts of a being which I call *myself*, my *mind*, my *person*.
3. Those things did really happen which I distinctly remember.
4. [The veracity of] our own personal identity and continued existence, as far back as we remember any thing distinctly.
5. Those things do really exist which we distinctly perceive by our senses, and are what we perceive them to be.

6. We have some degree of power over our actions, and the determinations of our will.
7. The natural faculties, by which we distinguish truth from error, are not fallacious.
8. There is life and intelligence in our fellow-men with whom we converse.
9. Certain features of the countenance, sounds of the voice and gestures of the body, indicate certain thoughts and dispositions of mind.
10. There is a certain regard due to human testimony in matters of fact, and even to human authority in matters of opinion.
11. There are many events depending upon the will of man, in which there is a self-evident probability, greater or less, according to circumstances.
12. In the phaenomena of nature, what is to be, will probably be like to what has been in similar circumstances.[27]

In contrast to self-evident propositions of necessary truth, these principles are clearly not self-evident according to the usual definition of the word. Reid acknowledges this difference, writing that the contingent principles do not have 'that kind of evidence which mathematical axioms have'.[28] The difference is this: whereas the contrary of first principles of necessary truth is impossible, the contrary of first principles of contingent truth is not. In consequence, Reid says that the truth of necessary first principles is absolutely certain, while the truth of contingent first principles is probable.

Reid's third proposition concerning first principles is that it would be immensely helpful in all areas of inquiry for our first principles to be explicitly enumerated. Here Reid's love of natural philosophy and mathematics, and the influence of Newton, are again apparent. Following Newton's suggestion in Query 31 of the *Opticks* – 'if natural Philosophy in all its parts, by pursuing this Method, shall at length be perfected, the Bounds of Moral Philosophy will also be enlarged' – Reid believed that if other branches of philosophy could agree on first principles, then those intellectual pursuits could be as successful as Newtonian physics.[29]

With the benefit of hindsight, this assessment appears foolishly optimistic. But despite his hopefulness for a philosophy in which we have agreement on first principles, Reid knew that the task of setting forth and agreeing on first principles in any line of inquiry is not, nor has ever been, simple. As history shows, even the recognition that reasoning requires first principles gains us little.

> The ancient Philosophers granted, that all knowledge must be grounded on first principles, and that there is no reasoning without them. The Peripatetic philosophy was redundant rather than deficient in first principles. Perhaps the abuse of them in that ancient system may have brought them into discredit in modern times.[30]

If first principles are self-evident, necessary to all knowledge and cannot be tested for accuracy by examining the reasons for them, then it may seem a puzzle how Reid can so confidently dismiss the veracity of Peripatetic, or indeed any, offered first principles.

Yet, although Reid grants that we cannot give more fundamental reasons for first principles, Reid's fourth proposition is that 'nature has not left us destitute of means whereby the candid and honest part of mankind may be brought to unanimity when they happen to differ about first principles'.[31] To this end, Reid proposes four ways in which first principles may be tested in the case of disagreement. First, Reid notes that it is 'a good argument *ad hominem* if it can be shewn, that a first principle which a man rejects, stands upon the same footing with others he admits'.[32] Second, as with mathematics, Reid writes that if denying a debated first principle leads to obviously absurd results, this gives us another good reason to hold it. Third, Reid appeals to the opinion of tradition, not because he believes the past was more enlightened than the present, but because he believes tradition records the opinions of other competent judges. And finally, Reid holds that when an idea appears absolutely necessary for the conduct of human life, such as those (like object permanence) reliably formed in early human development, this counts as a good reason to believe it.

The fact that Reid provides four ways of testing our judgement of self-evident principles may appear contradictory. If the ability to recognise first principles is intuitive, why would we ever get one wrong? Yet Reid never claims that we always succeed in correctly judging self-evident truths. On account of factors such as immaturity, prejudice and interest, we 'may, to the end of life, be ignorant of self-evident truths'.[33] If Reid believes this, though, why call these fundamental principles 'first'? The reason is not that Reid believes we always assent to first principles before we assent to any propositions which are rationally grounded upon them. On the contrary, not only may we be ignorant of first principles our whole lives, but also our assent to true propositions often swings free of rational justification.

This is especially true of children, who 'believe a thousand things before they ever spend a thought upon evidence'.[34] Reid does not think that the fact that children believe more than they can justify is a problem, because the reasoning faculties take time to develop, and, in order to function, children need to learn too many things too quickly to wait on evidence. Nature therefore supplies them with natural credulity and faith in their instructors. As Reid writes in the *Active Powers*:

> A person who has lived so long in the world as to observe that nature is governed by fixed laws, may have some rational ground to expect similar events in similar circumstances; but this cannot be the case of the child. His belief therefore is not grounded on evidence. It is the result of his constitution.[35]

The same is less true of mature human beings, according to Reid, but is not untrue. There are many things that we believe which we cannot at present justify, or can only partially justify, although they are rationally justifiable. For example, I believe that Fermat's Last Theorem has been proven true. But I could not begin to fill in the steps between the basic axioms of mathematics – which I also could not at present list – and the conclusion.[36] Thus, for Reid, first principles are not first because we assent to them first and the truths are drawn from them afterwards. They are, rather, first in the way that Aristotle and Wittgenstein indicate, being the foundation of all rationally justified belief.

Common Sense

According to Reid, then, there are different ways that we assent to true propositions. One obvious way is by assenting to propositions which are rationally entailed by prior justified principles. Another way, just discussed, is through natural credulity. In the first of these, we not only have true beliefs but are justified in holding them. In the second, we are not justified in our belief, even when it is true. For Reid, however, there is another way to hold a justified true belief, and that is through rational assent to first principles, on the basis of self-evidence. That human beings make such judgements is, according to Reid, a fact about our mental capacities, contingent in the sense that human beings could be otherwise created. But this faculty plays a large role in Reid's epistemology because it is necessary to our being rational creatures. Without this capacity we would have no first principles from which to reason. And this is the capacity that Reid frequently refers to as 'common sense'.

It is somewhat ironic, and unfortunate, that Reid is often remembered as a philosopher of common sense. In the first place, Reid was ambivalent about the phrase and considered using the less-common term 'common judgement' instead.[37] Second, while Reid both appealed to and defended common sense, he did not see these appeals or defences as the point of his philosophy, or of philosophy in general. It is true that, for Reid, philosophical investigation relies on the ability to make self-evident judgements, i.e. on principles of common sense. But this is true for all human knowledge. Thus, from Reid's perspective, it makes only slightly more sense to call him a philosopher of common sense as it does to call Newton a physicist of common sense, or Halley an astronomer of common sense, because they trusted in principles of common sense – e.g. the general veracity of their observations, the regularity of the laws of nature, the axioms of mathematics – and drew further inferences from them.

Why then, given the above, did Reid risk misunderstanding and call our faculty of judgement concerning non-propositional evidence 'common sense'? The reason is twofold. First, according to Reid, both reasoning with judgement and judgement without reasoning are properly termed exercises of reason. Yet, since we find 'in the greatest part of mankind no other degree of reason' than judgement without reasoning, only the latter is common.[38] Second, Reid wanted to rectify the use of the word 'sense' in contemporary philosophy. All senses, he complains, 'whether external or internal, have been represented . . . as the means of furnishing our minds with ideas, without including any kind of judgement'.[39] And this, as we saw in the last chapter, is precisely what Reid wants to deny. In contrast, Reid believes that 'in common language, sense always implies judgement', adding that our external senses are called senses by non-philosophers 'because we judge by them'.[40] In this vein, Reid wanted to emphasise that the capacity to make self-evident judgements – i.e. affirm first principles – was no less a mental faculty of human beings than our faculties of sight, sound, touch, smell or taste.

In my opinion, it may have been the better part of valour to abandon the overworn and ambiguous phrase 'common sense', rather than to use it in the idiosyncratic way Reid does. Calling it 'common judgement' would have avoided many misunderstandings because it would have emphasised the connection between this capacity and reason. Still, even this clarification would not solve all of the difficulties around the term 'common sense' in Reid's philosophy, because there are still several obscurities regarding its use in his philosophy.

Let us start with what is clear. By 'common sense' Reid means to denote the human capacity to make self-evident judgements.[41] As he writes in the *Intellectual Powers*, '[a]ll knowledge, and all science, must be built upon principles that are self-evident, and of such principles, every man who has common sense is a competent judge, when he conceives of them distinctly'.[42] Further, Reid believes that although the ability to judge on the basis of self-evidence varies from person to person, there is a 'certain degree of it which is necessary' to our being considered competent human beings.[43] What is not entirely clear is the extent of common sense. For example, under the ability to make judgements about 'principles that are self-evident', does he mean both contingent and necessary principles, such that we judge the truth of mathematical, geometrical and logical axioms by common sense in the same way that we make judgements about the properties of the external world? Further, are all of the immediate judgements of our perceptual senses included under the banner of 'common sense'; and if so, does Reid think of common sense as a class of mental faculties which includes but is not limited to the external senses, or is common sense a single faculty which our external senses somehow participate in or appeal to? Additionally, does Reid conceive of common sense as assenting to general self-evident propositions (e.g. those things do really exist which we distinctly perceive by our senses, and are what we perceive them to be) or to particular self-evident propositions (e.g. this table, which I distinctly perceive by my senses, exists and is what I perceive it to be) – or both?

Despite the acknowledged difference between the self-evidence of necessary and contingent propositions, the answer to the first question, regarding the extent of common sense, can only be 'yes'. If it were not, and common sense only extended to either contingent or necessary propositions, it would be hard to make sense of Reid's statement that '[a]ll knowledge and all science' is built upon first principles judged by common sense. Further, Reid explicitly connects our capacity to make contingent self-evident judgements and necessary self-evident judgements.

> The constitution of our understating determines us to hold the truths of a mathematical axiom as a first principle, from which other truths may be deduced, but it is deduced from none; and the constitution of our power of perception determines us to hold the existence of what we distinctly perceive as a first principle, from which other truths may be deduced, but it is deduced from none.[44]

Thus, when Reid writes that the 'sole province of common sense' is 'to judge of things which are self-evident', he means that it fills the province entirely.[45]

With respect to the question of the relation between the immediate deliverances of the five external senses and common sense, the answer also seems to be 'yes'. That the judgements of the external senses are deliverances of common sense is indicated by several things Reid says. They make judgements based on self-evidence, are necessary for all knowledge and science, and are necessary to being a competent human being: all hallmarks of common sense.

As for whether the ability of each sense to judge is included with other abilities under a category of judgements called 'common sense', or whether there is a faculty of judgement called 'common sense' which is exercised in each perceptual judgement, Reid does not say. Yet this may be intentional. According to Reid, we 'know nothing of our natural faculties but by their operations within us'.[46] Thus, when it comes to accounting for the overlap between the operations of perception and common sense, he does not attempt to account for the mind's internal structure. Rather, Reid has nothing more to say except to affirm that the immediate deliverances of the external senses are judgements of common sense.[47]

Still, perhaps we should not be so hasty to include the individual, immediate judgements of the external senses among the judgements of common sense. For, depending on how we read it, the fifth first principle of contingent truth may not mean that our individual perceptions of the external world are first principles. It may, rather, mean that it is a first principle that the world generally exists as we perceive it.[48] Perhaps, in other words, this first principle is a general self-evident judgement about perceptual judgements. This brings us to the third question asked above, as to whether the judgements of common sense are general or particular. On this topic, scholarship is divided. Keith Lehrer, for example, believes that both general and particular judgements are first principles, and therefore principles of common sense. Van Cleve disagrees and holds that only particular judgements ought to be considered true first principles. On this matter, I take the side of Lehrer, not because I think this position is without difficulty, but because it appears to be Reid's.[49] As he writes in the *Intellectual Powers*, 'the particular propositions contained under a general axiom are no less self-evident than the general axiom'.[50]

With these answers in mind, we can now see that by 'common sense', Reid means nothing more or less than the natural human capacity to make judgements regarding self-evidence. This is not to say that there are no further questions to be asked considering Reid's conception of common sense or his use of the term 'self-evident'. Indeed, it is a topic of much academic interest.[51] Yet, for our purposes here, we now have enough to attempt to explain why Reid believes our perceptions can be self-evident.

For Reid, our perceptions of the external world are first principles of contingent truth. When we encounter something in the external world, on this account, we non-inferentially interpret the sensation it causes and form a judgement about the object. Note that in this process we do not first form a judgement about the sensation and then form a judgement about the object from the prior judgement. That would make our perceptual beliefs inferential. Rather, as Wolterstorff puts it, on Reid's account '[o]ur perceptual beliefs are the products of the activation of dispositions, not the conclusion of inferences'.[52] And, as the ability to make these non-inferential judgements about the external world immediately – without 'searching for evidence' – is common to our condition as reasonable creatures, and forms the foundation about all our reasonings about it, its deliverances are first principles, meaning, principles of common sense.[53]

Reid and Scepticism

To summarise the above, Reid believes that perception of the outside world consists of two acts of the mind: first, getting a mental grip on an object through simple apprehension; and second, an intuitive and immediate judgement regarding the object. Clearly, this is a different account of perception than that of the way of ideas. Yet the question remains: if Reid rejected the way of ideas partly because it led to scepticism, does his account fare any better?

In the judgement of history, the verdict is mixed. Although Reid was widely hailed as a refuter of scepticism in his own time, the success of Reid's theory of perception was by no means obvious to his philosophical critics. Indeed, as the following exchange between the Scottish philosophers James Mackintosh and Thomas Brown shows, Reid was understood by some of his contemporaries not only to have failed in his effort to refute scepticism, but to have inadvertently entailed scepticism in his theory of perception.

> In 1812, as the present writer [Mackintosh] observed to him [Brown] that Reid and Hume differed more in words than opinion, he answered 'Yes, Reid bawled out, We must believe in an outward world; but added in a whisper, We can give no reason for our belief. Hume cries out, We can give no reason for such a notion; and whispers, I own we cannot get rid of it'.[54]

Given the stark differences between their theories of perception, this close analogy between Reid and Hume on the reliability of our perceptions should be surprising. Yet, as I read it, Brown makes this reply not because he finds Reid's account of perception unpersuasive – although he does – but on account of Reid's own statements about self-evident judgements, and especially those, like perceptual judgements, which regard contingent truth. As we saw above, Reid thinks that these truths are probable, and are intuitively judged on the basis of non-propositional evidence. This is, of course, what makes them contingent first principles. If they were necessarily true, they would not be contingent; and if they rested on prior principles, they would not be first. But it does nothing to ease the sting of Brown's barb. Just because we naturally make certain judgements about the world when presented with the evidence of sensations does not mean that those judgements are correct or justified. After all, even Hume grants that we typically act as if the external world exists in roughly the same way that we perceive it.

The idea that Reid and Hume disagree more in words than in substance is further strengthened by recent interpretations of Hume, according to which Hume's considered position is that the irresistibility of our perceptions counts as justification for them.[55] The interpretive issues here are complex, but if this is correct then it may seem that the disagreement between Hume and Reid regarding the justification of our perceptions is slight indeed. For myself, I do not find these revisionist readings of Hume convincing.[56] As I read him, Hume does not think that our natural tendency to believe our sensations counts as a reason to trust them. But for the sake of argument, let us accept that it is a plausible position to take within the ideal system. This being the case, if Reid wants to show that his theory of perception does not, like the ideal theory, entail scepticism – even the very mitigated scepticism according to which we unavoidably accept our perceptions without further justification – he must not only show that we *do* believe our perceptions, but that we are justified in doing so.

Ideally, in order to judge whether Reid's account of perception is more resistant to scepticism than Hume's, we would take the train of reasoning that Hume used to reach his sceptical conclusions and apply it to Reid. Yet this cannot be done because Hume arrives at his mitigated scepticism by carefully following the premises of the way of ideas to their logical conclusion – and Reid rejects these premises. What we need, therefore, is a general-purpose sceptical argument, which begins from premises Reid accepts, such as the limited nature and occasional unreliability of our perceptions, and ends with the same type of mitigated scepticism we find in Hume. One promising option which fulfils these requirements is an argument derived from the ancient Pyrrhonian sceptics. By applying this argument we will see that Reid's account of perception is not, as Brown believed, am implicit form of scepticism, because Reid's common sense is a form of epistemic externalism and not, like the way of ideas, a version of epistemic internalism.

The Sceptic's Net

Before proceeding to this Pyrrhonist argument, let us first acknowledge that both Hume and Reid rejected Pyrrhonism, as they understood it, for similar reasons. In the *Enquiry Concerning Human Understanding*, Hume complains that 'a Pyrrhonian cannot expect, that his philosophy will have any constant influence on the mind' because it is so contrary to experience.[57] By this acknowledgement, Hume makes it clear that he does not disagree with Reid regarding the general phenomenon of first principles. There are, he believes, certain propositions to which we naturally assent without prior reasons, and which are useful for life.[58] The point of Hume's scepticism, therefore, is not to so disbelieve the senses that we walk into fires and off cliffs, but to puncture intellectual hubris. In contrast, Hume asserts that the Pyrrhonist's scepticism is excessive because it holds that we should actively disbelieve our perceptions in ordinary life. Reid agrees, characterising Pyrrhonism as a philosophy that died away of itself by being, literally, unbelievable.[59]

Yet although they agree on this matter, both Hume and Reid in fact read the Pyrrhonists incorrectly. The primary aim of Pyrrhonism – at least according to Sextus Empiricus' collection of Pyrrhonist wisdom, *Outlines of Pyrrhonism* – was not a life lived contrary to useful but un-provable propositions, but 'equipollence'.[60] Equipollence, according to Sextus, occurs when judgement is suspended and the intellect is at a standstill, neither accepting nor rejecting anything. The Pyrrhonists hoped that in equipollence they would be free of all mental anguish caused by doubt. They would – in a manner not so unlike Hume's mitigated sceptic – go along with those things that seemed true while withholding rational assent to them.

According to Sextus, equipollence is achieved by the employment of several argumentative strategies, or 'modes', designed to show that, for any proposition, its opposite is also plausible. True to Pyrrhonist form, in the *Outlines*, Sextus appears to suspend judgement as to exactly how many such modes there are, giving at one place ten, at another five, and at another two.[61] It is, unfortunately, beyond the scope of this work to mediate among them. Conveniently, though, Jonathan Barnes has supplied a helpful reconstruction which he calls the 'The Three Modes' that succinctly captures the basic thrust of these methods, even if it does leave out a fair bit of interesting subtlety and complexity.[62] In short, it works as follows.

There are three modes – disagreement, infinite regress and circularity – and they work in concert. Whenever Pyrrhonists find themselves tempted to assent to a proposition instead of suspending judgement, or confronted with someone who does – a 'dogmatist' in Pyrrhonist parlance – the first step is to employ the mode of disagreement and assert a contrary proposition to the one considered. At this point, the original proposition, according to Barnes' reconstructed Pyrrhonism, could be supported in one of two ways. Either it could be described as self-supporting, or another reason could be given. In the case of the former, the sceptic ought to employ the mode of circularity, arguing that nothing stands on its own. If another reason, itself a proposition, is given, the

Pyrrhonist then immediately employs the mode of disagreement again and starts over. Should further reasons be given at every point of disagreement, the Pyrrhonist then asks where the argument ends, employing either the mode of infinite regress or circularity as the occasion requires.

Barnes aptly names this three-mode distillation the 'sceptic's net'.[63] For, by it, the Pyrrhonist starts with disagreement and, using the threat of infinite regress, tries to push the would-be dogmatist into circularity. With the toy example given above, this circularity was described as self-support, but an appeal to a previously given reason also does the trick, self-support merely being the circularity of a single proposition.[64]

Catalepsis

To see how the sceptic's net works in practice, let us apply it to the anti-sceptical arguments of the Pyrrhonists' contemporary opponents, the Stoics. According to the Stoic line – at least as presented in a modern reconstruction by R.J. Hankinson – one need not withhold assent from all propositions because it is possible to know, for a fact, that some are true. These true propositions were called, by them, 'cataleptic impressions'. A cataleptic impression satisfies the following criteria:

1: It derives from an existent object.
2: It accurately represents the object.
3. It is stamped on the sensoria.
4: It contains a sign of its truth that distinguishes it from non-cataleptic impressions.[65]

In the face of equipollence about, for example, the existence of a table offered for inspection, the Stoic would argue that a perceiver can know that the table exists because he or she has a cataleptic impression of it. When the Pyrrhonist then asks, 'How can the perceiver know that the perception of the table is a cataleptic impression?', the Stoic replies 'Because cataleptic impressions attest to their own truth'. They have a distinguishing feature, a distinctness, endurance or vividness, that non-cataleptic conceptions do not have. According to the Stoics, then, the sceptics are wrong to withhold assent from all of our beliefs, including our beliefs about the external world, because many of them are founded on the certainty of cataleptic impression.

Let us pause here to assess how well the Stoic is doing. The Pyrrhonist, it seems, is still owed a Stoic account of how cataleptic impressions are distinguishable in such a way that ensures they can be reliably distinguished from non-cataleptic ones. And until the Stoic provides this account in a fashion that escapes the sceptic's net, the Pyrrhonist will suspend judgement as to whether any supposedly cataleptic impressions are actually distinct from non-cataleptic ones.

On the other hand, the Stoic may concede that sometimes cataleptic impressions are not recognised as such, and may also concede that someone blinded by prejudice or defective in some other way may falsely identify a non-cataleptic impression as cataleptic. But they will still want to know why we must withhold assent from the impressions that seem obviously cataleptic. The critical question, in other words, is whether there are non-cataleptic impressions that are indistinguishable from cataleptic ones, and if so, whether we must suspend judgement.

At this point, even if this question can be answered, it seems fair to say that the Stoics are losing the battle against scepticism. The Pyrrhonists, after all, are not asking us to deny that we can have epistemically interesting perceptions. They are only asking us to suspend judgement. The Stoics, on the other hand, are demanding that we affirm as a fact our knowledge of certain impressions. As for how we can know that we have true impressions, the Stoics assure us, rather unconvincingly, that some impressions do bear in themselves the signature of truth.

Yet it is worth noticing that the Stoics, rather than affirm that we can have knowledge in the face of Pyrrhonist equipollence, a position which would free us from this suspension of judgement, have set the bar higher than is necessary. They seek to show not only that we have knowledge, but that we *know* that we have knowledge. To use the Stoic Zeno's analogy, knowledge of a cataleptic impression must be like one hand grasping the other hand, which bears a true impression.[66] One likely motivating factor for this high standard was the Stoic doctrine of the sage who never made a mistake. To never make a mistake, the Stoics thought, one must always be assured that the knowledge one has is true.

Perhaps this short reconstruction does not do the Stoic line enough justice, but I do not see how the strategy of founding beliefs on cataleptic impressions can avoid either disagreement at worst or circularity at best. It seems we must either just know certain impressions to be cataleptic – circularity – or know for a good reason, which pushes us deeper into the sceptic's net. And Reid, I think, would agree. As he writes in the *Active Powers*:

> [W]hen we attempt to prove by direct argument what is really self-evident, the reasoning will always be inconclusive; for it will either take for granted the thing to be proved, or something not more evident; and so, instead of giving strength to the conclusion, will rather tempt those to doubt of it, who never did so before.[67]

Externalism and Internalism

We can avoid these problems, however, if we make escaping the sceptic's net no harder than necessary. All we need to defeat scepticism is to show that our beliefs are justified, not that we are justified in our justification. Along these lines, Barnes contrasts internalist and externalist approaches to foundational beliefs, and suggests that one promising way to defeat the Pyrrhonist challenge is to adopt the latter. To make this case, Barnes asks that we consider the difference between these two statements.

A) Because I believe reason R, I believe proposition P.
AND
B) Because of reason R, I believe proposition P.[68]

The first case – which Barnes takes as a formulation of internalism – sounds like the Stoic line: because I believe that impression P is cataleptic, I believe that P. The second case – which Barnes offers as a formulation of externalism – sounds like a description of Reidian judgement based on non-propositional evidence. To see this more clearly, let us return once more to Reid's description of the first principles of contingent truths in the *Intellectual Powers*:

> the judgement follows the apprehension of them necessarily, and both [judgement and apprehension] are equally the work of nature, and the result of original powers. There is no searching for evidence, no weighing of arguments; the proposition is not deduced or inferred from another.[69]

It seems that Reid indeed gives us something like Barnes' suggestion. His approach is externalist by virtue of the fact that Reidian first principles of contingent truth are not believed for the sake of other beliefs, but for the sake of (self-)evidence. Applying this account to the first principle 'that the material world exists', Reid writes that we are so constructed that the immense amount of 'evidence discerned by us forces a corresponding degree of assent'.[70]

To see how Reid's externalism meets the Pyrrhonist's challenge, let us return briefly to the debate between the Stoic and the Pyrrhonist. When we paused the discussion, the Stoic owed us an account of how cataleptic impressions could justify themselves, and the Pyrrhonist owed us an explanation as to why we ought to withhold judgement from the great many impressions that seem to be cataleptic. Although we called the match for the Pyrrhonist above, the argument appears to favour the dogmatists when catalepsis is exchanged for Reidian self-evidence. Here the Pyrrhonist might reasonably question Reid's assertion that some propositions are intuitively accepted based on judgement from evidence, but Reid places a much larger burden on the Pyrrhonist by asking why we ought to suspend judgement on a proposition in the face of compelling evidence for it. Reid's strategy, therefore, is not to meet the sceptic head on, but to shift the burden of evidence.[71]

To see how this strategy works, consider again the perception of a table. Adapting an argument from Sextus regarding the existence of a tower, the Pyrrhonists could 'oppose what appears to what appears' and point out that the table looks differently when observed from different angles and at different distances.[72] Even if a Reidian were to consider this evidence against the existence of the table, they may oppose this sceptical argument by pointing to other factors which support a belief in the table's existence. Our senses of sight, touch, hearing and – should we be brave – taste and smell tell us it is there. Previous experience tells us it is there. Our fellow interlocutors tell us it is there. This seems to be compelling evidence, in two senses. First, it is naturally compelling in that there is so much evidence of its existence that, absent madness, we cannot act as if it isn't there. Lose focus for a moment and we will inevitably find ourselves walking around it, setting our tea on it, thinking about where it could be moved for greater convenience, wondering about the last time it was cleaned. Second, the preponderance of evidence seems to be on Reid's side. On the Pyrrhonist side is the regular and predictable (and, Reid would hasten to add, mathematically necessary and describable) phenomenon of visual perspective.[73] On the Reidian side, on the other hand, is the vast majority, if not the entirety, of our inferential and non-inferential judgements about the table before us. Even adding the likely Pyrrhonist arguments concerning the unreliability of testimony and the faithlessness of dreams, it seems the scales are more than slightly tipped towards the Reidian dogmatist.

If this is correct, then the equivalence Brown drew between Reid and Hume regarding scepticism is at least partially wrong. By appealing to the propositions immediately approved by judgement without reasoning, Reid may sidestep the sceptic's net in a way unavailable to proponents of the way of ideas like Hume, who, because of metaphysical orthodoxy, box themselves into the more difficult, internalist position of justifying all beliefs with other beliefs. As we saw with the Stoic doctrine of cataleptic impression, once we have abandoned non-inferential evidence, we have played into the Pyrrhonist's hands. There are only two directions, towards the infinite or in a circle. Reid, on the other hand, does not impose a similar burden on himself. Instead of taking the internalist position A, where because I believe in reason R, I believe in P, Reid holds the externalist position B, where reason R is non-propositional evidence, which requires no further justification.

Thus, for a narrow, Reidian definition of the word 'reason' – in which 'reason' means only the ability 'to draw conclusions that are not self-evident from those that are' – Brown was correct to say that Reid allowed that we have 'no reason for our belief' in the external world.[74] But this misses Reid's point. Reid admits that we do not believe in the veracity of our external senses on account of (propositional) reasons. Yet propositional reasons are not the only rational ground of belief. There is also evidence, and in the case of the existence of the external world, there is so much evidence for it, our belief is both justified and irresistible.

The above argument will not, of course, be wholly convincing to everyone. Sceptics will ask how we know that we need not justify every belief with another belief, and how we know that self-evident propositions are justified on account of evidence. They will also want more clarification of and justification for Reid's doctrine of self-evidence. Yet even if we have not, in the foregoing, defeated scepticism once and for all, we have at least gained some purchase on Reid's methodology, reasons for rejecting the way of ideas and epistemology. With these in hand, we now turn to our main topic, Reid's moral philosophy, starting with an examination of his arguments against moral subjectivism.

Notes

1. The same effect may be generated by focusing on something in the distance while placing our finger in the foreground of our visual field.

2. For a discussion of this topic, see Van Cleve, 'Reid on Single and Double Vision: Mechanics and Morals'; Foster, 'Reid's Response to Hume on Double Vision'; and Van Cleve, 'Double Appearances are Double Trouble: Reply to Foster'.

3. Reid, *Inquiry into the Human Mind*, p. 148.

4. Reid, *Essays on the Intellectual Powers*, p. 96. See also Broadie, 'Reid Making Sense of Moral Sense', p. 93.

5. Note that Reid lists three features of perception, separating the belief which accompanies conception and the immediacy of the belief into two. For the sake of simplicity, I have combined them into the single feature of immediate belief.

6. See Wolterstorff, *Thomas Reid and the Story of Epistemology*, p. 8.

7. Wolterstorff, *Thomas Reid and the Story of Epistemology*, pp. 8–11. In a later article, Wolterstorff returns to the topic of Reidian conception, and finds it more confusing that he previously allowed. See Wolterstorff 'Reason and Trust in Reid', pp. 187–188.

8. Reid, *Essays on the Intellectual Powers*, p. 296.

9. Wolterstorff, *Thomas Reid and the Story of Epistemology*, p. 10 and Reid, *Essays on the Intellectual Powers*, p. 295.

10. Reid, *Essays on the Intellectual Powers*, p. 408. Note that, according to Copenhaver, this does not mean that all of these judgements generate propositional attitudes, writing that 'belief or judgment represents the object apprehended by conception as being thus-and-such'. Of course, to express these judgements in words, we must take a propositional attitude toward them. See Copenhaver 'Reid on the Moral Sense', pp. 82–83.

11. Reid, *Essays on the Intellectual Powers*, p. 406.

12. See Reid, *Essays on the Intellectual Powers*, p. 434.

13. Reid, *Essays on the Intellectual Powers*, p. 422.

14. Reid, *Essays on the Intellectual Powers*, p. 422.

15. Reid, *Essays on the Intellectual Powers*, p. 433.

16. Reid, *Essays on the Intellectual Powers*, p. 452.

17. Reid, *Essays on the Intellectual Powers*, p. 452. For a concern about Reid's use of 'in itself' see Wolterstorff, *Thomas Reid and the Story of Epistemology*, p. 222.

18. Reid, *Essays on the Intellectual Powers*, p. 452.

19. See Van Cleve, *Problems from Reid*, p. 304.
20. Wolterstorff, 'Reid on Common Sense', p. 83.
21. Van Cleve, *Problems from Reid*, pp. 345–347.
22. Davis, *Thomas Reid's Ethics*, p. 68.
23. Reid, *Essays on the Intellectual Powers*, p. 453. While Reid frequently uses the terms 'first principle' and 'self-evident principle' as if they are exchangeable, his discussion of Newton's first laws of motion show that the latter are a subset of the former. Typically, that is, our intuitive judgements are based on self-evidence, but sometimes they are based on evidence gathered through experimentation. As Reid is clear that the first principles of morals are self-evidently true, and as it seems that, for Reid, the great majority of first principles are self-evidently true, I will use them synonymously, as Reid typically does. See Reid, '68. *To Lord Kames*', in *The Correspondence of Thomas Reid*, p. 124. See also Wood, 'Introduction', in *Thomas Reid on Mathematics and Natural Philosophy*, p. lx.
24. Wittgenstein, *Philosophical Investigations*, §1.
25. Reid, *Essays on the Intellectual Powers*, p. 455. See Aristotle, 'Posterior Analytics', p. 117.
26. Reid, *Essays on the Intellectual Powers*, p. 490.
27. Reid, *Essays on the Intellectual Powers*, pp. 470–489. Emphasis original.
28. Reid, *Essays on the Intellectual Powers*, p. 456.
29. Newton, *Opticks*, p. 405. See Reid, *Essays on the Intellectual Powers*, p. 458.
30. Reid, *Essays on the Intellectual Powers*, p. 454.
31. Reid, *Essays on the Intellectual Powers*, p. 459.
32. Reid, *Essays on the Intellectual Powers*, p. 462.
33. Reid, *Essays on the Active Powers*, p. 278.
34. Reid, *Essays on the Active Powers*, pp. 86–87.
35. Reid, *Essays on the Active Powers*, p. 88
36. One could object that my belief here is justified by expert testimony. And Reid would agree. Yet for a mathematical proof, such justification can be at best partial.
37. Reid, *Essays on the Intellectual Powers*, p. 427.
38. Reid, *Essays on the Intellectual Powers*, p. 433.
39. Reid, *Essays on the Intellectual Powers*, p. 424.
40. Reid, *Essays on the Intellectual Powers*, p. 424.
41. On other ways to understand the phrase 'common judgement', see Greco, 'Common Sense in Thomas Reid', pp. 143–145.
42. Reid, *Essays on the Intellectual Powers*, p. 426.

43. Reid, *Essays on the Intellectual Powers*, p. 426.
44. Reid, *Essays on the Intellectual Powers*, p. 100.
45. Reid, *Essays on the Intellectual Powers*, p. 433.
46. Reid, *Essays on the Active Powers*, p. 185.
47. Although, see Wolterstorff, 'Reid on Common Sense', p. 81.
48. *Mutatis mutandis,* the same distinction can be drawn with principles 1, 3 and 10 above.
49. See Lehrer, 'Chisholm, Reid, and the Problem of the Epistemic Surd', p. 40, and Van Cleve, *Problems from Reid*, pp. 308–326. See also Wolterstorff, 'Reid on Common Sense', pp. 91–95.
50. Reid, *Essays on the Intellectual Powers*, p. 521.
51. See especially Van Cleve, *Problems from Reid*, pp. 301–327 and Wolterstorff 'Reid on Common Sense'.
52. Wolterstorff, 'Reason and Trust in Reid', p. 186.
53. Reid, *Essays on the Intellectual Powers*, p. 452
54. Mackintosh, *Dissertation on the Progress of History*, p. 174a. See also Rysiew, 'Reid and Epistemic Naturalism', p. 30.
55. See, among others, Winkler, 'The New Hume'.
56. See, for example, Andreotta and Levine, 'Revisionism Gone Awry: Since When Hasn't Hume Been a Sceptic?'.
57. Hume, *Enquiry Concerning Human Understanding*, p. 160.
58. Hume, *Enquiry Concerning Human Understanding*, p. 161.
59. Reid, *Essays on the Intellectual Powers*, p. 461.
60. Sextus Empiricus, *Outlines of Scepticism*, p. 6.
61. Sextus Empiricus, *Outlines of Scepticism*, pp. 12, 40, 43.
62. Barnes, *The Toils of Scepticism*, p. 118.
63. Barnes, *The Toils of Scepticism*, p. 114.
64. This is all I will have space to say about Pyrrhonism, and in doing so I acknowledge that I am leaving quite a lot on the table – most urgently, whether the sceptic's net reconstructed by Barnes faithfully represents Pyrrhonism. See, for example, Burnyeat, 'Can the Sceptic Live his Scepticism?', pp. 32–35. According to Burnyeat, the modes are intended to be used not in concert, but as standalone rejoinders. In any case, whether or not Barnes' net is truly Pyrrhonist, it is an interesting sceptical argument, and a challenging one.
65. See Hankinson, 'Stoic Epistemology', p. 61.
66. 'Zeno used to demonstrate . . . with gestures. When he had put his hand out flat in front of him with his fingers straight, he would say: "An impression is like this". Next, after contracting his fingers a bit: "Assent is like this". Then, when he had bunched his hand up to make a fist, he would say that that was an "apprehension" or

"grasp". (This image also suggested the name he gave to it, *katalêpsis* [lit. grasp].) Finally, when he had put his left hand on top, squeezing his fist tight with some force, he would say that scientific knowledge was like that: a state none but the wise enjoyed.' Cicero, *On Academic Scepticism*, p. 84, §145.

67. Reid, *Essays on the Active Powers*, p. 270.
68. See Barnes, *The Toils of Scepticism*, p. 131.
69. Reid, *Essays on the Intellectual Powers*, p. 452.
70. Reid, *Essays on the Intellectual Powers*, p. 481.
71. See Harris, 'Reid on Hume on Justice', p. 205.
72. Sextus Empiricus, *Outlines of Scepticism*, p. 11.
73. See Reid, *Inquiry into the Human Mind*, pp. 103–112 and Reid, *Intellectual Powers*, pp. 182–183.
74. Reid, *Essays on the Intellectual Powers*, p. 433. Mackintosh, *Dissertation on the Progress of History*, p. 174a.

3

Reid's Arguments against Moral Subjectivism

In the previous two chapters we saw that Reid's epistemology is best understood as an attempt to replace the theory of ideas by describing perception not as the passive reception of impressions and ideas, but as the product of active apprehension and judgement. Further, we also saw that it was Hume's unflinching extrapolation from the way of ideas, and the conflict of those extrapolations with Baconianism, which spurred Reid to undertake this project. In turning to the chief topic of this book, we find a similar approach in Reid's moral philosophy. In parallel with his epistemology, Reid's moral theory is an attempt to oppose a passive account of ethical evaluation with an active account of moral judgement. And, in formulating this moral theory, Reid chiefly contrasts his account with the one we find in Hume.

In this chapter, we therefore begin with an outline of Hume's account of moral distinctions, which proposes that they arise from our sentiments and not our reason. We then examine the effectiveness of three counter-arguments which Reid levels against Hume's moral theory. By the end of this chapter, we will, I hope, not only see why Reid rejected Hume's account of moral distinctions, but also see that, despite several interpretive mistakes, Reid gives us good reasons to do the same.

Hume's Moral Theory

To give a full accounting of Hume's moral philosophy is difficult, for at least two reasons. First, like his epistemology, Hume's full moral theory is intricate and subtle, and resists easy summary. Second, in addition to various smaller essays, Hume presents his ethics twice, in Book III of the *Treatise of Human Nature*, and again in the *Enquiry into the Principles of Morals*. While both books lay out similar accounts, they clearly differ in their emphases and style.

On account of these factors, even when Hume is read carefully, his moral theory generates a large number of interpretations, of varying levels of compatibility.[1] Happily, despite these difficulties, the heart of Hume's theory – and, conveniently, also the chief issue with which Reid disagrees – is easily explained.

To see the central idea of Hume's ethics, consider this famous passage from the *Treatise*:

> In every system of morality, which I have hitherto met with, I have always remark'd, that the author proceeds for some time in the ordinary way of reasoning, and establishes the being of a God, or makes observations concerning human affairs; when of a sudden I am surpriz'd to find, that instead of the usual copulations of propositions, *is*, and *is not*, I meet with no proposition that is not connected with an *ought* or *ought not*. This change is imperceptible; but it is, however, of the last consequence.[2]

For this passage, and others like it, Hume is sometimes labelled a moral sceptic. But this label is imprecise. Hume explicitly affirms the reality of moral distinctions in both the *Treatise* and the moral *Enquiry*. Further, although this passage bears several incompatible interpretations among Hume scholars, its general meaning is clear. Hume doubts not the existence of virtue and vice, but rather the common account of their origin.

According to Hume, the popular account of morality goes roughly like this: human beings are a certain way, God – perhaps – is a certain way, therefore reason demands that we ought to act thus and so. For Hume, this account is illogical because it contains an illicit transition from description to normativity.

This transition from 'is' to 'ought' is unjustified, according to Hume, on account of his understanding of reason. Extrapolating from his epistemology, Hume writes that 'morals . . . cannot be deriv'd from reason because . . . [m]orals excite passions, and produce or prevent actions', while '[r]eason of itself is utterly impotent in this particular'.[3] In other words, reason is never strictly practical. The most it can do with respect to action is tell us how to achieve practical ends; it can never tell us which ends to choose. According to Hume, in this circumscribed arena, reason discovers the truth or falsity of propositions in two manners: either with respect to the actual existence and character of facts, or among relationships of ideas.[4] In the first case, reason chiefly deals with sensory impressions regarding the external world and internal impressions regarding our passions. And in the second, reason compares abstract ideas, as one does when computing sums or solving a mathematical equation. Thus, although reason may tell us that we feel a certain way, have a certain impression or recognise a certain relation, those deliverances of reason are purely 'is' statements. They report something about the world to us, but do not, absent a coinciding passion or desire, move us to action. Thus, we cannot move from 'is' to 'ought' on the basis of reason alone because normativity does not fall within reason's remit.

To illustrate his belief that moral normativity cannot be found among reason's first objects, 'matters of fact', Hume gives the following example:

> Take any action allow'd to be vicious: willful murder, for instance. Examine it in all lights, and see if you can find a matter of fact or real existence, which you call *vice*. There is no other matter of fact in the case. The vice entirely escapes you, as long as you consider the object.[5]

Entering into Hume's imaginative example draws a compelling picture. Paint in the details however you like. There is no property in a murder weapon (knife, steel, sharp, seven inches), a wound (between the seventh and eighth ribs on the left side), a dead body (five foot eight inches long, male, decreasing in temperature from 37 degrees Celsius to room level) or even the motion of stabbing (with the right hand, thrice), that signifies vice. Again, Hume is not denying that wilful murder is vicious. He believes it is. He is only claiming that the viciousness cannot lie in some real property of the murder.

Could moral normativity lie in reason's other object, 'relationships among ideas'? Given the way we often talk about linked ideas such as duty, autonomy and freedom, this option may seem more promising. Hume disagrees. Consider patricide, he offers. We blame the son who dispatches his father, but not the acorn that grows so tall it kills the oak from which it fell.[6] The two relations, claims Hume, are exactly the same. At first blush, this example appears less successful than the last. What about will? What about intention? The tree does what it does involuntarily, unintentionally. In the worst of circumstances, the son kills deliberately. Like the example of wilful murder above, Hume's point is not to deny that an instance of intentional patricide is blameworthy. His point is that telling a story about willing and intending to kill one's father does not change the relationship of 'child kills parent'. It merely describes a relationship of cause and effect, and this, like the relationship of parent and offspring, does not move us from description to normativity. Whatever normativity adheres among ideas – for example: sons ought not to kill their fathers – was, according to Hume, already there to be discovered. Reason may affirm that we feel the wilful murder of a father by a son to be vicious, but that is only the affirmation of truth, the denial of falsity. This is all that reason can do. It does not give us reasons for action.

If not reason, what then is the origin of the moral 'ought', examined by countless moralists, and powerfully motivating to (the vast majority of) human beings? Hume's answer is sentiment. 'Morality,' Hume famously declares, 'is more properly felt than judg'd of'.[7]

The position that moral distinctions are the product of our feelings and not of our reason is the heart of Hume's ethics, and also the chief point of contention between Hume and Reid. Yet Hume's sentimentalist moral theory immediately prompts a question. Assuming that moral distinctions are the product of our sentiments and not of our reason, what is it that our sentiments find appealing in those actions we consider moral? In the *Enquiry Concerning the Principles of Morals*, Hume tells us that all acts considered morally praiseworthy are so by virtue of being immediately agreeable (*dulce*) to human sentiment, or secondarily agreeable on account of being useful (*utile*) to ourselves or others.[8]

Regarding the first, Hume argues that it is just the case that certain qualities are immediately and naturally approved by sentiment. According to Hume, these immediately approved virtues may be further divided into two categories. Some qualities, such as cheerfulness, are immediately agreeable to ourselves. And some, such as good manners, are immediately agreeable to others.[9] These categories are not meant by Hume to be exclusive. For, by the functioning of sympathy, many immediately agreeable virtues, such as courage and utility, appear to straddle the line. Whatever their precise provenance, though, what these virtues have in common is that they are all approved on account of our basic human, or 'first' nature.

As for those virtues we approve due to their utility, Hume argues that, for the most part, we find them virtuous on account of the agreeableness of utility, the *dulce* of *utile*. Utility, as we just saw, is one of those qualities that Hume believes we naturally and immediately find sweet on account of our natural sympathy and concern for others and ourselves.[10] And so, by extension, those habits and actions which reliably render utility become sweet to us as well. Chief among the virtues approved on account of their utility is justice, which derives its moral approbation 'from its necessary *use* to the intercourse and social state of mankind'.[11] Thus, justice is approved in a second-order fashion. Only in the case that its conventions are useful is it approved, and then chiefly because usefulness, and not justice itself, is *dulce*. If the circumstances of human life were otherwise, so that previously useful virtues became useless, then they would not be approved. This is because, unlike immediately agreeable virtues such as cheerfulness and wit, the virtue of justice often directs us towards actions which seem inconvenient in the moment, until we consider their great overall utility.

This, in (very) short, is Hume's account. As with all of Hume's philosophy, there are many interpretations, but most agree that Hume is some version of a subjectivist sentimentalist: subjectivist in the sense that moral distinctions depend upon our responses, and sentimentalist in the sense that the relevant responses are, at bottom, emotive and not rational. What Hume is not, is a moral sceptic. He does not deny the existence of moral obligations in our social lives, or counsel us to ignore or strenuously doubt our moral inclinations. What he denies is that we originally become aware of, and are motivated to honour, moral norms through reason. Thus, while reason may point out to us various circumstances which give rise to moral distinctions – as when it tells us that *a murder has here occurred* – moral 'oughts' are not, ultimately, products of reason; they are first- and/or second-order natural sentiments of approbation or aversion.

Against Hume's subjectivist account there are several likely complaints. One shallow complaint is that Hume reduces justice to private utility. To this, Hume has an easy reply: Since, by the natural operation of sympathy, we approve of the utility of justice itself, and not merely first-personal utility, even onerous conventions of justice take on the lustre of goodness so long as they tend towards public good. As evidence of this tendency, Hume points to our approbation of those who act justly, even when they are our political enemies, or when their actions run counter to our personal self-interest.[12]

A second common complaint is that Hume's moral philosophy opens the door to relativism. If all 'ought' statements are based on how we feel, how do we adjudicate among conflicting feelings about what constitutes good manners and public utility? Do you have your morality and I have mine, in the same way that you prefer coffee while I prefer tea? This question does not appear to have seriously bothered Hume. While he grants that different people and communities may use different means to cultivate the agreeable character traits and produce the social utility of which we naturally approve, Hume believes that well-functioning human beings are, by and large, one way and not another. This does not mean that Hume intends to assert, against all evidence, that every moral issue can be resolved easily, or that the conventions of justice and manners are uniform across history and culture. He is well aware that, for example, some societies assert that polygamy is more appropriate than monogamy, while others take the opposite position.[13] Yet despite differences such as these, Hume believes that, so long as society does not suffer a critical failure, it is highly unlikely that murder, say, or rudeness, will suddenly become fashionable. When we can manage it, human beings are, according to Hume, just the sort of creatures that will eschew certain practices and approve others.

Some philosophers have found this reply to the accusation of relativism insufficient. Alasdair MacIntyre, for example, believes Hume's appeal to human nature is nothing more than a mask for the conventional values of the ruling elite in eighteenth-century Scotland.[14] There is, to be fair, some truth to MacIntyre's accusation. Hume's opinions on race and gender, for example, seem hopelessly outdated if not outright reprehensible today.[15] Yet, let this much be said in Hume's defence. If we grant his belief in the general agreement of human nature, then we have no special reason to fear radical relativism within his account. Regarding those virtues we naturally find sweet, if our very nature makes intelligence and wit pleasant to us as surely as dogs' very nature makes venison delicious to them, we should not expect that disagreements about what constitutes good manners will dissolve into mutual unintelligibility. Similarly, we need not fear radical relativism regarding justice. So long as the general run of circumstance makes certain conventions of human behaviour useful and therefore pleasant to us, we will continue to view intentional acts of theft and murder as vicious, while approving a limited range of social conventions. It will, according to Hume, almost always be useful and pleasant for us to be safe from arbitrary violence in the same way that it will almost always be more useful and pleasant for us to eat oats than ivy.

In sum, then, what we find in Hume is not an attempt to advance moral scepticism or moral relativism, or even to overturn the greater part of conventional morality. It is, rather, an attempt to ground our moral lives in the subjective experience of human beings. This is not to say that Hume thought his sentimentalist moral theory would have no effect whatsoever on moral practice. Hume believed, for example, that the naturalisation of moral distinctions would show the falsity of religious piety as manifested in what he called the 'monkish virtues': practices such as fasting, humility and celibacy, which receive moral approbation but are not immediately pleasing, and generate no social benefits.[16] Still, when contrasted with some of his contemporaries, who alternatively attempted to revolutionise moral practice by reducing all moral distinctions to considerations of benevolence or self-interest, Hume's ethics do not appear especially radical.[17]

Despite this apparent ethical moderation, Hume's theory of morals and rejection of pietistic virtues was widely condemned in his own time.[18] Reid himself seems to vacillate on the overall effects of Hume's ethics, at times downplaying the influence it is likely to have on popular morality, and at other times declaring that it has 'a tendency to subvert all faith and fair-dealing'.[19] As for particular complaints, Reid levels a great many, both large and small, against Hume's ethics. To canvass them all – even all the interesting ones – would take too much time and space. Yet we may form an accurate picture of Reid's reasons for rejecting Hume's moral subjectivism by examining three of Reid's larger complaints, given in the form of *experimenta crucis*, which seem to strike at the heart of Hume's conception of justice. They are: first, that Hume's moral theory contradicts his practical ethics; second, that Hume's theory runs counter to our moral practice in extreme situations; and, finally, that Hume's theory misdescribes our typical moral language.

Reid's First Argument: Hume Contradicts Himself

Reid's first argument attempts to show that Hume's moral theory and practical ethics are in conflict with each other. The focus of this argument is Hume's famous 'sensible knave' passage from the moral *Enquiry*.

> According to the imperfect way in which human affairs are conducted, a sensible knave, in particular incidents, may think that an

act of iniquity or infidelity will make a considerable addition to his fortune without causing any considerable breach in the social union and confederacy. That *honesty* is the best policy may be a good general rule, but it is liable to many exceptions and he, it may perhaps be thought, conducts himself with most wisdom, who observes the general rule and takes advantage of all the exceptions.[20]

This passage sets the matter before us. Hume does not deny that, at times, utility and the conventions of justice diverge. Immediately after this passage, however, he does deny that in those cases we ought always to prefer utility to conventional justice. To Reid, this seems to be a flat contradiction of Hume's understanding of justice, which, as we saw, is approved on account of its utility.

How can Hume state that justice is founded on utility, but that the knave ought to forego utility in the name of justice? As Reid puts it, 'the reasoning of the *sensible knave*' is 'justly founded upon the principles of the Enquiry and the Treatise of Human Nature'.[21] Indeed, as Reid observes, if we morally approve those actions which increase overall utility, then, so long as the knave's action leads to more utility for himself than those he victimises, violating the general conventions of justice in just the way the sensible knave proposes is more than sensible, it is morally required!

Note that this may be the case even if the utility in question is public utility. For, if the knave obtains more benefit than he produces harm for others – perhaps on account of their ignorance – he has increased public utility by increasing his own private utility. To dress the argument in modern clothing, Reid believes Hume is proposing an act-utilitarian theory of morals, according to which actions that increase public utility are always to be preferred over actions which decrease public utility or increases it less. Therefore, so long as the sensible knave's dishonesty leads to greater overall utility than the course of action proposed by conventional morality, disapproval of the sensible knave from this standpoint is irrational. As Reid sees it, this contradiction forces a choice upon Hume: he must either give up his argument that the sensible knave sacrifices his character by acting against the conventions of justice, or abandon the idea that '*justice is an artificial virtue, approved solely for its utility*'.[22] To do the former would require Hume to acknowledge that his moral theory leads to a moral practice radically at odds with conventional morality – something Hume seems reluctant to do. Yet to do the latter would be to give up his account of the nature of justice.

At first glance, Reid's argument against Hume may seem strong. Yet, some commentators hold that Hume's account of justice and his condemnation of the sensible knave are not, in fact, in tension, because he wisely separates the intention behind an act from an act's actual effects, and places the approbation of virtue on the former.[23] On this reading, what is most useful, and therefore approved, is the motive to act justly, not the immediate results of individual actions. Or, as Hume himself puts it in the *Treatise*, ''Tis evident that when we praise any actions, we regard only the motives that produced them, and consider the actions as signs or indications of certain principles in the mind and temper. The external performance has no merit.'[24] It is this evaluation of motive over immediate result that the sensible knave does not see.

In other words, by the light of this interpretation of Hume, the knave's mistake is to think that we ought to consider justice on a consequentialist and case-by-case basis, using our own best judgements about utility over and above the standard account of justice. To the sensible knave, what counts as justice is therefore neither conventional nor focused on motive, but narrowly results-oriented. Yet because the knave ignores intention, this is a mistake, and shows that the knave has a poor understanding of the usefulness of justice.

This interpretation of Hume is not without its problems. For one thing, it seems to run contrary to what he says about the relationship between virtue and justice in other places.[25] And for another, Hume clearly says that 'public utility is the *sole* origin of justice, and that reflections on the beneficial consequences of this virtue are the *sole* foundation of its merit'.[26] I will not attempt to address all these interpretive problems here. Yet, if Hume truly emphasises intention over result, then when Hume says that justice is approved for its utility, what he is really saying is that justice is considered a virtue because we approve of those who seek the good of society. We may therefore state the sensible knave's mistake succinctly: he exercises prudence when he ought to practice justice. And, in doing so, Hume writes, the knave has 'sacrificed the invaluable enjoyment of a character, with themselves at least, for the acquisition of worthless toys and geegaws'.[27]

If interpretation is correct, and Hume believes justice is worth pursuing based on the tendency of just intentions to secure the good of public utility, but not reliant on the utility of justly motivated actions in every particular case, then the sensible knave's practice is in conflict with Hume's moral theory. The knave has already granted that honesty is usually the best policy – already acknowledged that the just thing to do is act honestly – but decides not to act accordingly. He therefore has no excuse. Should the sensible knave press the point and insist that actual, instantiated public utility, and not the motive of justice, should be our guide to action, Hume can only shrug. To him, such an evaluation is both empirically inaccurate and practically unwise. As he sees it, human beings tend to approve of motives which secure utility in the long run rather than the consequences of any one action. On this reading, then, Hume has a ready reply to Reid's criticism of the sensible knave passage and can plausibly condemn the action of the sensible knave on his own principles.

Reid's Second Argument: Hume Misdescribes Moral Practice at the Margins

Reid's second argument against Hume's theory of morals is that, by founding justice on utility, he misdescribes our moral prac-tice in extreme circumstances. According to Hume, in cases of an extreme sort, justice as we know it loses its meaning. This, both Reid and Hume agree, is merely the logical consequence of Hume's belief that justice is desired on account of its utility. In the *Essays Concerning the Principles of Morals*, Hume argues that in the extreme conditions of paradise and crisis, the conventions of justice become incoherent.[28]

Regarding paradise, Hume explains that, should all want be relieved, either through a surplus of goods or the blossoming of universal and indefeasible benevolence, justice would be 'totally useless' and 'an idle ceremonial' with no 'place in the catalogue of virtues'.[29] Hume's reasoning here is straightforward. If all the goods that justice might secure in more difficult circumstances are easy at hand, or if everyone naturally acted according to universal benevolence, what possible purpose could the practices of justice serve? The intention to increase public utility is useless because public utility has already reached its maximum level.

Reversing the situation reveals the same result. What if the resources necessary for life became not inexhaustibly bountiful but dangerously scarce, as may happen in occasions of siege or ship-wreck? Hume suggests that on these occasions too, justice ceases to be a virtue. A person in great crisis will find that 'justice being no longer of use to his own safety or that of others, he must consult the dictates of self-preservation alone, without concern for those who no longer merit his care and attention'.[30] As with his two paradises, the reason is the same. The intention to increase public utility is a virtue only if public utility can actually be increased by the conventions of justice. In situations where they cannot, justice becomes useless at best and harmful at worst.

Hume emphasises the dissolution of justice in these circumstances for two reasons. First, he believes that they demonstrate the conventionality of justice. In circumstances where conventions of justice fail to produce (more) utility, those conventions are pointless. Second, Hume also believes that most people will agree with his assessment that, in paradise and crisis, the practices of justice are useless and therefore pointless.

Reid questions both these assertions. With respect to the proposed conventionality of justice, Reid makes four objections. First, Reid finds it puzzling that in Hume's first proposed paradise, an abundance of material goods is supposed to obviate the need for justice. Certainly, there are many persistent issues of justice which would no longer concern us in a condition of infinite material abundance; but not all, or even most. Even if Hume is correct about the conventionality of justice, in order to pursue Humean utility in such a state, we would still approve of the conventions of justice which prevent murder, slander and lying.[31]

Reid's recognition of Hume's oddly limited conception of justice calls into question Hume's first paradise – the paradise of plenty. But it does not affect Hume's second proposed paradise, a paradise of benevolence. Thus, against this paradise, Reid levels a second complaint against the proposed conventionality of justice, arguing that, just because we show benevolence to one person or group, does not mean that in doing so we practise justice with respect to all.[32] In a benevolent paradise, it may be the case that in acting benevolently we also act justly, but it is not necessarily so. Consider nepotism. Giving a member of your family more than he or she deserves is an act of benevolence to that person. Yet, this does not mean that the act is also just, since nepotistic benevolence is often accomplished by unjustly taking resources or opportunities from others who deserve them, as the generally negative connotation of the word implies.

Third, according to Reid, because the concept of benevolence is dependent on the concept of justice, even if we can assume general and total benevolence, we still need a good idea of justice in order to intentionally act benevolently.[33] Without knowing what each deserves by right, how could we know that we are giving more than justice demands to some while taking care not to do so by giving others less? The concept of supererogatory action, in other words, requires a prior conception of duty.

And fourth, as Reid sees it, Hume himself appeals to conceptions of justice within the example of crisis. For Reid, it is non-controversial that certain obligations relating to property and contract ought to be temporarily suspended in times of crisis, so long as those obligations are replaced by a regime in which 'an equal partition' is given to those in danger.[34] Even if this temporary disregard for property rights is enacted by force, Reid believes it is still just, so long as there is a retrospective accounting for damages to property. In this way, the suspension of property rights in crisis is only a temporary modification of justice during unusual circumstances. Under this rubric, when the enemy is at the gate, the government may commandeer the contents of your larder and distribute it to those in need without concern for your property rights, so long as you are fairly compensated after the siege has been lifted.

In turning to evaluate the quality of Reid's objections, it is clear that his first criticism of Hume's account of justice is strong. Reid is surely correct that, even in a society in which material goods are infinitely abundant, there would still be many opportunities for injustice. The crucial flaw in Hume's argument here is that Hume oddly confines his discussion of justice to economic relations. Thus, unless Hume can supplement his account of justice either to rule out injustices like murder or slander, or reasonably limit his account of justice to considerations of property, his first paradisical example does not show that justice is solely approved for its utility.

By contrast, Reid's second argument, concerning Hume's paradise of benevolence, does not seem to hit the mark. If Reid had correctly read Hume here, he would have seen that his counterexample misfires because Hume's second proposed paradise is a state where all, by dint of overflowing natural generosity, are benevolent to all. Reid's second objection therefore does not apply to this example because it is, by stipulation, impossible to be benevolent to one person while acting unjustly to another in Hume's paradise of benevolence.

Similarly, Reid's third criticism rests upon a misreading of Hume. Here, Reid proposes that in Hume's paradise of benevolence, we cannot have a conception of benevolence without a prior conception of justice. Yet Hume only asserts that, in the case of manifest general benevolence, we would have no conception of justice, not that we would have no conception of justice while at the same time having a conception of benevolence. Thus, Hume can easily grant that we must understand the concept of justice to understand the concept of benevolence, while still maintaining that we might live in a paradise of benevolence without having any idea that the world could be otherwise.

Since Reid's second and third complaints – that is, his complaints against Hume's benevolent paradise – fail, it seems that Hume's assertion that universal benevolence negates the need for justice is not as absurd as Reid would have it. The same is true with Reid's fourth complaint, regarding siege and shipwreck. As with his second and third complaint above, Reid misconstrues Hume's example, adding the stipulation that during a crisis, property rights may be temporarily ignored so long as goods are distributed equitably, and restitution is made upon the resumption of regular order. This is not, however, Hume's position. For Hume, when the siege begins or the ship flounders, all bets are off. The conventions of justice are wholly useless and not, as they are for Reid, merely adapted in order to render justice in extreme conditions. Reid's fourth complaint is therefore also invalid. Hume does not appeal to justice in crisis without acknowledgement.

In other words, according to Hume, the inapplicability of justice in either a benevolent paradise or in crisis is total and does not change with the perspective in which these circumstances are viewed. At the cessation of radically benevolent or difficult times – when the utility that justice secures is either more or less at hand, and justice once again becomes useful – there are no grounds for praising the justness of the benevolent or decrying the viciousness of apparently unjust acts. Since justice, in these exceptional times, is useless, its obligation is 'suspended'.[35] Such suspension is more than temporary forbearance or modification, where the obligations of justice are held pending. Following a Humean suspension, there will be no retrospective accounting when life as we know it resumes. Rather, in those times, when justice fails to increase public utility, we are granted a full and total holiday from its conventions.

Stepping back for a moment, it seems at this point that Hume's account of justice has held up rather well against Reid. For, while it is true that Hume's example of the abundant paradise does not recognise the full scope of justice, Reid's three latter complaints – which all accuse Hume of inconsistency – miss the mark. Just as Hume does not contradict himself when he admonishes the sensible knave, neither does he sneak conceptions of justice into his examples of paradise and crisis. Still, this only goes to show that Hume is internally consistent, and not that, as he asserts, his examples of ethics *in extremis* describe actual moral practice. For, despite Hume's confidence, it is not at all obvious that people do believe that crisis obliterates the obligations of justice.

Consider, for instance, the event immortalised in Théodore Géricault's *Raft of the Medusa*. On 5 July 1816, the French frigate *Medusa* wrecked off the coast of Mauritania. Because there were not enough lifeboats for everyone on board, 146 passengers and crew members were loaded onto a hastily built and thinly supplied raft. Those placed on the raft were twice promised by the leaders in the lifeboats that they would be towed to safety and provisioned out of the lifeboats' stores. Shortly after clearing the wreckage of the *Medusa*, however, the raft was cut loose and, lacking navigational aids or even a functioning tiller, those on it were left to die. After thirteen days on the open sea, only fifteen survivors were rescued. On account of both the incompetence of the *Medusa*'s captain and the cowardly actions of the lifeboat crews – who violated their oaths and sacrificed their fellows in an attempt to secure their own safety – the incident became a scandal that inspired not just Géricault's work, but an international outcry.[36]

The abandonment of the raft of the *Medusa* is only one instance, but both true and speculative examples of this type are easily provided.[37] Any instance of looting or murder during a natural disaster, crisis or military siege will do. By contrast, it is difficult to think of examples that fit Hume's theory. Certainly, many people do abandon their duties in dire circumstances. Yet, even if one has sympathy for those who act contrary to justice in crisis, these violations are rarely treated as morally neutral, let alone morally laudable acts. Rather, in both fiction and history, we more commonly find moral revulsion towards those who do not observe justice, and moral approbation for those who do, in situations of crisis.

Since Reid misreads Hume's discussion of siege and shipwreck, he does not make this exact complaint, as we have seen. But in his discussion of another of Hume's speculative examples, Reid advances a similar line. The section in question immediately follows the discussion of siege and shipwreck in the moral *Enquiry* and concerns the possible existence of 'a species of creatures inter-mingled with men, which, though rational were possessed of such inferior strength, both of body and mind, that they were incapa-ble of all resistance'.[38] Here, Hume suggests that, since members of this species have no ability to resist exploitation, they cannot be considered part of the community bound by the conventions of justice. That is not to say that we ought to be cruel to them. As with our dealings with non-rational animals, to whom Hume compares his imaginary *misérables*, our natural instincts of com-passion and kindness will often, and, in accordance with human nature, should often direct our actions. As for justice, though, its conventions are unintelligible since there is simply no public utility to be gained by being fair to such unfortunates.

In response to this admission, Reid writes that, had 'Hume not owned to this sentiment . . . I should have thought it very unchari-table to impute it to him'.[39] Yet Reid agrees with Hume that the consequence follows from his theory of justice. For this reason, it seems safe to assume that Reid would have made a similar com-plaint regarding Hume's description of justice during a crisis, had he read the relevant section on siege and shipwreck correctly. There is a ghastly parallel between Hume's rational but helpless species within society, and the fate of the weak – both 'of body and mind', as Hume says – when society breaks down. Though both groups are populated with rational agents, neither group, whether living among us or drifting windward on a makeshift raft, can resist the actions of the strong.

Reid considers Hume's declaration that we owe nothing by way of justice to those who are incapable of retaliation counterintui-tive enough to cast serious doubt on Hume's moral theory, but Hume anticipates this line of criticism, and supplies a reply. In the *Enquiry Concerning the Principles of Morals*, Hume grants that we often do consider justice in circumstances where no public util-ity can be obtained through its conventions, but believes that this is a mistake, caused by habit.[40] This is, essentially, an error theory, premised on the idea that sympathy with those in hopeless situa-tions is exceedingly difficult. According to this response, the fact that it is hard to come up with examples where the abandonment of justice in crisis was approved, and relatively easy to come up with examples where it was not, ought not to surprise us, as the majority of these judgements are made by those who are living in a state where the conventions of justice are useful. Thus, Hume could suggest that, absent the blindness caused by the present utility of justice, we would see that the crews of the *Medusa*'s lifeboats made the correct choice: taking advantage of the weak is the choice that we also would, and should, make in similar circumstances.

Reid's Third Argument: Hume Contradicts Common Language

Whether or not one accepts Hume's above response, it is a fair point that the circumstances under discussion are (blessedly) rare. And the exceptional nature of siege and shipwreck makes it hard to judge whether Reid or Hume more accurately describe our actual moral practice.[41] Reid's third argument against Hume's theory of morals, however, is not so constrained. For, as Reid points out, if we accept Hume's theory of morals, we cannot make good sense of our everyday moral vocabulary.

Reid's first example is the linguistic difference between 'hurt' and 'injury'.[42] A rock falling from a cliff may hurt us, but it does us no injury unless it was intentionally pushed upon us. The same holds true for 'benefit' and 'favour'. Whereas an injury is a hurt in which we receive less than justice demands, a favour is a benefit that gives us more than justice demands. According to Reid, these distinctions run contrary to Hume's account of justice. For, if it is the agreeableness of usefulness that leads us to approve of justice, we have no grounds to distinguish between hurt and injury, or benefit and favour. Finding a £20 note on the sidewalk is, after all, just as useful as receiving one as a gift.

Notice, however, that this complaint only applies in the case that Hume holds that we approve of just actions because of their actual utility. As we saw when we discussed the sensible knave passage above, though, this may not be Hume's considered position. Under the interpretation we offered there, Hume holds that we evaluate the morality of actions based on the intention behind them – in which case this criticism does not apply. Hume may account for the distinction between hurt and injury, and benefit and favour, by appealing to the intentionality of the latter of each pair.

The same reply is not available, however, in two further and related complaints that Reid makes. In the first, Reid claims, *contra* Hume, that we mean to express more than a like or dislike towards an act when we say it is morally praiseworthy or blameworthy. As Reid points out, it is in no way strange to reasonably disagree with the statement 'that is wrong', but it would be very odd for someone to disagree with the statement 'I don't like that'. Yet, according to Hume's theory, these statements ought to be practically synonymous, since moral distinctions are based on either immediate agreeableness or the agreeableness of the utility.

Relatedly, according to Reid, in all known languages there is a distinction between feeling and judging, arising from an introspectively perceivable difference in the quality of these mental acts. Thus, we would not accept, as Reid humorously points out, a change in terminology such that a court judge would now be called a 'feeler'.[43] Reid is aware that this argument is susceptible to an objection based on the Baconian concern for misleading terminology. Perhaps the terminological difference between feeling and judging is as useless and misleading as the theory of the luminiferous ether. Yet, while Reid grants that languages may include false or misleading distinctions, he finds it highly unlikely to be the case here. If there were not a real difference between the acts of feeling and judging, such divisions would eventually fall out of use or become interchangeable in an obvious way.[44] The near universality of the distinction, on the other hand, provides evidence 'sufficient to sink any philosophical opinion' such as Hume's.[45]

According to Terence Cuneo, however, all is not well with Reid's examples here. Against it, he believes that Hume could justly claim that a person who is offended by an objection to a statement reporting a feeling but not by a similar objection to a statement reporting a moral judgement, or who makes a strong distinction between a moral judgement and a moral feeling, is simply confused.[46] Even if the speakers do not think they are reporting their feelings when they speak of morality, it is still possible that they are. This, in short, is an argument for scepticism regarding the self-understanding of our expressions. If we actually do report our *pro* and *con* feelings in moral speech, even when we think we are reporting our judgements, then Reid's arguments here are insufficient.

There are two points of interest here. First, it is worth noticing that the suggestion that our understanding of our moral utterances is different than their actual meaning is similar to Hume's error theory regarding our intuitions about justice during crisis. In both cases, we are asked to trust the conclusions of moral theory over our moral experiences. Second, we ought also to observe that this error theory applies to both the linguistic distinction that Reid highlights between judgements and feelings, and the felt difference, observable by introspection, which he believes underlies it. Thus, according to this argument, it may be that introspection fools us into thinking that judgement precedes feeling, whereas, in fact, a more subtle feeling precedes the apparently initial judgement. Perhaps the subtlety of this initial feeling is to blame for the regular but false division we find in language – a hidden feature of the world that was long unnoticed, like the accelerative effect of gravity, until science and philosophy brought it into the light.

But as with Reid's response to the sceptic seen in the previous chapter, it seems natural to ask for evidence, which is not forthcoming. It very well may be that Hume is right and the general run of humanity is wrong regarding the artificiality of justice. But why should we accept Hume's hypothesis, and discount both our strongly felt intuitions and the evidence of everyday language, in advance of argument? To discount widely held views on the persistence and nature of moral obligations merely because it causes trouble for Hume's moral theory seems to be a reversal not only of Reid's preferred Baconian methodology, but of good sense.

Summary

In sum, then, we find that some of Reid's criticisms of Hume's subjectivist, sentimentalist moral theory may miss the mark. Hume may not be, as Reid reads him, a strict consequentialist about the utility of justice, and so Hume may both criticise the actions of the sensible knave and account for the differences between hurt and injury, and between benefit and favour, from within his moral theory. Yet some of Reid's other complaints raise real difficulties. What are we to say, for instance, when both majority opinion regarding moral behaviour in crisis and common linguistic distinctions around the actions of judgement and feeling run counter to Hume's account of ethics? Hume would have us prefer his theory, but this answer is not acceptable to a Baconian like Reid, who holds that

> whenever we find any disagreement between the practical rules of morality, which have been received in all ages, and the principles of the theories advanced upon this subject, the practical rules ought to be the standard by which the theory is corrected.[47]

Against this dictum, a Humean may reply that, whatever the difficulties of moral subjectivism and sentimentalism, they are both simpler and account for our moral practice better than other moral theories which, like Reid's, hold that we rationally perceive and are motived by objective moral distinctions. In the final chapters of this book, we will evaluate just this claim. Before we can compare Reid's and Hume's moral theories, however, we must first come to an understanding of what Reid proposes. The next three chapters are therefore devoted to Reid's account of the concept of duty, moral perception and moral motivation.

Notes

1. For a helpful overview, see Cohon, 'Hume's Moral Philosophy'.
2. Hume, *Treatise of Human Nature*, p. 469. Emphasis original.
3. Hume, *Treatise of Human Nature*, p. 457.
4. Hume, *Treatise of Human Nature*, p. 458.
5. Hume, *Treatise of Human Nature*, p. 468. Emphasis original.
6. Hume, *Treatise of Human Nature*, pp. 466–467.
7. Hume, *Treatise of Human Nature*, p. 470.
8. Hume, *Enquiry Concerning the Principles of Morals*, p. 270.
9. See Hume, *Enquiry Concerning the Principles of Morals*, pp. 250–267.
10. Hume, *Enquiry Concerning the Principles of Morals*, p. 231.
11. Hume, *Enquiry Concerning the Principles of Morals*, p.186. Emphasis original.
12. Hume, *Enquiry Concerning the Principles of Morals*, pp. 216–217.
13. See Hume, 'Of Polygamy and Divorces'.
14. MacIntyre, *After Virtue*, p. 231.
15. See Hume, 'Of National Characters' and 'Of the Study of History'.
16. Hume, *Enquiry Concerning the Principles of Morals*, p. 270.
17. See, for example, Hutcheson, *An Inquiry into the Original of our Ideas of Beauty and Virtue*, and Mandeville, *Fable of the Bees*.
18. For an excellent summary, see Heydt, *Moral Philosophy in Eighteenth-Century Britain*, pp. 107–112.
19. Reid, *Essays on the Active Powers*, p. 337.
20. Hume, *Enquiry Concerning the Principles of Morals*, pp. 282–283. Emphasis original.
21. Reid, *Essays on the Active Powers*, p. 308. Emphasis original.
22. Reid, *Essays on the Active Powers*, p. 308. Emphasis original.
23. For a compelling interpretation along these lines, see Cohon, *Hume's Morality*, pp. 161–214. See also Bowlin, 'Sieges, Shipwrecks, and Sensible Knaves', p. 257.
24. Hume, *Treatise of Human Nature*, p. 477.

25. See Hume, *Treatise of Human Nature*, p. 478.
26. Hume, *Enquiry Concerning the Principles of Morals*, p. 183. Emphasis original.
27. Hume, *Enquiry Concerning the Principles of Morals*, p. 283.
28. Hume, *Enquiry Concerning the Principles of Morals*, pp. 184–188.
29. Hume, *Enquiry Concerning the Principles of Morals*, p. 184.
30. Hume, *Enquiry Concerning the Principles of Morals*, p. 187.
31. Reid, *Essays on the Active Powers*, p. 319.
32. Reid, *Essays on the Active Powers*, p. 320.
33. Reid, *Essays on the Active Powers*, p. 320.
34. Reid, *Essays on the Active Powers*, p. 320.
35. Hume, *Enquiry Concerning the Principles of Morals*, p. 188.
36. For an excellent account of the wreck, Géricault's painting, and the public reaction see Miles, *The Wreck of the Medusa: The Most Famous Sea Disaster of the Nineteenth Century*.
37. See, e.g. Joseph Conrad's *Lord Jim*.
38. Hume, *Enquiry Concerning the Principles of Morals*, p. 190.
39. Reid, *Essays on the Active Powers*, p. 321.
40. Hume, *Enquiry Concerning the Principles of Morals*, p. 203.
41. Although see Solnit, *A Paradise Built in Hell*.
42. Reid, *Essays on the Active Powers*, p. 132.
43. Reid, *Essays on the Active Powers*, p. 358.
44. Reid, *Essays on the Active Powers*, p. 351.
45. Reid, *Essays on the Active Powers*, p. 351.
46. Cuneo, 'Reid's Moral Philosophy', p. 252. As Cuneo rightly points out, if Reid takes Hume to be a non-cognitivist, then Reid's argument does not address the position he is attempting to refute. However, as Van Cleve notes, a mistake by Reid here may be partially explained by Hume's apparent vacillation between a cognitivist subjectivist account and non-cognitivism. See Van Cleve, *Problems from Reid*, pp. 441–446.
47. Reid, *Essays on the Active Powers*, p. 291.

Part II

Reid's Account of Duty

4

Defining Duty

Central to Reid's moral theory is an objective account of moral obligation, which Reid calls 'duty'. In this chapter, we examine Reid's understanding of this concept in order to show that Reid can account for moral phenomena which he believed made trouble for Hume's theory of justice. To accomplish this, we will proceed in four parts. First, we will look at Reid's somewhat scattered remarks on moral philosophy. As we will see, although Reid's remarks are suggestive, they do not, by themselves, provide a clear idea of Reid's understanding of duty. In the second section we will therefore augment Reid's moral theory with the concept of the 'second-person standpoint', as proposed by the contemporary philosopher Stephen Darwall. To make sure that Reid can use the resources that Darwall provides, in the third section we will see if Reid's and Darwall's accounts of duty overlap, such that Darwall makes explicit what is implicit in Reid. Finally, we will return to Reid's challenges to moral subjectivism to see if his account of morals can meet the test which he set for Hume, without falling afoul of Hume's is/ought distinction.

Reid on Duty

At the outset of addressing Reid's moral philosophy, it is helpful to place Reid's reflections on duty within two contexts. The first is the context of his corpus. Reid's published remarks on moral obligation largely occur in two places within the *Active Powers*. The first is in Essay III.iii. In this section, entitled 'Of the Rational Principles of Action', Reid discusses the rational principles of action as distinct from the mechanical principles of action (those which operate automatically, such as instinctual respiration) and the animal principles of action (those which operate according to 'will and intention', and are necessary for the life of the individual and the species, but which are motivated by desire or passion).[1] According to Reid, there are two rational principles of action, which 'have no existence in beings not endowed with reason, and . . . require not only intention and will, but judgement or reason'.[2]

The first of these principles is our 'good on the whole', which he discusses in Chapters II through IV, and which he describes as the 'general and abstract notion' of whatever 'makes a man more happy or more perfect'.[3] The second rational principle of action is 'duty', also called 'rectitude, or moral obligation', which is the subject of Chapters V through VIII.[4] Both good on the whole and duty are, for Reid, rational and normative principles. And both, 'when rightly understood', lead to the same course of life, 'like two fountains whose streams unite and run in the same channel'.[5] In Reid's usage, however, only the latter principle of action, 'duty', is properly called 'moral'. Thus, Reid distinguishes himself from philosophers who include discussions of virtue and politics in their moral philosophy, writing that by 'the theory of morals' he means only 'a just account of the structure of our moral powers; that is of those powers of mind by which we have our moral conceptions, and distinguish right from wrong in human actions'.[6]

The second place Reid discusses moral obligation at length is in Essay V, entitled 'Of Morals'. Building off his general observations on duty in Essay III.iii, he addresses questions concerning the first principles of morals (Chapter I), systems of morals and natural jurisprudence (Chapters II and III), the relations between intention, judgement and moral approbation (Chapters IV and VII), the naturalness of justice (Chapter V) and the nature of contract (Chapter VI). Together, the latter half of Essay III.iii and the whole of Essay V of the *Active Powers* constitute Reid's most complete statement of his views on moral philosophy. They are not, however, always as systematic or thorough in presentation as one would wish, for at least two reasons.

First, as Terence Cuneo has recently pointed out, in the *Active Powers* Reid treats ethics generally – and the nature of moral obligation specifically – as a sub-topic related to the main issue which dominates the work: the nature of human agency.[7] Second, as Reid himself acknowledges, his published work on ethics was not as polished as he would have liked. As he writes concerning the final chapters of Essay V,

> the substance of the four following chapters was wrote long ago and read in a literary society, with a view to justify some points of morals from metaphysical objections urged against them in the writings

of David Hume, Esq. If they answer that end, and, at the same time, serve to illustrate the account I have given of our moral powers, it is hoped that the reader will not think them improperly placed here; and that he will forgive some repetition, and perhaps anachronisms, occasioned by their being wrote at different times.[8]

Even the chapters on duty in Essay III.iii appear to have been written in some haste. Although Reid lived another nine years after the publication of the *Active Powers* in 1787, we know from his correspondence that these chapters were some of the last ones written, and that Reid was concerned that he would not live to complete the project.[9] Thus, although in this book we will focus on Reid's remarks in the *Active Powers*, we will supplement and attempt to clarify Reid's moral philosophy by turning to other resources within and without his corpus.

The second context we ought to keep in mind when discussing Reid's account of duty is the way Reid thinks about the philosophical investigation of duty and our perception of it. Throughout his remarks on duty, Reid returns again and again to a distinction between what he calls the 'theory of morals' and what he calls 'practical ethics'. The theory of morals consists in the philosophical investigation of concepts like 'duties' and 'rights', and the faculty by which we perceive rights and duties, alternatively called the 'conscience' or 'moral sense'.[10] Practical ethics, on the other hand, is the systematic presentation of our rights and duties, which, when combined with mnemonic devices and illustrations, helps us to act well in the world. Together, these two divisions make up the field of moral philosophy.

For Reid, both moral theory and practical ethics seek first principles through observation and induction, but they are not equal partners. As we have seen, Reid is adamant that moral theory is subservient to practical ethics, and has 'little connection with the knowledge of our duty', adding that 'those who differ most in the theory of moral powers, agree in the practical rules of morals which they dictate'.[11] Further, while disagreement in theory does not often lead to disagreement in practice, an overemphasis on moral theory can be detrimental to our moral practice by leading us 'into this gross mistake . . . [t]hat in order to understand his duty, a man must needs be a philosopher and a metaphysician'.[12] Reid's moral theory is therefore a secondary science, which aims to account for our lived experience of moral practice. This is, naturally, a consequence of his Baconian method. Like his investigation of the external senses, Reid's moral theory is metaphysically and theoretically modest, attempting chiefly to describe and account for the regularities we find in moral language, moral behaviour and moral experience.

Given the priority Reid gives to practical ethics, and his warning about the dangers of moral theory above, it seems we need some reason to justify a book on Reid's moral theory; yet this reason is not hard to find. In his Introductory Lecture, printed in Knud Haakonssen's reconstruction of Reid's 'Lectures and Papers on Practical Ethics', Reid states that

> although it is true and ought to be understood that very different Theories in Morals do in most instances lead to the same practical Conclusions yet it must also be owed that there have been Licentious Theories advanced on this Subject that tend to overturn all good Morals, and that even of those Theories that do not deserve the Name of Licentious some have a happier influence upon morals than others, and there is no false theory whatsoever which may not in some cases at least mislead a Man in Practice.[13]

As Reid believed at least part of Hume's moral theory 'borders on licentiousness', it is no surprise that Hume's moral theory served as a foil for Reid's remarks on duty, just as Hume's scepticism spurred Reid to formulate his own theory of perception.[14]

Reid's Definition of Duty

With this context in hand, let us begin our discussion of Reid's moral theory with his description of the concept 'duty'. Reid explicitly addresses this topic in Chapter V of Essay III.iii in the *Active Powers*, entitled 'Of the Notion of Duty, Rectitude, Moral Obligation'. Here, Reid gives several general remarks concerning the nature of duty. For the sake of clarity, I have sorted them into six observations.

Reid's first observation is that duty is 'too simple to admit of logical definition'.[15] Reid's statement may initially give the impression that he finds duty to be a mysterious quality. Yet we need to be careful not to overstate Reid's intention here. When he says that duty does not admit of a 'logical definition', he does not mean that it cannot be defined at all; he simply means it cannot be defined according to Aristotle's method of genus and species.[16] Reid's attitude towards Aristotelian definition is of a piece with his concern about the overuse of the Aristotelian syllogism; just as Reid believes that not all philosophy must proceed by syllogism, so Reid also believes that there are many non-mysterious entities and qualities which, for various reasons, cannot be defined according to Aristotle's method. These include such mundane items as Aristotle's own categories, singular entities such as London and Paris, and individual colours.[17] The point is not that we are unable to competently distinguish these things. It is that Aristotle's method, though beloved of philosophers, is not always fit for purpose.

Thus, although we cannot define duty within the narrow confines of Aristotle's method, we may still define it, in the colloquial sense, by 'synonymous words or phrases, or by its properties and necessary concomitants'.[18] Reid therefore explicates duty as 'what we ought to do, what is fair and honest, what is approvable, what every man professes to be the rule of his conduct, what all men praise, and what is laudable, though no man should praise it'.[19] Even without the confines of Aristotelian definition, this description of duty is a philosophical failure. For one thing, it begs the question to say that duty is 'what we ought to do' and 'what is fair and honest', 'approvable' and 'laudable'. Second, the statement that duty is 'what all men praise' is both counter-factual and contradicted by the final clause of the definition!

Still, despite these substantial problems, we can find significant hints of Reid's position within this definition. From the first clause it is clear that duty, for Reid, is normative; it tells us not what is but what should be. From the second we learn that duty has to do with desert, with what is owed to others. The fourth clause indicates that duty is generally perceived by the bulk of humanity. The third, fifth and sixth clauses hold that the performance of duty is praiseworthy and confers worth upon the person who performs it. And the final clause holds that duty is objective in that its performance confers worth independent of its recognition. From these, we may attempt a first, revised definition of Reidian duty: *duty is a simple entity which provides to general humanity reasons for action having to do with desert, the performance of which is objectively laudable.* This definition is better than the one provided by Reid because it is neither circular nor contains a contradiction. But we can make it better still by incorporating the rest of Reid's observations.

Reid's second observation concerning duty contrasts his account with Hume's. According to Reid, the 'notion of duty cannot be resolved into that of interest, or what is most for our happiness'.[20] Here, Reid is tersely saying that duty is to be distinguished from all animal (and, by extension, mechanical) principles, and the other rational principle of action, 'good on the whole'. According to Reid, there was in his time a common confusion regarding duty's distinction from these other motives of action, for several reasons. One reason, which he addresses at length, is philological. As Reid notes, in *De Officiis* (*On Duty*) Cicero used the word '*officium*', which is often translated 'duty', to indicate two different but related concepts. The first concept is what Cicero calls 'complete duty' or '*honestum*'. *Honestum*, according to Cicero, is 'that which is of such a nature that, though devoid of all utility, it can be justly commended in and for itself apart from any profit or reward'.[21] The second concept of duty Cicero identifies is what he calls 'middle duty'. Middle duty, in contrast to complete duty, is merely 'that for which a persuasive reason can be given as to why it has been done'.[22] This latter type of duty is identified by Cicero as concerning '*utile*': that which produces either benefit or pleasure. According to Reid, Cicero unites the two concepts of *honestum* and *utile* under the single banner of *officium* because both are rational principles of action. As mentioned, this close association between the good and the useful is not abhorrent to Reid. Like Cicero, Reid believed 'duty' and 'good on the whole' were complementary rational principles of action. However, according to Reid, due to the confusion between these two distinct but related principles of action, the English word 'duty' is most properly applied to *honestum* alone.[23]

Reid's third observation concerning duty is that 'the abstract notion of duty . . . appears to be neither any real quality of the action considered by itself, nor of the agent considered without respect to the action, but a certain relation between one and the other'.[24] Duty is therefore not only a practical reason for action, but a certain type of relationship between agents and actions. In this latter respect, it is like other relations such as mathematical equality or proportionality. And, like these relations, it may be changed or nullified by a change in the entities – in this case the agent and the action – of which it is a relation.

The attributes of the actions and agents necessary for instantiating a duty-type relation are the subject of Reid's fourth and fifth observation, respectively. According to Reid, all acts required by moral obligation must be possible and voluntary. Furthermore, all agents bound by moral obligation must have understanding, free will and the ability to act. In these two points, we find Reid's libertarian understanding of free will, which holds that actions are only free if they are the actions of a causal agent, and agents are only free if they are, themselves, causes. That human beings are themselves causes – that they have what Reid called 'moral liberty' – is an important tenet of Reid's philosophy, to which he devoted the entirety of Book IV of the *Active Powers*.[25] As it bears most directly on Reid's understanding of moral motivation, however, I will not discuss this idea in detail here, but rather will postpone it until chapter six.

Reid's sixth and final observation is that the moral worth of an action is derived from the intention behind its performance. 'If [an agent] does a materially good action, without any belief of its being good, but from some other principle, it is no good action in him. And if he does it with the belief of its being ill, it is ill in him'.[26] Thus, although the same agent may perform the same action in two similar instances, a change in the intention of the agent may change the moral worth of the action.

Taking these all together we may augment our definition above and define Reidian duty as *a simple and objective relationship between voluntary actions and free and rational agents, which provides to those agents reasons for action having to do with desert, the performance of which is objectively laudable, so long as that action is intentionally performed on account of this relationship and not on account of any consideration of benefit or pleasure.*[27]

This definition is clearer than either Reid's own or the first attempt above, but there are still many questions. For example: What type of agents are we talking about? Under what conditions does this relationship adhere among such agents? And how can such reasons be motivating apart from considerations of benefit or pleasure? Reid does not clearly address these issues. Yet I believe we can begin to answer them by stepping away from Reid for a moment, to look for resources in the work of the contemporary moral theorist Stephen Darwall.

Darwall's Second-Person Standpoint

In *The Second-Person Standpoint*, Stephen Darwall attempts to bolster the case for an objective moral law by describing what he calls 'the felicity conditions' under which objective moral obligations arise.[28] According to Darwall, moral obligation is best seen an irreducible feature of certain kinds of relationships among agents, which occurs when one person addresses another, not as an object, but as an agent with reason and will. Because such relationships require the agents within them to treat the other as a 'second person', Darwall calls both these types of relationships and the reasons given in them 'second-personal'.[29]

To see the contrast between a properly second-personal command and a command that is acknowledged for non-second-personal reasons, Darwall points us back to Hume, this time to the famous example of the gouty toes. 'Would any man who is walking along, tread as willing on another's gouty toes, whom he has no quarrel with, as on the hard flint and pavement?', asks Hume.[30] The implied answer is, thankfully, negative, but Hume's reasoning for it, according to Darwall, is hard to countenance. It is, Hume supposes, the *dulce* of 'the good of mankind' that prevents us. We do not, without cause, willingly inflict discomfort on another because of our natural sympathy for human beings. The world, according to this sympathetic feeling, is more agreeable when gouty toes go untrodden.

On this account, then, when someone asks us to kindly remove our foot from their toes, we do so not because they have the authority to ask us to refrain and we have a responsibility to comply, but because they have informed us about the state of the world, and we naturally feel that the state of affairs will be better in the case that we halt our treading. This kind of reasoning, which in Darwall's terms would be 'third-personal', stands in contrast to second-personal reasoning because it does not rest upon the relationship between or among agents.[31] The particular agents do not actually matter in the calculation of sympathy, except insofar as they too are part of the world made better by stepping aside.

According to Darwall, this account is, simply, an implausible rendering of what actually happens when we choose not to harm other people. To him, it seems much more plausible, and true to experience, to say that when someone asks us to refrain from stepping on their sore feet, we comply with their request on the basis of the judgement that we owe them such respect, rather than any consideration of our own pleasure at the utility of untrodden toes.[32] Hume, of course, would be wary of the former account because it seems to move directly from description (foot on toes) to normativity (don't!). But Darwall believes that the is/ought distinction makes no trouble for his understanding of moral normativity, because it does not apply.

From Darwall's perspective, Hume's is/ought distinction gets this much right: you cannot derive moral normativity from a non-normative description of the world. But Darwall understands the relationship between these domains differently. Normative, second-personal reasons presuppose a certain kind of relationship built on obligation and respect, and operate within this relationship. They are, therefore, 'agent-relative'. Non-normative, third-personal reasons, on the other hand, are 'agent-neutral' because they regard the agents in the situation from a perspective outside of their relationship.[33] Since second- and third-personal reasons describe identical situations from contrasting perspectives, it is impossible to make second-personal reasons operate from a third-personal perspective, and vice-versa. You cannot get one from the other.

If you cannot get second-personal reasons from third-personal descriptions of the world, then what is their basis? We have already seen that Darwall considers them to be a feature of certain kinds of relationships among or between agents, but more explication of this relationship is necessary. To this end, Darwall makes three 'points'.

The first, which he calls 'Strawson's point', is that moral responsibility cannot be based on any consideration of desirability. 'When we seek to hold people accountable, what matters is not whether doing so is desirable . . . but whether the person's conduct is culpable and we have the authority to bring him to account'.[34] This point – named after P.F. Strawson's criticism of consequentialism in his essay, 'Freedom and Responsibility' – draws attention to the difference between moral praiseworthiness and utility. It could, though, very well be named 'Cicero's point', according to the definition of *honestum* Reid cited above.

For an example of Strawson's Point, consider the recent debate about embryonic stem-cell research.[35] Opponents of embryonic stem-cell research usually do not argue that the advances promised by the research are, overall, harmful or useless. Their argument is not that, if stem-cell research were to advance apace, public utility would be reduced. Rather, opponents of embryonic stem-cell research commonly argue that, in spite of the great promise of stem-cell research and the great utility of its expected advances, the acquisition and destruction of embryonic cells is morally prohibited. To them, utility and morality are not only non-identical but fundamentally intransitive. There simply is no amount of utility that could trump the moral prohibition.[36]

Darwall's second point – 'Fichte's Point' – is derived from J.G. Fichte's analysis of '*Aufforderung*' or 'summons' in *Foundations of Natural Right*. Here, Fichte contrasts the difference between summons and coercion. A summons, according to Fichte, appeals to the freedom and self-determination of an agent, while coercion forces compliance by overriding autonomy.[37] Because requests may be ambiguous, it is difficult to describe situations that perfectly capture each of these types of reason without providing substantial detail. One can get a good feeling for the difference, however, by considering the difference between the request 'come here, please' and the requests 'come here, or else' or 'come here, and I'll make it worth your while'. The first does not *prima facie* imply any coercion. The second demands compliance on pain of consequence. And the third appeals to a future benefit. For Darwall, the importance of this distinction is that a summons emphasises the second-personal status of the summoner and the summoned. In contrast to coercion and enticement, when I ask you to walk over to me, from a second-person standpoint, I am asking you to recognise my authority as a free and rational agent to request your compliance as a free and rational agent. To do this, though, I must also recognise your second-personal competence – that is, your ability to recognise second-personal forms of address – and your responsibility, assuming my request is proper, to comply.[38]

Darwall's third point addresses second-personal motivation and is called 'Pufendorf's Point', after the German theological voluntarist. Being a theological voluntarist, Pufendorf argued that all moral obligations are fundamentally derived from God's command. Interestingly, though, Pufendorf also argued that God's commands must address us as rational agents. For God's commands to be morally binding, the commanded agent must be internally motivated by a prior, rational acceptance of God's authority, and not by fear of punishment. As Darwall puts it, '[t]o be obligated by God's command, we must be able to take a second-personal standpoint on ourselves and be motivated by internally addressed demands whose (second-personal) authority we ourselves accept'.[39] The repetition of the phrase 'second-personal' in the previous sentence may make it seem gnomic or circular, but the meaning is clear enough. With respect to a fulfilled summons, to use Fichte's language, it is not enough that an agent be addressed in a second-personal manner. The agent who complies with the act must do so because he or she is motivated by the second-personal nature of the request, not by any third-personal fear of punishment or hope of reward.

Naturally, none of these points go uncontested. However, if Darwall is correct in identifying these points as felicity conditions necessary for moral normativity, then when we go looking for duty, we are looking for three things. First, we are looking for a type of reason that is irreducible to and incommensurable with considerations of benefit or pleasure. This is Strawson's Point. Second, we are looking for a property of relationships among agents that share second-personal authority, competence and responsibility, as outlined in Fichte's Point. And finally, according to Pufendorf's Point, we are looking for acts which are motivated by a recognition of the second-personal nature of the summons made upon them.

When thinking about these three points, it is important to note that they are overlapping. For, although Pufendorf's Point – that agents subject to moral obligations must acknowledge a second-personal responsibility to act according to duty – emphasises motivation, the concepts of second-personal authority, competence and responsibility are simultaneously implied. How could we be motivated by duty without also recognising the authority from which it flows? How could we act on a duty as a duty without having the competence to both recognise its distinction from interest and act from an intention to fulfil it? The concepts of second-personal reasons, authority, competence, responsibility and motivation are intertwined. They rely on each other for their own intelligibility.

Reid and Darwall

Darwall's framework is helpful because it gives a clear, objectivist account of the types of entities, relations and reasons involved in moral evaluations. If this framework is to be useful for Reid, however, we will need to find an affirmation of all three of Darwall's 'points' within Reid's moral theory. Only then can we use the second-person standpoint to augment our definition of Reidian duty.

Finding Strawson's Point is easy. As we have already noted, Reid makes the same distinction between acting from duty and acting for the sake of benefit or pleasure in Cicero's name above. Darwall notes the connection as well, explicitly linking his argument for

Strawson's Point to Reid's argument against Hume's account of justice. According to Darwall, Reid correctly discerns that Hume appeals to third-personal reasons – the 'wrong kinds of reasons' – in his moral philosophy.[40] Thus, we find a clear expression of Strawson's Point in the *Active Powers*, when Reid writes that those who have a proper conception of justice 'perceive its obligation distinct from its utility'.[41]

So much for Strawson. What of Fichte's Point, that second-personal address requires a relationship among agents sharing second-personal authority, competence and responsibility? When trying to show that Reid endorses this view, we immediately run into a difficulty. Reid tells us that duty is a relationship between agents and actions. Yet Fichte's Point speaks of relationships among agents. Does this mean that Darwall's view of duty is incompatible with Reid's? The answer, I think, is 'no'. The apparent conflict between Reid's position regarding agents and actions and Darwall's regarding agents and other agents occurs because Reid and Darwall are approaching the topic of moral obligation from different angles. Reid tells us what duty is, and describes it as a relationship among agents and actions, because duty obliges agents to do or to refrain from doing certain actions. Darwall, on the other hand, is giving us the 'felicity conditions' among which duty arises. He is therefore not saying that duty is a relationship among agents. He is saying it occurs as a product of a certain type of relationship among agents.

We can see that this is the case for two reasons. First, it is hard to image what 'duty' or 'moral obligation' would mean if it was a relationship among agents, as opposed to a relationship between an agent and an action. If someone said, 'You have a duty to me', and you replied, 'What actions are required or forbidden by that duty?', the answer 'No action at all' would be illogical. Second, Darwall agrees with Reid that duty is a relationship between agents and actions when he writes that moral obligation implies 'accountability-seeking demands', since a demand is a relation between an agent and an action.[42]

But does Reid also believe that duty arises among agents who have second-personal authority, competence and responsibility? Although Reid did not consider this question in precisely these terms, it seems so. According to Reid, 'every man . . . ought to consider himself as a member of the common society of mankind'.[43] Furthermore, this society appears to be second-personal. At the end of his discussion of animal principles of action, Reid imagines a being which has 'that superiority of understanding and that power of self-government which man actually has', but which lacks 'a conscience or sense of duty'.[44] According to Reid, this being would be 'more than a brute' because it 'would be capable of chusing some main end' of life, but would be excluded from the moral community.[45] Thus, Reid implicitly affirms Fichte's Point as well.

Finally, we find in Reid a clear endorsement of Pufendorf's Point in Reid's sixth observation noted above. There, Reid claimed that it is the intention of the agent which gives an action its moral denomination, and that if an action is done from any consideration other than the obligation of duty, it lacks moral worth. To put this in Darwall's terms, if the intention of an action is not second-personal, then it may result in an action which brings good or bad consequences from an agent-neutral perspective, but it could not be a morally worthy action.

Promise and Contract

We may further observe all three of these points working together in Reid's explanation of promise and contract. On this topic, once again, it is Hume who supplies the philosophical grist for Reid's mill. Hume believes that promises and contracts, being aspects of justice, are founded on convention and public utility, which in turn is pleasing. Before the establishment of this convention there is 'only a general sense of common interest; which sense all the members of the society express to one another, and which induces them to regulate their conduct by certain rules'.[46] This sense of common interest gradually creates stability, trust and the conventions of private property, only after which 'the ideas of justice and injustice . . . and [finally] *obligation*' arise.[47] On this account, without the existence of mutually beneficial society, there can be no promises or contracts since, without the influence of society, promises cannot be enforced.

Reid, on the other hand, believes that promises are not as Hume would have them. They are neither conventional nor require the enforcement of society to be intelligible. Rather, according to Reid, promises and contracts are inherently social and also natural, in the sense that human beings understand and are bound by them without the threat of outside compulsion. On Reid's account, the difference between his understanding and Hume's stems from a fundamental disagreement about the nature of the act of making a promise or compact.

According to Reid, Hume believes that promises are solitary acts of the mind which are then expressed, whereas Reid believes that promises are fundamentally social operations.[48] Given that the existence of society is a prerequisite for Hume's account, this may seem to be an odd criticism. What could be more social than an act that requires the existence of society for its intelligibility? The distinction that Reid is drawing, however, is not between acts intelligible before and after the advent of society, but between those acts which are possible while alone and those which require communication with another agent. As Reid puts it:

> I call those operations *solitary*, which may be performed by a man in solitude, without intercourse with any other intelligent being . . . [and] those operations *social*, which necessarily imply social intercourse with some other intelligent being who bears a part in them.[49]

As examples of solitary operations Reid lists the ability to see, hear, remember, judge and reason. As examples of the social operations Reid proposes the asking of a question, the giving of testimony, the giving of a command and the making of promises and contracts.

Reid's account of social acts is critical for understanding his account of promises. But Reid is simply wrong to accuse Hume of holding that 'a promise is some kind of will, consent, or intention, which may be expressed, or may not be expressed'.[50] According to Hume, it 'is evident, that the will or consent alone never transfers property, nor causes the obligation of a promise . . . but the will must be expressed by words or signs, in order to impose a tie upon any man'.[51] Hume therefore also understands promises to be social in just the way Reid does: not in the sense that we require the existence of a society before they can be performed, but in the sense that more than one agent is required to perform them.

Yet while Reid is wrong to accuse Hume of treating promises and contracts as solitary acts, Reid makes three further points of criticism against Hume's account which are worth considering. The first is Reid's claim that Hume appeals to the wrong type of reasons. Or, as Cuneo puts it, that '[t]he fact that actions of certain types tend to contribute to unfavorable distributions of pleasures and pains . . . is simply not the right sort of thing to explain why agents have rights to goods of a certain type'.[52] As evidence for this, Reid argues that, if Hume is correct and promises are valued solely for their utility, it is hard to explain how children, who are incapable of calculating social utility, can make and understand them.

> One boy has a top, another a scourge; says the first to the other, If you lend me your scourge as long as I can keep up my top with it, you shall next have the top as long as you can keep it up . . . This is a contract perfectly understood by both parties though they never heard [a philosophical definition]. And each of them knows, that he is injured if the other breaks the bargain, and that he does wrong if he breaks it himself.[53]

A Humean may reply that this phenomenon is explainable by the fact that children pick up the conventions of justice – which are justified by social utility – faster than they can learn to calculate that utility. They may, that is, be motivated to obey the conventions of justice without understanding the ground for it. Yet Reid would not find this rejoinder convincing, because it seems to misdescribe the situation. This Humean line proposes that children, like the ones in the example above, have an abstract sense of justice which they are able to apply to appropriate situations, even if they are unable to explain why certain actions are or are not just. By contrast, Reid's point is that children have a natural sense of what is fair in particular situations before they acquire an abstract understanding of justice. In other words, an appeal to third-personal reasons does not explain the observed phenomena of contract-making in human life, even if those reasons have been transformed into conventions of justice, because human beings demonstrate an immediate, instinctive ability to judge of what is and is not fair. What does explain it, according to Reid, is not the calculation of utility, but the natural human ability to recognise duties.

Reid's second point regards the intention behind a promise. According to Reid, what makes a promise is the intention to make the promise, and not, as Hume writes, 'a will or intention to perform what we promise'.[54] For Reid, then, whether or not one intends to fulfil a promise is immaterial to the binding nature of a promise. By contrast, to (socially) will the creation of an obligation does create that obligation. As a corollary to this idea, Reid notes that if a person wills to do a certain (non-morally obligatory) action in the future, absent a prior promise or contract, the completion of that action does not count as the fulfilment of a promise, even if that will was expressed to others. It is only when the third-personal intention to do a certain action is accompanied by the second-personal intention to be bound by promise or contract, that the performed action has moral worth.

Finally, Reid makes note of the type of society we find promises in. According to Reid, we can only find promises – and indeed all social operations – in communities of moral agents.[55] Dogs may have affection for their masters and foxes may evade hunters, but neither can make promises or tell lies. To make a contract or a promise, therefore, it is necessary for at least two beings to have the mental abilities to intend the promise and to make it by a social operation. The ability to communicate complex ideas and to have abstract thoughts is therefore necessary but not sufficient. For promises and contracts, the beings involved also must have the ability to understand, perceive and be motivated by considerations of duty.

Thus, in his discussion of Hume's account of promises, Reid makes Strawson's Point (that Hume appeals to the wrong type of reasons), Pufendorf's Point (that the moral worth of actions is dependent on their intention) and Fichte's Point (that promises require a community of morally authoritatively, competent and responsible agents). As Reid appeals to these points throughout his moral philosophy, examples could be multiplied. But the above gives us enough to warrant using the resources of Darwall's second-person standpoint to augment Reid's account of duty.

To this end, we may further modify our definition of Reidian duty given the above by substituting 'second-personal agents' for 'free and rational agents'. This modification is allowed because it is a specification: all second-personal agents must be free and rational. This modification made, we may finally define Reidian duty as *a simple and objective relationship between voluntary actions and second-personal agents, which provides to those agents reasons for action regarding desert, the performance of which is objectively laudable, so long as that action is intentionally performed on account of this relationship and not on account of any consideration of benefit or pleasure.*

At this point, someone familiar with Reid's corpus might offer an objection. In the above I have claimed that Reid believes that duty is a type of relation between second-personal agents and actions, which arise within communities of second-personal agents. In his 'Lectures and Papers on Practical Ethics', however, Reid notes three categories of duties: duties to God, duties to ourselves and duties to others. Duties to others is clearly second-personal. Similarly, since Reid believes that God is a second-personal agent, there is little difficulty with duties to God. With respect to 'duties to ourselves', however, it seems fair to note that one person is not, by definition, a community. Does Reid then disagree with Darwall's assertion that moral obligation always arises within a community of second-personal agents?

Once again, the answer is negative, for two reasons. First, Reid tells us that, since 'no man is born for himself', the cultivation of the 'virtues of self-government' (i.e. duties owed to ourselves) allows us to discharge the duties we owe to society.[56] Second, the fulfilment of duties to ourselves is also the fulfilment of our duties to God. 'All the powers & abilities of body & mind fortune or Station which a man is possessed of . . . are the talents God has given them,' he writes in the 'Practical Ethics'.[57] Therefore, 'using our talents in a right manner this God requires of us as our Duty, and we must be accountable to him for the proper Discharge of it'.[58] As a consequence, these three categories of duty – God, self and others – ought not to be taken as clear signifiers of Reid's moral theory. Rather, they are, for him, a convenient pedagogical tool for the teaching of practical ethics.[59]

Questions and Challenges for Reidian Duty

By adding the clause regarding second-personal agency to Reid's definition of duty, we now have the resources both to begin to answer the questions asked and to meet the challenges posed above. Reviewing these questions, we asked: 1) What type of agents are we talking about? 2) Under what conditions does a duty-type relationship adhere among such agents? and 3) How can such reasons be motivating apart from considerations of benefit or pleasure? To the first question, we may now reply 'second-personal agents', that is, agents who have second-personal authority, competence and responsibility. The answer to the second question is that duty-type relationships arise in communities of second-personal agents. Finally, the answer to the third is that reasons arising in these communities are normative because they are agent-relative, arising from within relationships of obligation and respect.

By helping us to answer these questions, Darwall's second-person standpoint proves useful in understanding Reid's account of duty. But can Reid's account stand up to the challenges he proposes to Hume and also to Hume's is/ought distinction? It seems that it can. Recall that, for Reid, one problem with Hume's moral theory is that it holds that justice becomes unintelligible where it is not useful. This, though, is not what we actually find in human behaviour. Even in severe crisis, and even when power differentials are so great that one party need never fear reappraisal for unjust actions, human beings recognise duties of equity and fair treatment. Unless we advert to an error theory, this phenomena needs to be explained – and Reid, with Darwall's help, can explain it.

For one thing, duty is not founded on any considerations of benefit or pleasure. Thus, the threat of retribution or the prospect of benefit is not needed for us to act according to the obligations of duty. Second, duty arises among communities of second-personal agents, who share second-personal authority, competence and responsibility. Nothing else is required. Thus, to ask whether prospects of success or survival are good or bad, or whether our fellow agents are weak or strong, is beside the point.

Similarly, the second-person standpoint helps us account for Reid's observation that languages tend to make a distinction between expressions of preference and expressions of moral approbation and disapprobation. Specifically, to try to collapse the latter into the former is to violate Strawson's Point and appeal to reasons of the wrong sort. This explains why people are not offended by moral disagreement in the way that they are if told they are unreliable reporters of their own feelings. Expressions of preference are first-personal and subjective. To say that someone is mistaken about these is to accuse them of lying or severe confusion. Moral judgements, by contrast, are second-personal and objective. To disagree with a statement about these judgements is just to say that someone has gotten it wrong.

Finally, Darwall's second-person standpoint allows Reid to avoid the challenge of Hume's is/ought distinction. Although Hume tells us that he is 'surpriz'd to find, that instead of the usual copulations of propositions, *is*, and *is not*, I meet with no proposition that is not connected with an *ought* or *ought not*', Darwall and Reid tell us that, so long as it is done correctly, this move from 'is' to 'ought' is not surprising at all. Indeed, so long as our descriptive statements are describing the existence of second-personal agents, it would in fact be surprising not to find 'ought' statements in close proximity, because ought statements – in the strong sense of *honestum* – only arise in such communities.

To find statements concerning specific duties alongside descriptions of second-personal agents and relationships is therefore no more surprising than finding descriptions of free-throws and three-pointers among discussions of basketball teams. Where else would you find them?

Notice that this type of movement from the descriptive to the normative does not violate Darwall's belief that we cannot move from agent-neutral to agent-relative reasoning. Both agent-relative description and agent-relative normativity are second-personal all the way down. It is therefore no more illogical, from Darwall's perspective, to say 'here is a moral community, therefore one ought to obey the duties that entails' than for Hume to say something like 'humans like utility, therefore we ought to follow the dictates of justice when it is useful'. Neither statement violates the is/ought distinction as I, following Darwall, have interpreted it. The point is not that you can never follow an 'is' statement with an 'ought' statement. It is that the move must be justified by an implicit or explicit appeal to a motivating force. For Hume that force is sentiment. For Reid, like Darwall, it is the fundamental normativity of agent-relative reasons. By Darwall's and Reid's lights, then, we are fully warranted in condemning sons who murder their fathers, but not trees which topple their sires, because fathers and sons make a second-personal community, while trees never do.

Yet here one might object: it is all very good to say that second-personal reasons arise among second-personal agents in second-personal relationships, but this appears to conjure normative, objective morality out of thin air by supposing that it is a feature of the world. To actually make the objectivist case, this is not enough. You have to show that second-personal reasons, agents and relationships exist.

Specifically, regarding the relation between mind-independent moral relations and the agents who observe them, we might first ask: how do we recognise second-personal agents and reasons? Which is to say, what is it about an agent that tells us they have second-personal authority, competence and responsibility, and what is it about an act which signals that it is obligatory or forbidden? Further, regarding motives, we might also ask how the normative features of second-personal relationships motivate us to action. By what mechanism, in other words, does the normative force of a moral proposition motivate us to action? Posing these questions this way moves from a discussion of the concept of duty itself to a discussion of moral perception and moral motivation. In the next two chapters, we therefore turn to Reid's treatment of these topics.

Notes

1. Reid, *Essays on the Active Powers*, p. 92.
2. Reid, *Essays on the Active Powers*, p. 152.
3. Reid, *Essays on the Active Powers*, p. 154.
4. Reid, *Essays on the Active Powers*, p. 168.
5. Reid, *Essays on the Active Powers*, p. 173.
6. Reid, *Essays on the Active Powers*, p. 282.
7. Cuneo, *Thomas Reid on the Ethical Life*, pp. 1–2.
8. Reid, *Essays on the Active Powers*, pp. 289–290.
9. Haakonssen and Harris, 'Editor's Introduction', in Reid, *Essays on the Active Powers*, xvi–xvii. See also Reid, '86. To James Gregory' and '96. To James Gregory', in *The Correspondence of Thomas Reid*, pp. 166 and 180.
10. See Reid, *Essays on the Active Powers*, p. 175.
11. Reid, *Essays on the Active Powers*, pp. 282–283. See also Reid, 'Lectures and Papers on Practical Ethics', in *Thomas Reid on Practical Ethics*, pp. 10–12.
12. Reid, *Essays on the Active Powers*, p. 283.
13. Reid, 'Lectures and Papers on Practical Ethics', *Thomas Reid on Practical Ethics*, p. 12.
14. Reid, *Essays on the Active Powers*, p. 341.
15. Reid, *Essays on the Active Powers*, p. 169.
16. Reid, *Essays on the Intellectual Powers*, pp. 18–20.
17. See Reid, *Essays on the Intellectual Powers*, p. 18 and Reid, *Thomas Reid on Logic, Rhetoric and the Fine Arts*, pp. 109–112.
18. Reid, *Essays on the Active Powers*, p. 169.
19. Reid, *Essays on the Active Powers*, p. 169.
20. Reid, *Essays on the Active Powers*, p. 169.
21. Cicero, *De Finibus*, II.xiv; quoted in Reid, *Essays on the Active Powers*, p. 302; translation by Haakonssen and Harris. In Essay III. iii.5 Reid quotes Cicero's definition of *honestum* from *De Officiis*, but as the definition given in *De Finibus* (*On Ends*) more clearly illustrates the distinction Reid is trying to draw here, and as Reid quotes the above passage from *De Finibus* in Essay V.5, I have substituted it here.

22. Cicero, *On Duties*, I.8.
23. Reid, *Essays on the Active Powers*, p. 172.
24. Reid, *Essays on the Active Powers*, p. 173.
25. Reid, *Essays on the Active Powers*, p. 196.
26. Reid, *Essays on the Active Powers*, p. 174.
27. For a complete definition, we ought also to include the observation that duty may require us to refrain from action, but for the sake of simplicity I have stated the definition positively.
28. Darwall, *The Second-Person Standpoint*, p. 3.
29. Darwall, *The Second-Person Standpoint*, pp. 3, 8.
30. Hume, *Enquiry Concerning the Principles of Morals*, p. 226.
31. See Darwall, *The Second-Person Standpoint*, p. 9.
32. Darwall, *The Second-Person Standpoint*, pp. 5–10.
33. Darwall, *The Second-Person Standpoint*, p. 9.
34. Darwall, *The Second-Person Standpoint*, p. 15.
35. See Nwigwe, 'Embrionic Stem Cell Research: An Ethical Dilemma', for an overview.
36. It is also worth noting, and also further evidence of Strawson's Point, that proponents of embryonic stem-cell research, no less than the opponents, adopt a second-personal stance. That is, proponents of stem-cell research typically do not argue that the utility of such research is so great that it should be pursued despite a moral prohibition against killing human beings in the course of scientific research. Rather, they argue that embryonic stem-cell research simply does not violate any rights claimed by members of the moral community. The debate, in other words, is not about the relationship between utility and duty, but whether this research does or does not violate the rights of (potential) human beings.
37. Fichte, *Foundations of Natural Right*, p. 41; quoted in Darwall, *The Second-Person Standpoint*, p. 21.
38. Darwall acknowledges that coercion and enticement can, in some cases, be second-personal, so long as the threats or rewards offered are extended by someone who has the second-personal authority to bestow punishment or reward. Further, defining the exact boundary between second- and third-personal coercion and enticement is not always clear. This, however, does not change the fact that, in certain situations, the motive force of a request entirely relies on the interest or benefit to the requested agent. See Darwall, *The Second-Person Standpoint*, pp. 49–52.
39. Darwall, *The Second-Person Standpoint*, p. 23.
40. Darwall, *The Second-Person Standpoint*, p. 185.

41. Reid, *Essays on the Active Powers*, p. 306.
42. Darwall, *The Second-Person Standpoint*, p. 95.
43. Reid, *Essays on the Active Powers*, p. 274.
44. Reid, *Essays on the Active Powers*, p. 149
45. Reid, *Essays on the Active Powers*, p. 149. See also p. 190.
46. Hume, *Treatise of Human Nature*, p. 490.
47. Hume, *Treatise of Human Nature*, pp. 490–491. Emphasis original.
48. Reid, *Essays on the Active Powers*, p. 342.
49. Reid, *Essays on the Active Powers*, p. 330. Emphasis original.
50. Reid, *Essays on the Active Powers*, p. 342.
51. Hume, *Enquiry Concerning the Principles of Morals*, p. 199n.
52. Cuneo, 'Does Reid Have Anything to Say to (the New) Hume?', p. 243.
53. See Reid, *Essays on the Active Powers*, p. 329.
54. Reid, *Essays on the Active Powers*, p. 342.
55. Reid, *Essays on the Active Powers*, pp. 330–333.
56. Reid, *Essays on the Active Powers*, p. 274.
57. Reid, 'Lectures and Papers on Practical Ethics', in *Thomas Reid on Practical Ethics*, p. 26. Punctuation and syntax original.
58. Reid, 'Lectures and Papers on Practical Ethics', in *Thomas Reid on Practical Ethics*, p. 26.
59. Reid, *Essays on the Active Powers*, p. 282.

5

Moral Perception

In the previous chapter we saw that, for Reid, duty is a simple and objective relationship between voluntary actions and second-personal agents, which provides to those agents reasons for action regarding desert, the performance of which is objectively laudable, so long as that action is intentionally performed on account of this relationship and not on account of any consideration of benefit or pleasure. Complex as this definition is, we also saw that, by taking this stance, Reid can account for a significant slice of human moral behaviour and speech which Hume cannot, while also avoiding the challenge posed by Hume's is/ought distinction. This definition, however, gave rise to two further questions. First, how is it that we perceive second-personal agents and reasons? And second, even supposing that there are features which mark out second-personal agents and reasons, in what manner do the latter, arising from relationships among the former, motivate us to act? Holding the second question for the next chapter, we will here attempt to answer the question regarding moral perception by examining Reid's account of the moral sense.

The Moral Sense as a Sense

As with the concept of duty, Reid begins his discussion of moral perception by pointing to synonymous words for the faculty of moral perception: 'moral sense, the moral faculty, conscience', and the *'sensus recti et honesti'*.[1] Reid uses all but the last of these names throughout his work, but most revealing of his position is the first.

As Reid well knew, the affirmation of a moral sense was common in his lifetime. Yet, according to Reid, there were, in his day, generally two competing accounts of the moral sense. One account, which Hume endorses, holds that our emotional reactions are the ultimate ground of our moral distinctions. The other account, which Reid endorses, holds that we perceive moral good and evil by an 'original power or faculty' in human beings.[2] Thus, although Hume and Reid both count themselves as proponents of moral sense, they mean different things. For Hume, 'moral sense' means something like 'moral sensibility'; it denotes a subset of our pleasant or unpleasant responses to perceived agents or actions. For Reid, on the other hand, the moral sense is a faculty of perception which perceives truths about the world in a manner analogous to the operation of our external senses. According to Reid, then, the moral sense is not a subset of emotive responses. It is a special faculty of the mind.

Reid's analogy between the external senses and the moral sense is provocative. Immediately, one wants to know how this moral faculty could act as a faculty of perception, since it seems to be different than our five external senses in several important ways. For one thing, there are no sensations associated with the moral sense. We have names for the sensations which accompany many of the perceptions of our external senses – e.g. lightness, darkness, sweetness, sourness, hardness, softness, smoothness, roughness, loudness, quietness – but nothing like for moral perception. For another, there is no organ of sensation obviously associated with the moral sense, as there is for sight, sound, taste, touch and smell.

Regarding the first of these apparent disanalogies between the moral sense and the external senses, Reid acknowledges that there is no sensation associated with moral perception, but this lack does not trouble him because the same can be said for certain forms of external perception. We can see that this is the case by noting that there are not one but two ways, according to Reid, that the external senses function. One obvious way that our perceptions arise is on account of sensations, which, according to Reid, serve as non-representational signs of the things signified. For instance, the pressure sensation of hardness – though not itself hard – gives us the perception of solidity. In his book on Reid's epistemology, Wolterstorff calls this account of perception the 'standard schema' since it is typically how Reid describes perception.[3]

Yet, as Wolterstorff notes, Reid also proposes an 'alternative schema' of perception, in which apprehension and judgement are not based on sensation.[4] Take, for example, our visual perception of shape. As we noted in chapter two when discussing the perception of a rectangular table, Reid believes that the perception of an object's physical shape, which he calls 'real figure', can be occasioned by sight.[5] The process by which this happens is quite complex, but essential to it is a concept which Reid calls 'visible figure': essentially, the projection of the three-dimensional space we have in view upon the two-dimensional areas of our retinae. Yet Reid writes that there 'seems to be no sensation appropriated' to this visible figure.[6]

Some Reid scholars have argued that in making this declaration, Reid is not speaking about the actual fact of human perception. According to Yaffe, for example, Reid is here conducting a thought experiment concerning what might have been – but is not – the case with human beings.[7] Similarly, Chris Shrock suggests that Reid is not claiming that there is no sensation associated with visible figure, but rather that there is no 'characteristic sensation' since 'visible figure is perceived in virtue of a variety of sensation types, visual and tactile'.[8] I will not attempt to adjudicate the issue here, nor is it necessary to do so. For, whether Reid believes a visible figure is or is not perceived by actual human beings on account of a sensation, he clearly believes that perception without sensation is possible. What we have, then, is a second Reidian account of perception, in which we (may) perceive objects in the real world without the occasioning sign of a sensation. The fact that the signs which the faculty of moral perception senses are not sensations, therefore, seems not to preclude Reid from calling it a 'sense'.

Still, even if there is no difficulty for Reid in acknowledging that there are no accompanying sensations which give rise to moral perceptions, there is another obvious distinction between our conscience and external senses: the moral sense has no organ of perception. At least in the perception of objects in our visual field, we know that it is occasioned through the operation of the eyes. But with the moral sense there is no specific organ of perception associated with moral perception. Our eyes and ears are probably the most common organs of perception associated with moral judgements, but it is easy to think of examples where moral perception is occasioned by others. A whiff of unfamiliar perfume may tell of infidelity as clearly as a photograph.

To address this discontinuity between the moral sense and the external senses, it is important to note two things. First, although Reid believes we perceive the figure, magnitude and position of objects in the external world through the organ of the eye, sight is not the only means by which we may perceive them. Inspired by his acquaintance with the blind mathematician Nicholas Saunderson, Reid notes that we may also perceive real figure, magnitude and position through the sense of touch.[9] By handling an object or tracing a line, that is, we may perceive its size and shape, and the relative position of various points. Thus, the fact that there is no one organ of sense associated with moral perception does not seem to be at odds with Reid's account of external perception.

Still, even with these points of connection granted, there appear to be further discontinuities between the moral sense and our physical senses, which are not so easily dismissed. For example, while the perception of figure, distance and position can be perceived by more than one sense, they are not as variously perceived as the perception of duty, which seems to supervene on perceptions of all of the external senses. Further, returning to one of Hume's objections, our external senses seem to tell us about facts regarding the material world, while Reid's account of duty describes it as a relation – as something, that is, strictly, inchoate. Reid does not deny that there are differences between the external senses and the moral sense. Yet Reid defends his use of the term 'moral sense' by stating that it gets its name 'from some analogy' to the external senses.[10] It does not, he grants, function exactly like the external senses. But the analogy is apt, Reid writes, because,

> as by [our external senses] we have not only the original conceptions of the various qualities of bodies, but the original judgments that this body has such a quality, that such another; so by our moral faculty, we have both the original conceptions of right and wrong in conduct, of merit and demerit and the original judgments that this conduct is right, that is wrong; that this character has worth, that, demerit.[11]

Reid never explicitly tells us what he means by 'original conceptions' and 'original judgment' here; and he uses these terms sparingly in his corpus.[12] Yet, as conception and judgement are the essential components of perception, we may, I think, confidently interpret Reid to be claiming that both the external senses and the moral sense generate what he calls 'original perceptions', which he describes extensively. On this reading, Reid is merely breaking the larger term, 'original perception', into the component parts of 'original conception' and 'original judgement'.

Taking this to be his meaning, let us recall that, according to Reid, all our external senses generate original perceptions. These perceptions are 'original' because they occur naturally and unavoidably, and cannot occur by any other means. A blind mathematician, for example, may be able to perceive that a ball is spherical just as well as a seeing person, on account of an original perception of touch. But they cannot tell us what colour it is, nor – should they be blind since birth – even conceive of what a 'colour' is, because colour is an original perception of our sense of sight.[13]

Contrasted with original perception, for Reid, is 'acquired perception'.[14] These latter perceptions follow after, are built upon original perception and are gained through experience and habit. For example, under the standard schema, the perception that there is a sweet smell is an original perception automatically prompted by a certain sensation in those with functioning olfactory systems, but unperceivable by someone born with anosmia. The recognition that a given sweet smell is associated with a particular type of plant – e.g. 'this is the smell of a rose' – is, by contrast, a perception we acquire through experience with flowers.[15]

The same can be said for perceptions plausibly falling under the alternative schema, like the visible perception of figure, magnitude and position. In all three we learn by experience that certain visible figures bear a (mathematically describable) relationship to real figures in the real world. Thus we learn, for example, that a given small and trapezoidal object in our visual field is actually a large, rectangular table at a distance.

Acquired perception is therefore a product not only of our external senses, but also experience and judgement. Interestingly, once we have become habituated to an acquired perception, according to Reid, the acquired perception typically effaces the original such that we have a hard time attending to the original perception without the acquired perception intruding upon our thoughts. Thus, once we have the perception 'this is the smell of a rose', we have a hard time sensing its sweet smell without immediately perceiving it under that aspect; and we may miss the fact that many roses smell like raspberries. Or, to give one of Reid's examples, once we acquire the visual perceptions of real figure, magnitude and distance, it is incredibly difficult to attend to our original perceptions of light, shade and colour – so difficult, in fact, that artists must train themselves not to see these acquired perceptions if they wish to paint convincing pictures.[16]

With the contrast between original and acquired perception in mind, we can see why Reid calls the moral faculty a 'sense', if only analogously. For Reid, the concept of duty, though describable by synonyms, is not divisible into simpler concepts. It is itself simple and cannot be perceived except by an original perception. Thus, if someone were to lack a moral sense – and some unfortunate people seem to have exactly this infirmity – they could never form the concept of 'justice', any more than a blind man could form the concept of 'red'. Similarly, while we might praise or punish animals for benevolent or malevolent qualities and actions, we do not treat them as moral agents. As anyone who has ever housetrained a dog knows, we do, of course, frequently try to teach animals by associating desirable or undesirable actions with good or bad consequences. But we do not put them on trial, or make contracts with them because, as Reid says, 'in man . . . natural affection is accompanied with a sense of duty, but in the dog, it is not'.[17]

What the Moral Sense Senses

In the above I have claimed that Reid posits a striking analogy between the moral sense and the external senses. Here, however, we might ask just how close this analogy between the moral sense and the external senses really is for Reid. Gordon Graham, for example, thinks that it is not a close analogy – though it may be a misleading one – writing that it is chiefly with respect to the '*feature of judgment* and not with respect to sensory input, that Reid thinks there is an analogy to be drawn' between the external senses and the moral sense.[18] This account of Reid's moral sense is not exactly contradictory, but it runs contrary to the one I have been advancing. In favour of Graham's interpretation are Reid's own worries about calling the moral faculty a 'sense': 'It is of small consequence what name we give to this moral power of the human mind . . . I find no fault with the name *moral sense*, although I think this name has given occasion to some mistakes concerning the nature of our moral power'.[19] Furthermore, Graham is certainly correct that, for Reid, the ability to make judgements is a key similarity between the moral sense and the external senses. And he is also correct to point out that Reid does not think of the moral sense as a kind of sixth external sense. As discussed, the moral sense does not take sensory input; it makes judgements about relations, not about sensations.

Yet, regarding Reid's concern about calling the conscience a 'moral sense', as Copenhaver points out, Reid fears that people will think that he is saying that the moral faculty is a passive sense of the type proposed under way of ideas.[20] This worry is therefore the opposite of Graham's concern, because Graham believes that it is only the capacity for judgement which underlies analogy between the external senses and the moral sense in Reid. Yet, as we have seen, this analogy does not end with judgement; it extends also to original conception. For the moral sense not only makes judgements about duty, it also gets a (moral) grip on the world by bringing it under conception. And it is for this reason – or so I suggest – that Reid frequently writes not just of moral judgement but of moral 'perception'.[21] According to Reid, perception is not just an act of judgement. For both our moral and our external senses, it is an act of both conception and judgement.

If this is Reid's position, then it leads us back to the question with which we began this chapter: how is it that the moral sense perceives second-personal agents and actions? This question may be taken in two ways. First, applying it to Reid's account of perception, it may be taken to ask what conceptions and judgements are produced by the moral sense. Second, it may also be taken to ask what it is in the world, and by what signs, the moral sense forms its conceptions and judgements. The close interaction of each of these four facets of perception in Reid make it difficult to talk about them in isolation from each other. But let us start at the end, with the things in the world, and work our way to signs, to conceptions and finally to judgements.

What in the World the Moral Sense Perceives: Signs and the Things Signified

Reid, as we have seen, is a moral objectivist, who believes that there are moral truths independent of our acknowledgement of them. Being thus mind-independent, these truths must be 'in the world'. But how is duty 'in the world'? As Hume astutely pointed out, you can examine a murder however you like, and you will never find its wrongness in the material facts of the murder. Such wrongness lacks what Hume calls 'real existence'.[22] In the previous chapter, we saw that Reid responded to the immateriality of moral obligation by describing it as a relation among entities which are physically manifest in the world. These entities, according to the definition of duty we above attributed to Reid, are second-personal agents and actions. These, then, are the entities in the world, the entities with 'real existence', among which the relation of duty arises.

This being the case, though, we may still wonder how we perceive second-personal agents and actions. What, in other words, are the signs of the thing signified? According to Reid, it is a first principle of contingent truth – that is, a principle of common sense – that 'certain features of the countenance, sounds of the voice, and gestures of the body, indicate certain thoughts and dispositions of the mind'.[23] There are, in other words, certain signs which prompt us to attribute certain mental capacities and mental states to beings we encounter. Many of these signs, according to Reid, are natural; the connection between them and the perceptions they prompt is not acquired by experience. Of the natural signs which indicate the contents of other minds, Reid writes that there is

> a connection established by Nature between certain signs in the countenance, voice, and gesture, and the thoughts and passions of the mind . . . that by our constitution, we understand the meaning of those signs, and from the sign conclude the existence of the thing signified.[24]

Thus,

> It is not by reasoning, that all mankind know, that an open countenance, and a placid eye, is a sign of amity; that a contracted brow, and a fierce look, is a sign of anger. It is not from reason that we learn to know the natural signs of consenting and refusing, or affirming and denying, of threatening and supplicating.[25]

Nor is there any necessary connection between these signs and what they signify. Their connection is contingent on our nature, as is our reliable interpretation of them.

Artificial signs, such as language or affected looks and gestures, also prompt an understanding of their meaning and an appreciation for the capacities of other minds. These signs are more varied and complicated than natural signs and are able to convey subtleties beyond the capacity of natural signs. Yet they are built upon the natural signs, and could not exist if we did not have the natural signs to function as a foundation upon which the artificial signs may be built. This, according to Reid, is how children learn language. Although they are born without knowledge of artificial signs, they learn the rudiments of language by associating certain sounds with the meaning of corresponding natural signs.[26] Taken together, these observations concerning natural and artificial signs lead Reid to assert, as a first principle of contingent truth, that 'certain features of the countenance, sounds of the voice, and gestures of the body, indicate certain thoughts and dispositions of the mind'.[27]

Reid does not explicitly make the connection, but since natural and artificial signs can convey the contents of other minds, they can also function as the signs by which we perceive intention and, by extension, moral agency. Returning to Darwall's definition of moral agency, this means that when these signs disclose second-personal authority, competence and responsibility, we naturally take the person under view to be a moral agent. Furthermore, when an act appears to be intentionally performed in virtue or violation of a second-personal reason, we take that act to be morally significant.

Our judgements concerning the agency and intentions of others are, of course, fallible. Sometimes we are deceived, and sometimes we merely get it wrong. Still, on Reid's account, without contrary evidence and absent pernicious prejudice, when we encounter someone who looks, talks and acts in a second-personal way – for example, they appear to make moral judgements, be swayed by moral arguments and engage in moral discourse – we take them, on good evidence, to be a moral agent. Similarly, when we observe the actions of someone whom we have judged to be a moral agent, we interpret them according to the intentions disclosed by natural and artificial signs. Reid thus proposes a kind of Turing test *avant la lettre* for moral agency. If a given entity displays convincing signs of such agency, we are justified in treating that entity as a moral agent and interpreting their actions according to their apparent intention.

What the Moral Sense Generates in the Mind of the Perceiver: Conception and Judgement

If the above is correct, then, according to Reid, the moral sense perceives relations among second-personal agents and actions through the mediation of natural and artificial signs, which reveal the second-personal capacities of those agents and disclose the intentions behind their actions. Here, though, we may ask, 'What do these signs generate in the mind of the perceiver?'.

As we saw in chapter two, perception, for Reid, is comprised of two features. There are conceptions (by which the mind gets a grip on percipients) and immediate judgements (in which we affirm their existence). Since they are simpler, let us start with moral conceptions before proceeding to moral judgements.

Moral Conception

In keeping with his belief that the moral sense is a sense, Reid describes the moral sense as a source of original conceptions. At the end of his chapter 'Of the Moral Sense' in the *Active Powers*, Reid writes that 'by an original power of mind, which we call *conscience, or the moral faculty*, we have conceptions of right and wrong in human conduct, of merit and demerit, of duty and moral obligation, and our other moral conceptions'.[28] A few chapters later, in 'Observations concerning Conscience', Reid further elaborates:

> By [the moral sense] solely we have the original conceptions or ideas of right and wrong in human conduct. And of right and wrong, there are not only many different degrees, but many different species . . .
>
> The conception of these as moral qualities, we have by our moral faculty; and by the same faculty, when we compare them together, we perceive various moral relations among them. Thus, we perceive, that justice is entitled to a small degree of praise, but injustice to a high degree of blame; and the same may be said of gratitude and its contrary. When justice and gratitude interfere, gratitude must give place to justice, and unmerited beneficence must give place to both.
>
> Many such relations between various moral qualities compared together, are immediately discerned by our moral faculty.[29]

From these statements we may make two observations regarding original moral conceptions. The first is that they are conceptions of evaluation. They imply, for example, that one thing is required and another is not, that one thing is more obligatory and thus more laudable than another. The second observation is that original moral conceptions are conceptions of relation. They either describe a relation between an agent and an action (that it is required or forbidden) or an agent and various actions (that some are to be preferred to others).

Put in these terms, Reid's point may seem obscure, but it is simple enough in application. Recalling that, for Reid, having a conception may merely mean having a mental grip on an idea and not necessarily a word or phrase to apply to it, what Reid is saying is that our moral faculty naturally and immediately prompts us to see certain agents as moral agents and certain actions performed by those agents as morally obligatory, forbidden, laudable, blameable or indifferent.

If this is right, then concepts like Darwall's moral authority, competence and responsibility are likely acquired; we come to them through the experience of having our original moral conceptions and extrapolating from them to certain categories of agents and actions. As Reid is nowhere explicit about acquired moral conceptions, this classification is admittedly contestable.[30] Still, although I think this is a plausible interpretation of Reid's thoughts on moral conception, not much hangs on it. For, although acquired conceptions must be the product of reason and experience, once we become habituated to their use we apply them immediately, just as we do original conceptions. Either way, concepts like second-personal authority, competence and responsibility all ultimately originate from the power of the moral sense to generate original conceptions.

Moral Judgements

So much for moral conceptions, what of moral judgements? In his chapter 'Of the Sense of Duty', Reid writes that 'I think all we can properly call moral judgements are reducible' to the judgement 'that such conduct is right, and deserving of moral approbation, or that it is wrong, or that it is indifferent, and, in itself, neither morally good or ill'.[31] From the way Reid writes about these judgements, it is evident that this is true upon the perception of both individual events and general statements.[32] Thus, the moral sense may deliver the judgement 'this is forbidden!' both upon the observation of a thief stealing someone's purse, and upon considering the question 'is stealing permitted?'. Similarly, it delivers the judgement 'you must help!' both when one sees a drowning man, and upon considering the question 'must we help those in peril?'.

For Reid, whether general or specific, most moral judgements are immediate and self-evident. They are all, therefore, first principles, because they spring from judgements of self-evidence and not from reasoning. As a result, there are at least as many moral first principles as there are possible actions taken in a community of second-personal agents: a potential infinity. However, 'without pretending to a complete enumeration', Reid supplies a list of those first principles from which he believes 'the whole system of moral conduct follows so easily, and with so little aid of reasoning, that every man of common understanding who wishes to know his duty, may know it'.[33]

In the *Active Powers*, Reid divides these first principles of morals into three general classes. The first class concerns those first principles of morality that 'relate to virtue in general'. They are:

1. There are some things in human conduct that merit approbation and praise, others that merit blame and punishment; and different degrees of either approbation or blame are due to different actions.
2. What is in no degree voluntary, can neither deserve moral approbation or blame.
3. What is done from unavoidable necessity may be agreeable or disagreeable, useful or hurtful, but cannot be the object of either of blame or of moral approbation.
4. Men may be highly culpable in omitting what they ought to have done, as well as in doing what they ought not.
5. We ought to use the best means we can to be well informed of our duty, by serious attention to moral instruction.
6. It ought to be our most serious concern to do our duty as far as we know it, and to fortify our minds against every temptation to deviate from it.[34]

The second class regards particular principles of duty.

1. We ought to prefer a greater good, though more distant, to a less; and a less evil to a greater.
2. As far as the intention of nature appears in the constitution of man, we ought to comply with that intention, and to act agreeably to it.
3. No man is born for himself only. Every man, therefore, ought to consider himself a member of the common society of mankind, and of those subordinate societies to which he belongs, such as a family, friends, neighbourhood, country, and to do as much good as he can, and as little hurt to the societies of which he is a part.
4. In every case we ought to act that part toward another, which we would judge to be right in him to act toward us, if we were in his circumstances and he in ours.
5. To every man who believes the existence, the perfections, and the providence of God, the veneration and submission we owe to him is self-evident.[35]

Finally, Reid provides two first principles regarding the relationship among virtues in those situations where the performance of one precludes the performance of another. First, 'unmerited generosity should yield to gratitude and both to justice'.[36] Second, 'unmerited beneficence to those who are at ease should yield to compassion to the miserable, and external acts of piety to works of mercy'.[37]

Problems with Reid's First Principles of Morals

There are four noteworthy features of this collection of lists. The first is that it is rather motley. The moral sceptic or subjectivist may well ask why we should accept a list which follows no clear order. Yet the disorder of the lists is, for Reid, merely the nature of morality. As Reid says, a

> system of morals is not like a system of geometry, where the subsequent parts derive their evidence from the preceding, and one chain of reasoning is carried on from the beginning . . . It resembles more a system of botany, or minerology, where the subsequent parts depend not for their evidence on the preceding.[38]

And this is reflected in the variety of the first principles of morals as well.

A second noteworthy feature of this list, and one that reverses his comparison with botany and geometry above, is that Reid holds that these first principles of morals are not contingent but necessary truths. This may at first seem highly improbable given how chancy and disputed moral judgements often seem. Consider, for example, the Reidian moral truth 'murder is wrong'. Most people agree that it is, in fact, wrong. But there have been many people in history who have been uncertain whether, or even denied that murder is wrong, if not *tout court*, then in certain circumstances. And, of course, there have also been a great many murders! If the wrongness of murder is uncertain and disputed, and if it is possible to commit a murder, how can 'murder is wrong' be one of the types of propositions which 'yield conclusions that are certain' and whose contraries are impossible?[39]

Reid answers this challenge on three levels. First, regarding the apparent tension between the asserted necessity of the first principles of morals and the contingency of some judgements of the moral sense, Reid holds that, although the first principles of morals are necessary truths, some judgements made by the moral sense regarding their application are contingent.

> Thus, a Magistrate knows that it is his duty to promote the good of the community which hath entrusted him with authority . . . [b]ut whether such a scheme of conduct in his office, or another, may best serve that end, he may in many cases be doubtful . . . [H]e can very rarely rely on demonstrative evidence.[40]

This is not an unusual position to hold. For we find the same to be the case regarding the application of other necessary truths to contingent situations. Take the Pythagorean Theorem. That, for all right triangles, the sum of the squares of their base sides is equal to the square of their hypotenuse is a necessary truth in the form of a general proposition. Similarly, it is also a necessary and particular truth that, for a given right triangle, the sum of the squares of its base sides is equal to the square of its hypotenuse. But whether the triangle we are examining is a right triangle, and therefore the sum of the squares of its base sides is equal to the square of its hypotenuse, is a contingent truth.[41] Yet the contingency of this final proposition does not negate the necessity of the Pythagorean Theorem, or the axioms of geometry. In the same way, there seems to be little difficulty in Reid simultaneously claiming that the first principles of morals are necessary truths while also holding that some judgements of the moral sense are contingent.

Second, regarding the possibility of dispute, Reid does not deny that the principles of morals, or indeed any truths necessary or contingent, are ever disputed. What he denies is that one can rationally dispute them. Being an objectivist regarding truth, Reid does not believe that our subjective attitude towards the world changes its truth.

Third, Reid readily acknowledges the ability of human beings to behave contrary to morals; but this does not contradict his statement that the truths of morals are necessary, because morals 'shew us, not what man is, but what he ought to be'.[42] Thus, first principles of morals are necessary in the sense that they tell us that certain obligations arise from certain relationships among agents and actions, not that those obligatory actions are necessarily performed.

If the above is correct, then it seems that Reid's belief that the first principles of morals are necessary truths is not philosophically troublesome. However, a third noteworthy feature of Reid's list is that it seems to oppose his own definition of 'moral'. To see this tension, compare Reid's extremely narrow definition of a properly 'moral' proposition – that is, only those propositions which tell us 'that such conduct is right, and deserving of moral approbation, or that it is wrong, or that it is indifferent, and, in itself, neither morally good or ill' – to his first four first principles of virtue in general.[43] These principles are not strictly normative. Unlike all the rest of his moral first principles, they do not tell us what we ought or ought not to do. They therefore fall short of properly 'moral' propositions.

Reid seems to be unaware of this tension – he never mentions it or tries to justify the inclusion of these principles under moral first principles – but it needs to be addressed. We have three plausible options. The first is to assume that these first four propositions actually are normative. To take this line is to say that the apparent tension between these principles and Reid's understanding of properly moral principles is the product of grammatical unclarity, which can be fixed by reformulating them so that they are obviously normative. Thus, proposition two – 'what is in no degree voluntary, can neither deserve moral approbation or blame' – may be rewritten as 'we ought not to ascribe moral approbation or blame to that which is in no degree voluntary'.

Yet there are two problems with this strategy. First, although propositions two through four may be plausibly, if somewhat awkwardly, rewritten in this way, it is hard to come up with a normative version of proposition one: 'there are some things in human conduct that merit approbation and praise, others that merit blame and punishment; and different degrees of either approbation or blame are due to different actions'.[44] Second, even if we were able to recast these propositions into a normative form, the normativity invoked seems to be that of truth, not morality. One could, without loss of accuracy, rewrite the mathematical axiom 'equals added to equals yields equals' as 'one ought to consider equals added to equals as equals', but the addition of the word 'ought' does not transform the mathematical first principle into a moral one. It only obscures its meaning. The same thing applies to the rewritten form of proposition two listed previously. Depending on circumstance, we might merit moral disapprobation by blaming someone for an involuntary action. But this type of moral error does not seem to be Reid's chief target. The error he is warning against here is ignorance, not vice. And this appears to be the case with all four of these propositions.

A second strategy is to say that Reid has blundered here and included non-moral first principles among his lists of moral first principles. A mistake of this kind is certainly possible but calls for explanation. One intriguing possibility is that Reid has made the same error he attributes to other philosophers, who include what Reid calls 'metaphysical' truths in their discussion of moral truths. The mistake is an easy one to make, according to Reid, because metaphysical truths and moral truths closely resemble one another. Take, for example, Locke's assertion that 'no government allows absolute liberty'.[45] Metaphysical truths like this one, according to Reid, are similar to moral truths in that they are necessary truths.[46] Further, metaphysical truths, like Locke's previously stated, may include moral concepts like justice, which are generated by the moral sense. Yet, despite these similarities, they are not like moral truths in this important regard: they are not normative.

If it is the case that Reid has accidentally included metaphysical propositions among his moral first principles, the proper action seems to be to cut them out of his lists of the first principles of morals. Yet this seems too high a price to pay. Excluding all of them shortens the list of first principles relating to 'virtue in general' from six to two. It is certainly possible that Reid both fell into the same error he identified in Locke, and also mistook the nature of two-thirds of the principles on his first list, but the evidence required for so uncharitable a reading seems high.

Third and finally, we could try to solve this puzzle by accepting these propositions as strictly non-normative – as metaphysical – and then attempting to justify their inclusion in a list of the first principles of morals. This option is like the one previously mentioned, except that it allows a certain subset of properly 'metaphysical' propositions to operate as first principles of morals. On this interpretation, we should read Reid's phrase 'the first principles of morals' as meaning something closer to 'first principles about morals' and not 'moral propositions which are also first principles', the former being a more inclusive category.[47]

This last option is, I believe, the best for two reasons. First, it relieves the burden of explaining how Reid could make a great blunder. Second, it helps us to make sense of a fourth noteworthy feature of Reid's lists of first principles of morals, which is that they do not tell us about specific duties. That this is the case is evident when we compare Reid's lists of first principles to any list of basic duties, such as the second table of the decalogue. In the latter we are famously told that murder, adultery, stealing and false testimony are forbidden, but we find nothing like this in Reid's lists of the first principles of morals.

That Reid does not include such principles prompts two questions. First, why doesn't he include them? And second, how is it that the principles he does include function as a foundation 'on which all moral reasoning is grounded' and from which 'the whole system of moral conduct follows'?[48] After all, if Reid believes that principles like the ones found in the decalogue are also first principles of morals, in that they are immediately judged by the moral sense without reasoning, it seems that we have scant need for foundational first principles outlined in Reid's three lists. There is little to deduce in morals because most moral judgements are first principles.

As I read them, both questions can be answered by interpreting the first principles of morals given in Reid's three lists as operating constitutively. By this I mean that they do not contain our basic duties – don't murder, steal, etc. Rather, they describe the arena in which moral judgement and reasoning occurs, and how to adjudicate among various moral judgements. In this, they bear some analogy to the rules of chess.[49] They are not moves within the game; they circumscribe the area in which the game is played and tell us how to figure out which move is best in a given circumstance.

If this is the case, then it makes sense that Reid does not include basic moral judgements like 'murder is forbidden' in his list of moral first principles. For, even though 'murder is forbidden' is both a moral proposition and a first principle, it is a move within the arena of morality, not one of its constitutive rules. It also explains why, as I argued above, Reid includes some metaphysical principles in the first principles of morals. For these metaphysical principles are constitutive in this way: they tell us that moral judgements apply to human actions which are free and voluntary, and apply to 'acts' of omission, as well as commission. They give us the rules of the game.

Similarly, seeing Reid's lists of the first principles of morals in this light also explains how they can function as a kind of foundation for morality. They do not, like the axioms of geometry, provide all the subject's first principles, from which every other principle is deduced. But we need them to know when a moral judgement is appropriate and how to adjudicate among various conflicting moral judgements. They thus serve as a necessary foundation to 'moral reasoning', which Reid says is 'brought to prove that such conduct is right, and deserving of moral approbation, or that it is wrong, or that it is indifferent, and in itself neither morally good nor ill'.[50] In a simple instance, where the choice is whether or not to hand someone over to unjust death, the moral judgement 'abetting a murder is wrong' suffices. There is no need for moral reasoning. The same is true of the moral judgement 'lying is wrong' if the choice is simply whether or not to lie. But in a complex situation – like the famous Nazis-at-the-door example, when deciding the culpability of a person who killed their abuser, or at what point life support may be withdrawn from a dying patient – we need more than immediate moral judgements such as 'murder is wrong' and 'lying is wrong'. Specifically, we need to know the exact parameters under which moral judgements are appropriate, and how to choose among conflicting moral judgements. And that is where Reid's lists of the first principles of morals prove essential.

Notes

1. Reid, *Essays on the Active Powers*, p. 175.
2. Reid, *Essays on the Active Powers*, p. 175.
3. Wolterstorff, *Thomas Reid and the Story of Epistemology*, p. 96.
4. Wolterstorff, *Thomas Reid and the Story of Epistemology*, p. 136. Cuneo similarly calls this the 'non-standard schema'. See Cuneo, 'Reidian Moral Perception', p. 233.
5. See especially Reid, *Inquiry into the Human Mind*, pp. 95–98.
6. Reid, *Inquiry into the Human Mind*, p. 101.
7. Yaffe, 'Reid on the Perception of Visible Figure'.
8. Shrock, *Thomas Reid and the Problem of Secondary Qualities*, p. 108.
9. Reid, *Inquiry into the Human Mind*, pp. 65–67 and *Essays on the Intellectual Powers*, pp. 233–225.
10. Reid, *Essays on the Active Powers*, p. 175.
11. Reid, *Essays on the Active Powers*, p. 176.
12. See Reid, *Essays on the Active Powers*, p. 195 and Reid, *Thomas Reid on Logic, Rhetoric, and the Fine Arts*, pp. 167, 170, 172.
13. Reid, *Inquiry into the Human Mind*, p. 51.
14. Reid, *Inquiry into the Human Mind*, p. 171.
15. Reid, *Essays on the Intellectual Powers*, p. 235.

16. Reid, *Inquiry into the Human Mind*, pp. 101–102.

17. Reid, *Essays on the Active Powers*, p. 305. See also pp. 189–190, and 225.

18. Graham, 'Was Reid a Moral Realist', p. 49. Emphasis original.

19. Reid, *Essays on the Active Powers*, p. 300. Quoted in Copenhaver 'Reid on the Moral Sense', p. 81.

20. Copenhaver 'Reid on the Moral Sense', p. 81.

21. See Reid, *Essays on the Active Powers*, pp. 175, 178, 180, 190, 195, 217, 276, 277, 285, 300, 304, 306, 309, 311, 335 and 'Lectures and Papers on Practical Ethics', in *Thomas Reid on Practical Ethics*, pp. 43, 55, 57, 78, 110.

22. Hume, *Treatise of Human Nature*, p. 468.

23. Reid, *Essays on the Intellectual Powers*, p. 484.

24. Reid, *Essays on the Intellectual Powers*, p. 487. See also *Inquiry into the Human Mind*, pp. 58–61. For an enlightening discussion on the nature of the natural signs involved in Reid's account of moral perception see Kroeker, 'Reid on Natural Signs, Taste, and Moral Perception'.

25. Reid, *Essays on the Active Powers*, p. 332.

26. Reid, *Essays on the Active Powers*, p. 331.

27. Reid, *Essays on the Intellectual Powers*, p. 484.

28. Reid, *Essays on the Active Powers*, p. 180. Emphasis original.

29. Reid, *Essays on the Active Powers*, p. 195.

30. See Copenhaver 'Reid on the Moral Sense', pp. 92–100.

31. Reid, *Essays on the Active Powers*, p. 177. See also Reid, *Essays on the Intellectual Powers*, pp. 550–551.

32. See, e.g. Reid, *Essays on the Intellectual Powers*, p. 521.

33. Reid, *Essays on the Active Powers*, pp. 270 and 277.

34. Reid, *Essays on the Active Powers*, p. 271.

35. Reid, *Essays on the Active Powers*, pp. 272–276.

36. Reid, *Essays on the Active Powers*, p. 276.

37. Reid, *Essays on the Active Powers*, p. 276.

38. Reid, *Essays on the Active Powers*, p. 281.

39. Reid, *Essays on the Intellectual Powers*, p. 455.

40. Reid, *Essays on the Intellectual Powers*, pp. 552–553.

41. For an alternative account of relationship between necessary and contingent propositions affirmed by the moral sense see Cuneo 'Reid on the First Principles of Morals', pp. 103–105. Cuneo has, I think, confused the necessity of moral principles with the contingency of the entities which entail them.

42. Reid, *Essays on the Active Powers*, p. 179.

43. Reid, *Essays on the Active Powers*, p. 177. See also Reid, *Essays on the Intellectual Powers*, pp. 550–551.
44. Reid, *Essays on the Active Powers*, p. 270.
45. Locke, *An Essay Concerning Human Understanding*, p. 550. Quoted in Reid, *Essays on the Intellectual Powers*, p. 550.
46. Reid, *Essays on the Intellectual Powers*, p. 495.
47. See Cuneo, 'Reid on the First Principles of Morals', p. 107.
48. Reid, *Essays on the Active Powers*, pp. 270 and 277.
49. Unlike Reid's first principles, the rules of chess are not, of course, necessary truths.
50. Reid, *Essays on the Active Powers*, p. 177.

6

Moral Motivation

In the previous chapter we saw that, according to Reid, the moral sense bears an analogy to the external senses in that it apprehends natural and artificial signs, produces original conceptions and makes original judgements.[1] Yet, despite the analogy between the moral sense and the external senses, the moral sense clearly differs from them in this important way: the moral sense not only tells us about the state of the world, it motivates us to act.

The purpose of this chapter is to explain how, according to Reid, the moral sense prompts us to act. This is a challenge in two ways. First, in his own day, Reid's theories of moral perception and moral motivation were opposed by moral sentimentalists like Hume, who held that all motivations were, at bottom, passions. Second, today there are two conflicting interpretations of Reid's response to the sentimentalist challenge. Some commentators – most notably James Van Cleve – argue that Reid accepts the sentimentalist belief that the faculty of reason is inert, and that only affective states like passions or desires can move us to act.[2] According to this interpretation, Reid holds a semi-sentimentalist position in which our duties are perceived by reason, but require the influence of the passions to motivate action. Others, like William Rowe, agree that Reid is a rationalist with respect to moral perception, and that he affirms the existence of moral affections, but also holds that the moral sense moves us to act through the influence of rational motives. On this account, we perceive our duties by reason, but are motivated to act both by the emotions those perceptions excite and through the rational influence of those perceptions themselves. In my opinion, the latter interpretation is correct. In this chapter I will therefore try to explain why we ought to see Reid's account of moral motivation as proceeding along two simultaneous tracks: motivational rationalism and motivational sentimentalism.

Hume's Challenge to the Rational Motivation of Morality

To see the distinction between motivational rationalism and motivational sentimentalism, it is helpful to start with Hume's classic argument for the latter. According to Hume, the apparent fact that our moral perceptions move us to action is good evidence against moral rationalism. As Hume puts it in the *Treatise*:

> Since morals . . . have an influence on the actions and affections, it follows that they cannot be deriv'd from reason; and that because reason alone, as we have already prov'd, can never have such influence. Morals excite passions and produce or prevent actions. Reason of itself is utterly impotent in this particular. The rules of morality, therefore, are not conclusions of our reason.[3]

Hume's conclusion clearly relies on a prior argument for the inertness of reason, which we will address in chapter eight. But even incomplete, Hume's argument is helpful because it serves as a foil for moral rationalism. To this end, Van Cleve has helpfully schematised Hume's argument as follows:

1. Moral evaluations are necessarily motivating.
2. No judgement of reason (such as the supposed judgement that one ought to do A) is necessarily motivating.
3. Therefore, moral evaluations are not judgements of reason.[4]

Note that this argument is related to, but not identical with, Hume's is/ought distinction. In the is/ought distinction, Hume argued that we cannot move from a description of the way things are ('is') to normativity ('ought') by reason alone. In chapter four we addressed this concern by appealing to Stephen Darwall's second-person standpoint, which holds that normative, second-personal reasons for acting arise among communities of second-personal agents. Hume's argument here, by contrast, addresses not the normative status of reasons but the rational faculty. For Hume, because our judgements cannot move us, there must be something else which moves us from an understanding about the way things are to a practical attitude about the way things should be. For Hume, this 'something else' is sentiment.[5] In the argument schematised by Van Cleve as presented here, Hume uses the clear normative status of our moral attitudes and the supposed inertness of our rational faculty to bolster his argument for moral perceptual sentimentalism.

Reid, of course, cannot accept that morality is 'more properly felt than judg'd of': that moral motivational sentimentalism funds moral perceptual sentimentalism.[6] As we have seen, Reid's entire account of moral perception is dedicated to showing that morality is indeed 'judg'd of' by the moral sense. He must therefore deny or modify at least one of Hume's premises to make the case for moral rationalism. But which? And how?

Reid and Motivational Sentimentalism

According to Van Cleve, Reid responds to Hume by rejecting the first of these premises – moral evaluations are necessarily motivating – and modifying the second such that it reads 'no judgement of reason is morally motivating *by itself*'.[7] This allows Van Cleve to propose an interesting interpretation of Reid's position. According to this interpretation, Reid's considered position is that the moral sense is a rational faculty of perception which is capable of prompting affective, motivating responses. On this reading, then, Reid is a rationalist with respect to moral perception, but a sentimentalist with respect to moral motivation; he accepts the inertness of reason without abandoning moral perceptual rationalism. Thus, the perception of morality by itself does not motivate us to act. It only does so by the aid of our passions.

Reid as a Motivational Sentimentalist

As evidence for his sentimentalist interpretation of Reid, Van Cleve points to a passage in the *Active Powers* where Reid notes the close relationship between our moral judgements and our attitudes of moral approbation and disapprobation. According to Reid:

> Our moral judgements are not like those we form in speculative matters, dry and unaffecting, but, from their nature, are necessarily accompanied with affections and feelings.
>
> It was before observed, that every human action, considered in a moral view, appears to us good, bad, or indifferent. When we judge the action to be indifferent, neither good nor bad, though this be a moral judgement, it produces no affection nor feeling, any more than our judgements in speculative matters.

But we approve of good actions, and disapprove of bad; and this approbation and disapprobation, when we analyse it, appears to include, not only a moral judgement of the action, but some affection, favourable or unfavourable, towards the agent, and some feeling in ourselves.[8]

In this passage Reid proposes that the perception of duty prompts 'affections and feelings' of approbation and disapprobation which motivate us to act. For Reid, affections and feelings are different but related phenomena. An 'affection' is an animal principle of action directed towards a person or animated being.[9] A feeling, on the other hand, is an agreeable or uneasy emotion. According to Reid, all affections are accompanied by corresponding feelings.[10] Thus, when we consider an action morally praiseworthy, positive feelings about that action naturally arise within us, on account of our esteem for the agent which performed the action. Similarly, when we consider a morally blameworthy action, negative feelings naturally arise within us, on account of the disapprobation we feel towards the agent which performed the action. Van Cleve's position therefore has textual support.

Further, this textual support is not limited to the passage just cited. Recall, for instance, our definition of duty back in chapter four. There we noted that Reid believed the performance of duty to be both laudable and typically lauded. This seems to imply that there is a close connection between our perception of duty and the generation of affective responses – a connection Reid makes explicit when he claims that positive and negative affections and feelings accompany our perception of virtue and vice on account of 'the constitution of our nature'.[11]

Yet, as Van Cleve recognises, there are also passages in Reid's works regarding the nature of this connection which cause trouble for this position. For Reid not only describes a natural connection between our moral perceptions and moral sentiments, he also indicates that there is a 'necessary' connection between our moral perception and moral sentiments.[12] This is a puzzling thing for Reid to assert. For one thing, it seems to fly in the face of his statement that duty is what is 'laudable though no man should praise it'.[13] If the connection between the perception of duty and a feeling of approbation is necessary, how could we not praise it?

According to Van Cleve, we can explain this puzzling claim by treating it as an exaggeration. Since Reid does not try to justify a logically or metaphysically necessary connection between moral judgements and feelings, and since he more frequently describes the connection between moral judgements and feelings as contingent upon our nature, Reid's considered position, according to Van Cleve, is that our moral perceptions typically but not infallibly generate motivating feelings. Interpreting Reid in this way bolsters Van Cleve's argument for interpreting Reid as a moral motivational sentimentalist. For, if moral judgements and moral affections were logically or metaphysically necessarily connected, then Reid would not deny but endorse Hume's first proposition. Moral evaluations, for him, would be necessarily motivating.

As for the second proposition of Hume's argument – that no judgement of reason is necessarily motivating – Van Cleve argues that Reid partly agrees, insofar as he holds that reason is, as Hume puts it, 'utterly impotent'.[14] If Van Cleve is correct about this, then Reid is half a moral rationalist and half a moral sentimentalist. For, while Reid cannot accept Hume's theory of moral perception, he does accept Hume's theory of moral motivation, bridging the gap between these two seemingly contradictory positions by positing natural affective responses occasioned by our rational moral judgements. Such a position is unusual and, as Van Cleve notes, would put Reid out of step with other moral rationalists such as his contemporary Richard Price, who believed that moral perceptions were themselves motivating. Yet, for the reasons given above, Van Cleve believes this to be the best rendering of Reid's position regarding moral motivation.

Van Cleve's interpretation is both textually supported and interesting. And, in one sense, it works. It both honours Reid's rationalist account of moral perception and answers Hume's challenge to rational moral perception. Still, while it is an answer to Hume's challenge, I do not think it is Reid's. As I see it, Reid is a rationalist with respect to both moral perception and moral motivation. To make this case, let me start by noting one point in which I agree with Van Cleve. Reid clearly believes that our rational moral perceptions typically and naturally occasion affective responses. This, however, is not the entirety of Reid's account. As I see it, Reid's sentimentalist account of moral motivation runs in parallel, and not in contrast, to a rationalist account of moral motivation. To make this case, however, we must turn from the immediate matter at hand, and say a little about Reid's theory of human agency more generally.

Reid's Theory of Human Agency

Reid's theory of human agency is difficult to summarise, for at least two reasons. First, Reid is not always consistent or clear in his terminology. Second, the widely acknowledged complexity of human action, and Reid's Baconian suspicion of theoretical simplicity, led him to propose an intricate, subtle and admittedly incomplete account of human agency. In order not to stray too far from the topic of moral motivation, I will therefore not attempt to give a full account of Reid's understanding of agency, or of his defence of free will.[15] Instead, I will try to outline the points most important for our purposes by contrasting Reid's account of agency with the account he wished to deny, paying particular attention to Reid's two distinct uses of the word 'motive'.

To this end, let us start with the account of human agency Reid rejects. According to Reid, there was, in his day, a growing belief that human actions are not, in a robust sense, free. As he saw it, philosophers like Locke, Hume and Joseph Priestley held that the actions of human beings are determined by forces outside their wills. While arguing for a libertarian notion of freedom in the *Active Powers* and his late essay 'Some Observations On the Modern System of Materialism', Reid acknowledges that each of these philosophers' arguments for necessity had their own emphases and subtilties.[16] Yet, for simplicity's sake, we may borrow a distillation of these arguments from Terence Cuneo.

According to Cuneo, Reid believed the basic argument for necessity consisted of three premises.

1. Every human action has a sufficient cause.
2. Provided normal background conditions obtain, the sufficient cause of a human action is its motive, which is a mental state of an agent.
3. Every human action is subsumable under a law, which specifies that for any agent S, set of motives M, and action A at t, necessarily, if S performs A, then there is some member of M that is S's strongest motive, which causes S to perform A at t.[17]

The upshot of this argument is that all our actions are determined by motives which are not otherwise under our control. We act according to the strongest motive within us at a given time, but we have no choice regarding what motives we have or their relative strength, except that they can arise from situations influenced by previous actions, which were, in turn, determined by prior motives.

Against this account of human action, Reid argued for a libertarian version of free will, according to which our actions are determined not by motives, but rather by ourselves. Again, Cuneo has helpfully summarised Reid's position, which I have produced below with a little emendation.

1. Every human action has a cause, which in the case of free human action is not itself a motive, but the agent himself.
2. Motives [in the narrow sense] are not mental states but the ends for which an agent acts.
3. Human action is nomic [i.e. subject to general laws] only to this extent: If an agent fails to exercise autonomy when deliberating (and he is not in a state of indifference), then his strongest desire to act in a certain way will prevail. If he exercises autonomy when deliberating, however, then he will act on the motive that seems to him most rationally appropriate.[18]

This account of human agency clearly contrasts with that of necessity, but may be confusing at first glance. On the one hand, the first two clauses tell us that 1) human actions are not determined by motives, and 2) that motives to action are not mental states like desires. On the other hand, it tells us 3) that sometimes – specifically, when we do not act autonomously and are not in a state of indifference – our actions are motivated by our strongest desire. There therefore seems to be some complex interaction among the ideas of causation, agency, motive and desire that produce human actions. But what that consists of requires further explanation.

Going step by step, we can clarify the first proposition above by getting a good handle on Reid's use of the word 'cause'. According to Reid, only free agents are, properly, 'causes'. Autonomous human beings and God, on this account, are therefore causes. But one billiard ball hitting a second is not truly the cause of the latter's movement. In this case, the true causes of the second ball's movement are the human being who struck the first billiard ball with a cue stick, and God, who is the agent behind all the regularities we observe in the universe, such as the laws of motion. Thus, while Reid grants that we loosely call phenomena like gravity or oxidation 'causes' in physics or chemistry, he believes they are not properly so called. Rather, they are the effects of God's causal agency.

On Reid's understanding, then, the terms 'agent' and 'cause' are, when precisely used, synonyms.

In line with this strict use of the words 'agent' and 'cause', Reid carefully delineates the power of determining the will from motives – that is, from all of the types of influences which suggest actions to us. According to Reid,

> [t]he advice given to a man [by motives] and his determination consequent to that advice, are things so different in their nature, that it would be improper to call them modifications. In like manner, the motives to action, and the determination to act or not to act, are things that have no common nature, and therefore ought not to be confounded under one name.[19]

In other words, well-functioning and mature human beings – agents – have the power to choose whether to act according to various motives, or even to act without one. As such they have what Reid calls 'active power'.

Frustratingly – though much in keeping with his typical method – Reid refuses to define 'active power'.[20] But Cuneo supplies a helpful description: 'active power is the executive practical capacity we exercise in order to regulate principles of action', like desires and judgements about duty.[21] Otherwise 'active' beings which do not have active power – like animals, infants and madmen – on the other hand, lack agency because they do not have the ability to choose from among motives and thereby determine their will. This means that although these latter beings make changes in the world – sometimes to great effect – they are not, for Reid, causes in the proper sense, because their wills are determined by forces outside themselves.

As for the second proposition of Cuneo's formulation above, my emendation 'in the narrow sense' is necessary because Reid uses the word 'motive' in two ways. First, as Cuneo notes, Reid often uses the word 'motive' in a 'wide' sense, to include both rational ends apprehended by reason and mental states like desires.[22] Yet Reid also uses 'motive' in a narrower sense, to mean only the former. Thus, while the wide use of the word 'motive' incorporates both animal and rational principles of action, the narrow sense only denotes the rational principles.[23] And it is in this narrow sense only that Reid can claim that motives are not mental states, but rather ends for action.

By contrast, under the wide use of the term 'motives', Reid calls inducements to action from mental states like desire and affection 'animal motives'.[24] These motives are 'not addressed to the rational powers', but their 'influence is immediately upon the will'.[25] By the word 'immediate' here, Reid does not mean that such motives are always acted upon. Although human beings 'feel their influence and judge of their strength, by the conscious effort which is necessary to resist them', we can choose not to follow them.[26] However – to make the same comparison as above – animals, infants and madmen cannot resist these motives and always act upon the strongest one at any given time.

Animal motives are the only type of motives which influence active but non-agential beings. In addition to animal motives, though, well-functioning human beings may be influenced by what Reid calls 'rational motives'. These are the type of motives which are exclusively identified under the narrow sense of 'motive', and 'do not give blind impulse to the will as animal motives do', but '[t]heir influence is upon the judgement, by convincing us that such an action ought to be done'.[27] When it comes to a competition among rational motives, Reid writes that 'it is evident, that the strongest, in the eye of reason, is that which it is most our duty and our real happiness [i.e. in accordance with the two rational principles of action] to follow'.[28] Likewise, when there is competition between rational and animal motives, Reid claims that 'every man, endowed with reason, is conscious he ought to pursue [rational motives] in preference to all others', even though the strongest concurrent animal motives occasionally point in the opposite direction.[29]

Finally, in the third statement in Cuneo's formulation of Reid's position regarding human action, we see that Reid does not completely reject the system of necessity. Rather, he constrains it, holding that the system of necessity well-describes the activity of beings like animals and infants, which lack active power. According to Reid, these beings have perceptions and will, but lack understanding. They therefore act according to the strongest current (animal) motive. And the same can be said for well-functioning human beings who – perhaps on account of a fit of passion, exhaustion or moral frailty – fail to exercise the power they have over their wills. Yet, when well-functioning human beings exercise the power of determining their wills by choosing to act according to rational motives – and/or according to the animal motives which best accord with their rational motives – they act as true causes and agents.

Thus, in summary, what we have in Reid is a complicated account of human action. When human beings act autonomously – as agents – they determine their own will under the influence, but not the direction, of both rational and animal motives. These motives operate on the will in different ways: the rational motives presenting ends, and the animal motives pushing us towards or pulling the will away from certain behaviours. However, human beings may also 'act', in the sense of manifesting behaviour, according to the strongest current animal motive. When behaviour is produced in this way, it is not properly the action of that human being, because they are functioning like non-agents. They are, in this case, not properly the cause of their own actions, but rather passive instruments of other causes.[30]

Reid and Motivational Rationalism

Throughout his accounts and defences of free will Reid justifies his libertarian position in the Baconian manner we discussed in chapter one: through appeals to observed language, behaviour and introspection. Of course, these appeals are not indefeasible, as the wide variety of philosophical opinions on free will shows. On the other hand, and to be fair to Reid, we have not yet come up with a better method of justifying various accounts of free will, and Reid's is *prima facie* plausible. Regardless of one's judgement regarding the accuracy of Reid's understanding of free will, with it before us we can now return to the central issue of this chapter, Reid's account of moral motivation.

To reiterate, Van Cleve holds that Reid has a rationalist account of moral perception but a sentimentalist account of moral motivation. According to Van Cleve, this position allows Reid to provide an interesting and cogent response to Hume's argument – which uses the assumption of moral motivational sentimentalism to argue for moral perceptual sentimentalism – by contending that there is a natural connection in human beings between our rational moral perceptions and our sentimental moral motivations. But, in order to claim that Reid believes there is only a natural, nomological connection between rational perception and sentimental motivation, Van Cleve was forced to override the plain meaning of several texts where Reid writes of a necessary connection between moral perception and moral motivation. By adopting a dual-track account of moral motivation, according to which we are moved to moral action by both rational and animal motives, however, we need not radically reinterpret these passages as Van Cleve does.

One of the advantages of a dual-track interpretation of moral motivation is that it can affirm the ways in which Van Cleve's interpretation is clearly correct. In recognition of the occasional mismatch between our moral judgements and the passions they prompt, Reid holds that the connection between them is 'physio-nomological', not 'logico-metaphysical'.[31] Thus, according to Reid, perceptions of virtue typically, but not invariably, generate positive affective responses within human beings, just as percep-tions of vice typically, but not invariably, generate negative affec-tive responses. Yet, according to this dual-track interpretation, there are two other possible ways that there can be a connection between moral perception and moral motivation, which honour Reid's use of the word 'necessary'.

One of the possible necessary connections between moral per-ception and moral motivation is moral normativity.[32] Reid does not make this point explicitly, but he affirms the connection in various ways. For example, Reid describes duty as that which is 'laudable, though no man should praise it'.[33] Further, for Reid it is a first principle of moral truth that there 'are some things in human conduct that merit approbation and praise, others that merit blame and punishment; and different degrees of either approbation or blame are due to different actions'.[34] These quota-tions do not contradict Van Cleve's observation that our moral judgements and our moral affections are occasionally at odds. Yet they also seem to indicate that we are morally required to have emotions of moral approbation and disapprobation in accordance with our moral judgements. And, being a moral requirement, the connection between them is thus a necessary one on Reid's view.

Interpreting Reid as holding that there is a necessary norma-tive connection between moral perception and affective response makes good sense of some of the passages which Van Cleve finds puzzling. For example, in response to Reid's assertion that 'we can-not conceive a greater depravity in the heart of man, than . . . to see and acknowledge worth without feeling any respect to it; or to see and acknowledge the highest worthlessness without any degree of dislike and indignation', Van Cleve writes that 'no one would denounce as depraved what he regards as logically impossible'.[35] Of course, no one would. And it is further true that although we are naturally inclined to praise the morally worthy and feel indignation

towards the morally vicious, there are times when human beings
fail to do so. Yet there is nothing strange about finding this behaviour depraved if the conceptual connection between the perception
and the affective response is moral necessity – if it is something we
morally ought to do, and are inclined to do, but sometimes do not.
Nor is there anything strange about taking pains to cultivate our
affections and passions so that they align with and reinforce our
best moral judgements. As Reid says in his gloss on his sixth first
principle of morals regarding virtue in general, we 'may fortify our
minds against every temptation to deviate from' duty

> by maintaining a lively sense of the beauty of right conduct, and of
> its present and future reward, of the turpitude of vice, and of its bad
> consequences here and hereafter; by having always in our eye the
> noblest examples; [and] by the habit of subjecting our passions to the
> government of reason . . .[36]

If moral normativity were the only necessary connection
between moral perception and moral motivation, then Van Cleve
could still be right in claiming that there is no logical or metaphysical connection between our moral judgements and affective
responses. And, if this is the case, he could also be right in claiming that, for Reid, our moral judgements require the aid of our
passions to be motivated. Yet, *contra* Van Cleve, Reid seems to
also hold that there is a logical connection between moral perception and moral motivation. Consider this passage, in which Reid
discusses the connection between desire and the perception of
our other rational principle of action, 'good on the whole'.

> I am very apt to think, with Dr Price, that, in intelligent beings, the
> desire of what is good, and aversion to what is ill, is necessarily con-
> nected with the intelligent nature; and that it is a contradiction to
> suppose such a being to have a notion of good without the desire of
> it, or the notion of ill without the aversion to it.[37]

Taken at face value, this passage seems to contradict the point at
which I agreed with Van Cleve in the previous pages: that Reid
believes there is no necessary, non-moral connection between
our moral perceptions and our actual affections. It seems, rather,
to say that there is more than a morally necessary connection
between them.

Van Cleve addresses the difficulty of this passage by interpreting Reid's use of 'necessarily connected' loosely. By 'necessarily connected', that is, Van Cleve reads Reid as claiming that it typically occurs. Yet this passage presents another problem for Van Cleve, which is that it seems to align Reid's response to Hume with Richard Price's. The difficulty here, as Van Cleve acknowledges, is that Price clearly accepts Hume's first premise (moral evaluations are necessarily motivating) while rejecting the second (that no judgement of reason is necessarily motivating). In response to this problem, Van Cleve argues that this is another place where Reid's considered view differs from the one he appears to endorse.[38]

Taking such a drastic interpretive line is, however, unnecessary, so long as we make a smaller interpretive move and read Reid's use of the words 'desire' and 'aversion' here to mean something other than affective response. Instead, I propose that we interpret Reid's use of 'desire' and 'aversion' in this instance as indicating the state of being motivated towards or away from something in Cuneo's narrow sense – that is, towards an end and not on account of an affective state. In this, I agree with William L. Rowe that Reid sometimes uses the word 'desire' to indicate a 'rational desire' – that is, an inclination towards or aversion to an action or person which is rational as opposed to passionate.[39]

Van Cleve could reply that to interpret the word 'desire' in this way flies in the face of Reid's explicit classification of 'desire' as an 'animal principle', which he defines as principles that 'operate upon the will and intention, but do not suppose any exercise of judgment or reason', and is therefore no less drastic a reading than his reading of 'necessary' as 'frequently'.[40] Yet there are two reasons, beyond Reid's inexact terminology, that we might prefer this line. First, it maps on to Reid's distinction between rational and animal motives. If the influence of a rational motive 'is upon the judgment by convincing us that such an action ought to be done', then there is a necessary connection between the judgement that a certain action tends towards our good on the whole or is our duty and a motive towards it.[41] If we can be influenced by rational motives, as Reid says, then it is, in his own words, 'a contradiction' to come to judge that 'this should be done' without that judgement having some motive influence. As we are both free and prone to forfeit our self-governance in the face of strong animal desires, having this motive does not, of course, entail that we act according to it. But if human beings are influenced by rational motives, it is impossible to conceive what it would be like to come to hold a normative judgement without it having any motive influence. What would it be like to rationally assent to a proposition like 'I should pay what I owe' and not be rationally motivated to pay what you owe?

Second, if we do not read Reid's use of the word 'desire' here to indicate the state of having a rational motive, then it undermines Reid's frequent contrast between our rational and animal motives. For example, just above the previously quoted passage Reid writes:

> I observe . . . [t]hat as soon as we have the conception of what is good or ill for us upon the whole, we are led, by our constitution, to seek the good and avoid the ill; and this becomes not only a principle of action, but a leading or governing principle, to which all our animal principles ought to be subordinate.[42]

The most straightforward reading of this passage implies that Reid is contrasting the motive connected to the 'conception of what is good for us upon the whole' with 'animal principles'. That motive would therefore need to be a rational principle of action, instead of an animal principle of action.

One taking Van Cleve's line could argue that, in this contrast, Reid is not differentiating rational and animal motives, but rather arguing that the perception of good upon the whole generates an affective response, to which all our other animal principles ought to be subordinate. On this reading, our rational faculty subordinates our non-moral affections to moral affections by performing a regulative function: blocking some affective responses while allowing others to influence our will. If this is the case, then we need not attribute motivational rationalism to Reid. Reason would function as a kind of gate for our motivations, which could then all be sentimental.

Reid does indeed believe that the rational principles of action are 'given us by God to regulate all our animal affections and passions'.[43] Yet, when it comes to motivation, any account which constrains reason to a regulative function encounters several difficulties. First, it needs to explain why Reid says that there are rational motives. Second, it needs to show that Reid in fact denies that we can be motivated by reason alone. Third, it needs to explain why Reid says our moral sense is 'both an active and an intellectual power of the mind'.[44] Given the textual resources we have, none of these tasks seem easy. Further, we may clearly see that Reid endorses motivational rationalism – and even moral motivational rationalism – by looking at his understanding of a moral agent who, on Reid's account, cannot be influenced by passion, and who always acts in accordance with reason: God.

On the Moral Motivation of the Deity

According to Reid:

> The moral perfection of the Deity consists, not in having no power to do ill, otherwise, as Dr Clark justly observes, there would be no ground to thank him for his goodness to us any more than for his eternity or immensity; but his moral perfection consists in this, that, when he has power to do every thing, a power which cannot be resisted, he exerts that power only in doing what is wisest and best.[45]

Should it be supposed that God's actions are not influenced by motives, Reid uses this description of divine power to make the point that '[t]o be subject to necessity is to have no power at all . . . We grant, therefore, that motives have influence, similar to that of advice or persuasion; but this influence is perfectly consistent with liberty, and indeed supposes liberty'.[46] God, in other words, is a free being with active power.

Could it be, then, that God is perfectly motivated to act according to God's perfect moral perceptions by perfect moral affections? Certainly, there are passages in the Bible – which Reid, as a Church of Scotland minister, endorsed as a source of knowledge about God – that make this suggestion plausible when they speak of God's wrath and pleasure. Yet we have good reason to believe that Reid would read these passages metaphorically and would not accept the attribution of passion to the deity. According to George Baird's notes on Reid's 'Lectures on Natural Theology', given during Reid's last year of teaching in 1779–1780, Reid said this concerning the nature of God:

> Is there anything in the deity analogous to moral character in man? Here it ought to be observed that there are various principles of action in man which appear suited only to our dependent nature and to [a] state attended with imperfection. These we never can suppose to

belong to the supreme being. Thus, we never possibly can ascribe to him those instincts of which we see common[47] in men and the lower animals, which lead them blindly to certain actions necessary for such imperfect creatures as we are, but to a being so perfect as the supreme being cannot belong. Neither can we ascribe to him those impulses which men receive from *passions*, these were given to man to supply the defects of reason and the moral faculty. It is only what belongs to man as a rational creation that we must ascribe to deity.[48]

Thus, while Reid affirms a close connection between God and humanity in their moral and rational faculties, he excludes from deity the possibility of affective response. As Reid believes God is an agent *par excellence*, Reid clearly endorses the motive force of reason.

Reid's Response to Hume's Argument against Motivational Rationalism

Given this, it appears that Reid does, in fact, agree with his fellow rationalist Richard Price in this much: he accepts Hume's first proposition and rejects his second. That is, he accepts that the connection between moral judgement and moral motivation is necessary, and he denies that reason cannot motivate us. Further, in addition to the rational motives necessarily connected to moral judgement, it seems Reid also believes we are constituted such that our moral perceptions naturally give rise to affective responses which produce coincident animal motives. This means that the animal motives occasioned by moral perceptions are in some sense redundant. A perfectly rational being, like God, does not require them. Yet, while not strictly necessary for moral action, Reid is clear that these naturally occurring affective responses play a key part in our moral lives.

According to Reid, God has given us affective responses to bolster and support our rational moral motives.[49] 'It is true,' he writes, 'that perfect virtue, joined with perfect knowledge, would make both our appetites and desires unnecessary encumbrances of our nature; but as human knowledge and human virtue are both very imperfect, these appetites and desires are necessary supplements to our imperfections.'[50] Reid's theory of moral motivation is best seen, therefore, not as rationalist with respect to perception and sentimentalist with respect to motivation, but rationalist with respect to perception, and both rationalist and sentimentalist with respect to moral motivation.

Still, just because Reid provides an answer to Hume's challenge does not mean that it is a good one. For one thing, we may note that Hume's argument includes the claim that he had 'already prov'd', that reason alone can never motivate action.[51] If Hume is able to conclusively show that reason cannot motivate us, then Reid's account of moral motivation is stopped before it gets going. At the close of this chapter, let us therefore see if Reid can respond to this supposed proof of the impotence of the reasoning faculty.

Hume's chief argument for the impotence of reason is found Book II of the *Treatise*, and can be schematised as follows:

1. There are two different types of reasoning: demonstrative and probable.
2. Demonstrative reason does not motivate us, as shown by the example of mathematics.
3. Probable reasoning does not motivate us, as shown in the example of the discovery of cause and effect.
4. Therefore, reason cannot motivate us.[52]

Put this way, Hume's argument appears question-begging and thus unconvincing. Why are there only two types of reason? And why is practical reason – a concept of venerable philosophical heritage – excluded? Here a supporter of Hume may respond in two ways. First, as given in the *Treatise*, Hume's argument against rational motivation assumes his theory of impressions and ideas, which, if correct, justifies clauses one, two and three. Second, Hume additionally appeals to the phenomenology of motivation in his argument for confining reason to an instrumental role in motivation. We are, Hume points out, often moved by desires and passions, and this is especially evident in the case of moral motivation. As I have already stated at length in chapter two my case for preferring Reid's epistemology over Hume's, we do not need to address the first of these objections here. As for the second, the apparent fact that we are motivated by passions and desires, and that such affective states often accompany the perception of moral distinctions, is easily accounted for by Reid's dual-track account of motivation. Hume's argument for the impotence of judgement therefore does not seem to be particularly troubling for Reid.

Yet let us say this much in favour of Hume's sentimentalist account of motivation: It is much less complicated than Reid's, which proposes that we both do and do not act autonomously under the influence of conflicting (types of) motives and upon the perception of certain special types of relationships among certain special types of agents and actions. Such a complicated account is naturally susceptible to many objections and questions. In the next chapter, therefore, we turn to objections proposed by the contemporary subjectivist ethicist J.L. Mackie, who finds objectivist accounts of duty and rationalist accounts of moral perception and motivation unconvincing on account of the commonness of moral disagreement and strangeness of the moral properties they propose.

Notes

1. As Copenhaver, among others, points out, Reid draws an even closer analogy between the moral sense and the sense of aesthetic taste. Since, however, Reid's objectivist account of aesthetic taste is as controversial as his objectivist account of the moral sense, I have chosen to emphasise its connection to the external senses. See Copenhaver, 'Reid on the Moral Sense'.

2. Van Cleve cites Broadie's 'Making Sense of the Moral Sense' and Cuneo's 'Reid's Moral Philosophy' as influences. As I read Broadie, however, while he acknowledges sentimentalist aspects of moral motivation in Reid's moral philosophy, he does not do so to the exclusion of a parallel rationalist account. Further, as we will see, Cuneo's most recent work seems to complicate the motivational account Van Cleve adopts.

3. Hume, *Treatise of Human Nature*, p. 457.

4. Van Cleve, *Problems from Reid*, p. 452.

5. Somewhat confusingly, Reid uses the word 'sentiment' to mean 'judgement accompanied with feeling'. See Reid, *Essays on the Active Powers*, p. 353. Here, I use the word as Van Cleve and Hume do, to refer only to affective responses.

6. Hume, *Treatise of Human Nature*, p. 470.

7. Van Cleve, *Problems from Reid*, p. 453. Emphasis original.

8. Reid, *Essays on the Active Powers*, p. 180. Van Cleve quotes the first part at Van Cleve, *Problems from Reid*, p. 453.

9. See Reid, *Essays on the Active Powers*, p. 107.

10. See Reid, *Essays on the Active Powers*, p. 183.

11. Reid, *Essays on the Active Powers*, p. 181.
12. Reid, *Essays on the Active Powers*, p. 156. Note that this reference is in regard to the perception of the other rational principle of action Reid identifies, our 'good on the whole'. I agree with Van Cleve, however, that, *mutatis mutandis*, it applies also to the perception of duty. See Van Cleve, *Problems from Reid*, p. 453.
13. Reid, *Essays on the Active Powers*, p. 169.
14. Hume, *Treatise of Human Nature*, p. 457.
15. For an excellent and relatively short treatment see Harris, *Of Liberty and Necessity*, pp. 179–202. See also Yaffe, *Manifest Action*, and Rowe, *Thomas Reid on Freedom and Morality*, pp. 57–121.
16. See Reid, *Essays on the Active Powers*, pp. 221–259 and Reid, 'Some Observations On the Modern System of Materialism', in *Reid on Animate Creation*, pp. 173–241. For conjectures about latter's composition, see Wood's 'Introduction', in Reid, *Reid on Animate Creation*, pp. 30–41.
17. Cuneo, 'Reid's Ethics', §1.
18. Cuneo, 'Reid's Ethics', §1.1.
19. Reid, *Essays on the Active Powers*, p. 47.
20. Reid, *Essays on the Active Powers*, pp. 7–20.
21. Cuneo, *Thomas Reid on the Ethical Life*, p. 7.
22. See Cuneo, *Thomas Reid on the Ethical Life*, pp. 35–37.
23. Cuneo also says the wide understanding of motive includes mechanical principles of action, but as these are not mental states and do not operate on the will, I do not think this is correct. See Cuneo, *Thomas Reid on the Ethical Life*, p. 36.
24. Reid, *Essays on the Active Powers*, p. 218.
25. Reid, *Essays on the Active Powers*, p. 218.
26. Reid, *Essays on the Active Powers*, p. 218.
27. Reid, *Essays on the Active Powers*, p. 218.
28. Reid, *Essays on the Active Powers*, p. 218.
29. Reid, *Essays on the Active Powers*, p. 218.
30. Note that, although Reid believes we are not strictly culpable for actions irresistibly motivated by animal principles, he believes we are culpable for actions – like excessive drinking – which prevent us from exercising our rational faculties. See Reid, *Essays on the Active Powers*, pp. 238–239.
31. Van Cleve, *Problems from Reid*, p. 453.
32. See Cuneo, 'Reid's Moral Philosophy', p. 256.
33. Reid, *Essays on the Active Powers*, p. 169.
34. Reid, *Essays on the Active Powers*, p. 271.

35. Reid, *Essays on the Active Powers*, p. 181. Van Cleve, *Problems from Reid*, p. 454.

36. Reid, *Essays on the Active Powers*, p. 271. See also Reid, *Essays on the Active Powers*, p. 234 and Kroeker, 'Reid's Moral Psychology: Animal Motives as Guides to Virtue', p. 134

37. Reid, *Essays on the Active Powers*, p. 156. Quoted in Van Cleve, *Problems from Reid*, p. 453.

38. Van Cleve, *Problems from Reid*, pp. 454–455.

39. Rowe, *Thomas Reid on Freedom and Morality*, p. 137.

40. Reid, *Essays on the Active Powers*, p. 92.

41. Reid, *Essays on the Active Powers*, p. 218.

42. Reid, *Essays on the Active Powers*, p. 156.

43. Reid, *Essays on the Active Powers*, p. 304.

44. Reid, *Essays on the Active Powers*, p. 193.

45. Reid, *Essays on the Active Powers*, p. 215. See also Samuel Clarke, *Demonstration of the Being and Attributes of God*, Section XII.

46. Reid, *Essays on the Active Powers*, p. 215.

47. This word is unclear in the manuscript.

48. Baird, *Notes from the Lectures of Thomas Reid*, v. 5, p. 133. See Foster, *Reid on Religion*, pp. 102–103. Emphasis original.

49. See Kroeker, 'Reid's Moral Psychology: Animal Motives as Guides to Virtue', pp. 130–135.

50. Reid, *Essays on the Active Powers*, p. 102.

51. Hume, *Treatise of Human Nature*, p. 457.

52. See Hume, *Treatise of Human Nature*, pp. 413–414.

Part III

Objections to Reid's Account

7

The Argument from Strangeness

Questions for Reid

In the preceding chapters we have gained a good idea of what duty is for Reid, and how he believes we perceive and are motivated by it. In short, Reid believes that duty is an abstract, objective and normative relation between second-personal acts and agents, which we perceive through the moral sense, and which motivates us both rationally and through the affective states it naturally prompts. Furthermore, throughout our discussion so far, we have seen that Reid largely establishes his position in contradistinction to other moral theories, and especially the moral subjectivism and sentimentalism of Hume. In all this, Reid has been largely on the offensive, asking pointed questions, pointing out difficulties and showing how his moral theory avoids the problems of others. But, as Reid acknowledges, in philosophical disputes 'it is easier to overturn all the theories . . . than to defend any one of them'.[1] With Reid's account of duty and the moral sense now largely before us, it is time to ask challenging questions of him, in order to see if Reid's account of duty can withstand the same critical probing he applies to others. Due to the extent of his influence, the clarity of his arguments and the similarity between his moral theory and Hume's subjectivist sentimentalism, we therefore turn, in this chapter and the next, to the objections against moral objectivism raised by J.L. Mackie.[2]

In his 1977 work *Ethics: Inventing Right and Wrong*, Mackie takes up Hume's subjectivist mantle in order to challenge accounts like Reid's, which hold that moral truth is objective. Against this position, in all its variety, Mackie argues that morality is subjective. By 'subjective', Mackie does not mean that there is nothing called 'morality' worth talking about, that 'all this talk of morality is tripe'.[3] That position, which Mackie describes as 'first order' subjectivism, seems implausible to him for empirical reasons. Human beings, Mackie observes, do appear to make moral distinctions, and to intend something specific by those distinctions. Rather, Mackie advances what can be called 'second order' subjectivism.[4]

Mackie's sentimentalist moral theory is therefore similar to Hume's, which holds that moral distinctions are real, but ultimately based on our desires. As for what exactly differentiates 'moral' categories from other categories of desirable qualities, Mackie does not explicitly say. Plausibly, though, he may take the same line that Hume takes in the fourth appendix to the moral *Enquiry*. According to Hume, the difference between virtues (like justice and prudence) and talents (like charisma and facility with mathematics) is chiefly verbal.[5] There is therefore no definite distinction or hard line between the 'moral' and the merely agreeable, only the tendency of our language to call some things the one and some things the other. In whatever manner Mackie intends to use the word 'moral', though, he draws the distinction between his subjectivist sentimentalism and the moral objectivism he opposes by appealing to Kantian language. For Mackie, there are no categorical imperatives, no unqualifiedly prescriptive obligations. There are only hypothetical imperatives, which depend on the prior, affective endorsement of their underlying end.[6]

To make trouble for moral objectivism and show the explanatory advantage of second-order moral subjectivism, Mackie advances two arguments: 'the argument from relativity' and what I will call 'the argument from strangeness'.[7] According to the first of these, moral rationalism is implausible because the diversity of moral belief is both quantitatively and qualitatively different from disagreement about objective topics. In history and science, disagreements are relatively few in number, and tend to be fully resolved over time. Poor theories are tried, found wanting and discarded, rarely to surface again. Moral disagreements, on the other hand, are both common and intractable. Further, while disagreements in history and science are largely bloodless, moral disagreement is frequently accompanied by violent expressions of emotion. This, at least, is Mackie's account. And for these reasons, Mackie believes disagreements in history and science are best understood as arising from an unclarity of relevant current evidence, while moral disagreements are better explained 'by the hypothesis that they reflect [different] ways of life than by the hypothesis that they express perceptions, most of them seriously inadequate and badly distorted, of objective values'.[8]

The second argument, which I am calling 'the argument from strangeness', presses moral objectivists on the matter of moral properties. For moral subjectivists like Mackie and Hume, moral properties are reducible to evaluations of desirability. True, Mackie believes, they often denote a special type of desire, specifically socially useful desire, where the payoff to the individual is frequently obscured.[9] Yet there is nothing strange about either their nature or their perception. So long as you have a theory of desire and/or a theory of the ends desired by individuals and society, you have a theory of morals. By contrast, the moral objectivist's belief in both the objectivity and normativity of moral properties makes these properties startlingly dis-analogous to other kinds of properties. The overall goal of the argument from strangeness, then, is to force moral objectivists to admit that if moral distinctions correspond to objective, prescriptive and observable properties, those properties must be very odd. Thus, whereas the argument from relativity argues that moral objectivity ill-describes the observed phenomena of moral disagreement, the argument from strangeness accuses moral objectivism of conceptual superfluidity. Why hold on to the strange idea of objective moral properties if common, everyday, subjective desires describe human moral experiences as well or better?

For two reasons, these are especially good arguments with which to test Reid's theory of duty. First, Mackie understands these arguments not as his own invention, but as a summation of subjectivist challenges to moral objectivism, from the Greek sophists to Hume.[10] Second, as we have seen, Reid is fond of both of these types of argument. Just as Reid accuses the way of ideas theorists of proposing unjustified 'hypotheses' which posit the strange, pseudo-physical existence of impressions and corresponding ideas, so Mackie's augment from strangeness accuses moral objectivists of metaphysical excess. And, just as Reid is fond of proposing *experimenta crucis* to show that the way of ideas misdescribes perception, so Mackie's argument from relativity accuses moral objectivists of misdescribing moral experience. If Reid's account of duty is to be convincing, it ought at least to rise to the level of his own philosophical standards.

The Argument from Strangeness

The Two Parts of the Argument from Strangeness

For reasons that will become obvious later, let us start with the second of Mackie's arguments, the argument from strangeness.

This argument has two parts: a 'metaphysical' and an 'epistemological' part.[11] In the former, Mackie reformulates Hume's argument against the real existence of moral properties. I have already quoted this argument in chapter two, but for the sake of clarity, it is worth reproducing.

> Take any action allow'd to be vicious: willful murder, for instance. Examine it in all lights, and see if you can find that matter of fact, or real existence, which you call vice. In which-ever way you take it, you find only certain passions, motives, volitions and thoughts. There is no matter of fact in the case. The vice entirely escapes you, as long as you consider the object. You can never find it, till you turn your reflection into your own breast, and find a sentiment of disapprobation, which arises in you, towards this action. Here is a matter of fact; but 'tis the object of feeling, not of reason. It lies in yourself, not the object.[12]

As I read him, in *Ethics*, Mackie distils Hume's expansive prose into two simple premises:

1) If moral properties exist objectively, they must exist in the same way as physical properties.
2) Moral properties and physical properties are disanalogous by virtue of the fact that moral properties are normative, while physical properties are causal.[13]

This is a good argument against moral objectivists who agree that objects of moral approbation are qualities that exist in the same way as physical properties. Mackie is aware, however, that most moral objectivists attempt to evade Hume's argument by denying the first proposition. These evasions, Mackie indicates, can be roughly divided into three camps. First, intuitionists postulate the existence of a special faculty of moral perception which perceives what are now commonly called 'non-natural properties' – that is, properties, like those indicated in Strawson's Point, which are not reducible to non-moral properties. Second, Platonists like Richard Price believe that moral properties are not physical but metaphysical. Third, rationalists like Kant take the latter half of Hume's famous fork between 'matters of fact' and 'relations of ideas', and describe moral properties as relations which are perceivable by reason. Mackie finds the first two positions highly implausible on their face, but to further strengthen his argument he also makes explicit another idea found in Hume: that if moral norms are relations, not physical qualities, they can be either objective or prescriptive but not both.[14]

Here, the meaning of 'objective' is clearly important, yet this word can be troublingly equivocal. Recognising both the importance of the term to his argument and the general lack of philosophical consensus over what it means, Mackie supplies a detailed definition. Mackie begins by saying what he does not mean. The word 'objective' is sometimes used to merely mean truth-apt, in the sense of admitting of truth and falsity. This is a first-order question, and so not the sense of objectivity that concerns him. There is, he thinks, nothing strange in attributing objectivity in this sense to moral statements, since truth-aptitude is not only the obvious intention behind our assertion of moral approbation and disapprobation, but also a common feature of many subjective evaluations. As examples, Mackie asks us to consider the grading of livestock, clothing or produce. Clearly, he believes, by grading a cut of meat 'Select' we intend to make a truth-apt statement based on an evaluative standard. Further, Mackie observes, this evaluative standard is based on desirability.[15] On Mackie's account, then, truth-apt evaluations such as these are not only ordinary, they also provide a model for evaluative moral statements. If, therefore, a would-be moral objectivist contends that moral norms are objective in only this way, then Mackie has no complaints.

Yet this is not what most self-understood moral objectivists hold. They contend that the standards of moral evaluation are both truth-apt and categorically imperative; in Mackie's words, 'action-directing absolutely, not contingently . . . upon the agent's desires and inclinations'.[16] They are therefore objective in the sense that they are normative features of the world which are not reducible to human desire. As Mackie sees it, the problem with this description of moral normativity is that, although we are familiar with action-directing properties (like the quality standards mentioned above) and objective, mind-independent relationships (like mathematical and logical relations), duty, on the objectivist account, is both an objective and a normative property. It is therefore strange.

The second, epistemological part of the argument from strangeness comes to the same point from a different angle. Even if one were to grant that there are such things as metaphysical moral properties or objective and prescriptive moral relations, how could we perceive them? Mackie knows that moral objectivism is not lacking in accounts of moral perception, but believes they only heighten the argument from strangeness by pointing out how different moral perception must be from other types of perception.

The best answer that objectivists can muster, Mackie believes, is of the type made by Price, who tried to avoid moral strangeness by suggesting that empiricism fails to properly account for any of our perceptions of properties, whether they be physical, mathematical or moral. If all properties are epistemically strange to empiricism, then none are. Mackie naturally finds this reply unconvincing, but at least it forces the issue back upon the moral subjectivist. The worst answer, on the other hand, is given by the moral intuitionist, who insists that 'moral judgements are made or moral problems solved by just sitting down and having an ethical intuition'.[17] This is, in Mackie's words, a 'travesty of moral reasoning'.[18] Yet even this reply, he believes, is helpfully clarifying. No matter what tack the objectivist takes – Platonism, rationalism or intuitionism – they will have to grasp the nettle of strangeness eventually. It is essential to their position. To be a moral objectivist is to say that there are moral properties or relations in the world which are different from objective and inert properties or relations like 'red' or 'equal' because their perception is motivating, and different from subjective and motivating evaluations like 'Grade A' because they are objective. That is what makes them uniquely moral on the objectivist account.

Applying the Argument from Strangeness to Reid

Because Mackie's argument from strangeness is intended to address multiple forms of moral objectivism, before attempting a reply it is worth taking a moment to determine exactly how Mackie's argument applies to Reid. Let us start with the metaphysical half. Immediately, we may rule out the Platonist option. To see this, consider the contrast between Reid's position and that of Richard Price, Mackie's model, though still mistaken, moral objectivist.

According to Price's Platonist views, all abstract ideas exist metaphysically as 'aspects of universal reason and real objects of the understanding'.[19] Since Price also believed that moral norms are abstract relations immediately perceived by the understanding or intelligence, he naturally held that moral goodness exists in the same way. Reid, as we have seen, counted Price as an ally in his struggle against moral subjectivism.[20] But on the issue of Platonism, Reid strongly disagreed. According to Reid, all versions of Platonism are mistaken because only particulars, not universals, have what Reid calls 'real existence'.[21] By this term, Reid, like Hume, means physical existence in time and space. For Reid, the source of Platonism's error is an illegitimate extension of the manner in which physical objects have real existence to abstractions. This leads the Platonists to paradoxically posit the existence of particular universals: a mistake which is easily avoided once we recognise that the word 'existence' has multiple yet only loosely analogous uses. For Reid, the existence of universals is 'nothing but predictability, or the capacity of being attributed to a subject'.[22] Thus, although Reid affirmed the 'existence' of universals like moral obligation and moral goodness, he did not mean that they exist like physical objects, or even in a way similar to physical objects.

Beyond declining the Platonist option, though, what is Reid's position concerning the reality of moral truth? To answer this question, we first need to make a crucial distinction. Mackie addresses his objections to all versions of moral objectivity, writing that his 'claim that values are not objective . . . is meant to include not only moral goodness, which might be most naturally equated with moral value, but also other things that could be more loosely called moral values or disvalues' such as duty and obligation.[23] The distinction between these two concepts – which, for clarity's sake, I will call 'moral goodness' and 'moral obligation', respectively – is vitally important for the correct application of Mackie's challenge. Yet because moral goodness and moral obligation are closely related, the distinction between them is sometimes hard to see.

Take, for example, Reid's own description of duty: 'what we ought to do, what is fair and honest, what is approvable, what every man professes to be the rule of his conduct, what all men praise, and what is laudable, though no man should praise it'.[24] Although this is a description of duty – of moral obligation – it includes within it a description of moral goodness: 'what all men praise, and what is laudable, though no man should praise it'. The close association between moral obligation and moral goodness is also present in the definition of duty we constructed in chapter four: *a simple and objective relationship between voluntary actions and second-personal agents, which provides to those agents reasons for action regarding desert, the performance of which is objectively laudable, so long as that action is intentionally performed on*

account of this relationship and not on account of any consider-
ation of benefit or pleasure. Here the contrast is even clearer. Moral
obligation is fundamentally the 'objective relationship between voluntary actions and second-personal agents, which provides those
agents reasons for action regarding desert'. Yet, honouring Reid's
close association between moral obligation and moral goodness,
our constructed definition of Reidian duty also notes that our
actions are morally good – 'objectively laudable' – when they are
done for the sake of duty.

That there is a distinction for Reid between these two concepts
is made clear in a late chapter of the *Active Powers*. Here, Reid
is concerned with Hume's argument that those who deny that the
virtue of justice is based on utility are frequently guilty of circular
reasoning.

> I conclude, that the first virtuous motive, which bestows a merit on
> any action, can never be a regard to the virtue of that action, but
> must be some other natural motive or principle. To suppose the mere
> regard to virtue of the action is what rendered it virtuous, is to rea-
> son in a circle. Before we can have such a regard, the action must be
> really virtuous; and this virtue must be deriv'd from some virtuous
> motive: And consequently the virtuous motive must be different from
> the regard to the virtue of the action.[25]

To put this argument in the terms of the distinction being posited
here, Hume is arguing that the moral goodness of an action cannot be dependent on it being performed for the sake of its moral
goodness, because an action must be morally good before we can
be motivated by its moral goodness. There must therefore be some
other basis – e.g. the motive to increase utility – which makes the
action virtuous.

Reid is susceptible to this argument because he holds that
actions are only morally good insofar as they are motivated by a
desire to act from duty. Yet this is where the distinction between
moral obligation and moral goodness comes in. According to Reid:

> A good action in a man is that in which he applied his intellectual
> powers properly, in order to judge what he ought to do, and acted
> according to his best judgement . . . But what do we mean by good-
> ness in an action considered abstractly? To me it appears to lie in this,
> and this only. That it is an action which ought to be done by those

who have the power and opportunity, and the capacity of perceiving their obligation to do it.[26]

Reid's point is that the apparent circularity identified by Hume dissolves once we make a proper distinction between moral goodness and moral obligation. This is, I think, hard for Hume to see because he is a virtue theorist for whom moral obligation is derived from moral goodness. Thus, it is the moral goodness of utility, and the desire to attain this good end, which makes certain actions morally obligatory. For Reid, on the other hand, it is moral obligation which is primary. Moral goodness is therefore strictly a quality not of actions but of agents, and indicates the excellence of their moral agency in the sense that they both correctly perceive duties and act upon them. Actions are also sometimes called morally good, but only in a secondary and derived sense – 'by a figure ascribed to the action', to use Reid's words.[27] Hume's proposed circularity is, thus, a mirage generated by obfuscating the difference between the moral obligation of an action and its derived moral goodness. For Reid, actions may be called good because they are obligatory, but they are not obligatory on account of their (figurative) goodness.

In addition to providing a reply to Hume, noting the primacy of moral obligation in Reid's moral theory also clarifies the way in which the argument from strangeness applies to him. We may therefore reformulate our question above to fit with Reid's moral theory: what is Reid's position concerning the reality of moral obligation? How, for Reid, is duty objectively in the world?

Despite the fact that, for Reid, duty is a relation between things that have real existence – between second-personal agents and voluntary actions – this is not an easy question to answer. Most interpreters of Reid – such as Broadie, Roeser and Cuneo – call Reid a 'realist' with respect to duty.[28] Gordon Graham, on the other hand, thinks he is not.[29] Both positions are plausible. In favour of Reidian moral realism is Reid's clear opposition to Hume's subjectivist ethics and assertion that moral truths are necessary truths. Against it is Reid's metaphysical modesty, both in general and with respect to duty. Indeed, on the question of the ontology of duty, Reid is almost coy. As far as I can determine, the closest he comes to giving an opinion is in the passage quoted in our prior discussion of Platonism. According to Reid, the 'existence' of a universal is 'nothing but predictability, or the capacity of being attributed to a subject'.[30] Since Reid explicitly tells us that 'moral relations . . . have no existence but between moral agents and their voluntary actions' and 'the abstract notion of duty . . . appears to be neither any real quality of the action considered by itself, nor of the agent considered without respect to the action, but a certain relation between one and the other', his answer seems to be that duty exists in the world only in the sense that it can be correctly or incorrectly predicated of certain actions.[31] According to Reid, as we have seen, whether something is or is not our duty is mind-independent in Mackie's sense. So Reid is certainly a moral objectivist. But whether this position counts as 'realism' depends on one's definition of 'real'.

Situating Reid's response to the epistemological part of the argument from strangeness is similarly tricky. Certainly, he is not a Platonist. And just as certainly – given his epistemology and identification of duty as a non-natural property – intuition plays a large role in his moral epistemology. Yet, as discussed in chapter two, Reid's intuitionism is a rational intuitionism, according to which our intuitive moral beliefs are judgements about evidence. True, these judgements are often immediate and address self-evidence. But this feature, for Reid, does not reduce their rationality. On the contrary, judgements of self-evidence are the foundation of all reason. Thus, I think that Van Cleve is correct when he calls Reid a 'cognitivist of the objective non-naturalist variety'.[32] That is, for Reid, moral obligation is something irreducible to non-moral properties (non-naturalism), about which we have judgements (cognitivism) which are true and false independent of our feelings about them (objectivism). Not only does this description capture the essential parts of Reid's moral epistemology, it takes no affirmative position about the metaphysics of duty, which Reid, in Baconian fashion, seems to avoid. In Mackie's taxonomy, then, Reid counts as partly an intuitionist and partly a rationalist.

Reid's Reply to the Argument from Strangeness

Having Reid's metaphysical and epistemological positions before us, let us turn to Reid's replies to the corresponding parts of Mackie's argument from strangeness, starting with the former. As we saw in chapter five, Reid draws an analogy between mathematical and moral propositions. If moral propositions are analogous to mathematical propositions in that both describe necessary relations between entailing entities, then we may look to mathematical propositions to help explain why the supervenience of abstract moral relations on second-personal agents and actions is less than strange. There is nothing strange about the fact that abstract mathematical and geometrical relations are necessary truths entailed by contingent entities which may exist in the world: these countable objects, that set of points. Why, then, should the abstract relations of morality which are entailed by contingent agents and actions be considered odd?

In short, Reid argues that moral obligations are objective in the same way as mathematical and geometrical propositions; they are entailed by certain instantiating entities. As for how any of these supervenient relations exist in the world, Reid refuses to speculate. This may seem to be a dodge to the first half of the argument from strangeness, but Reid is consistent in this attitude. For him, all we can justifiably say about the existence of objective relations is that we predicate them to things in the world and our judgements about them are either true or false. This is, then, a version of the argument Mackie attributed to Price, given previously. It deflates the first half the argument from strangeness by arguing that those who find the existence of objective moral relations strange must have similar difficulties accepting the existence of other objective relations which supervene upon things in the world. There is still, of course, the matter of the distinctiveness of moral relations, which, according to Reid, are not only descriptive but also normative. Yet we can best understand Reid's account of this feature of duty by turning to the second half of the argument from strangeness.

To begin Reid's answer to the second, epistemological part of the argument from strangeness, we may observe that, for Reid, moral relations are perceived in a way similar to the perception of mathematical relations: by a rational faculty of judgement. Therefore, on the question of objectivity, unless one also wished to assign strangeness to everyday mathematical perception and reasoning, the perception of moral relations is not especially strange. This is, however, only half the battle. What remains to be shown is that we have good reason to conclude that the perception of moral relations can motivate us independently of our desires. And from Mackie's perspective, Reid's insistence on the close analogy between mathematical and moral objectivity only heightens the strangeness of moral normativity. The perception of a mathematical relationship leads only to the judgement that such a relationship exists (in Reid's non-metaphysical sense). By contrast, the perception of a moral norm leads both to the judgement that there is a relevant moral relationship and to motivating belief that an action ought or ought not to be done.

As we have seen, Reid's general answer to this discontinuity between the perception of mathematical and moral reasoning is twofold. First, the propositions perceived by the moral faculty are normative in the sense that they are agent-relative. They arise in second-personal relationships among second-personal agents and actions. Second, while the general faculties of abstraction, judgement and reason by which we perceive mathematical relations are, according to Reid, only intellectual powers, the moral sense is both an intellectual and an active power. That is, Reid holds that our moral judgements motivate the will directly, without requiring the mediation of non-rational active principles.

Subjectivist Objections to Reid's Account of the Nature and Perception of Moral Obligation

This, then, is how Reid accounts for the dual nature of moral obligation. Metaphysically, moral obligation is a normative, objective relation which exists among certain entities in the world in a way similar to mathematical relations. Epistemologically, these relations are perceived by the moral sense, which is not only an intellectual but also an active power, and which therefore presents rational ends to the will. To a second-order subjectivist, however, these answers are less than convincing.

Consider the nature of duty itself. Although the self-evident necessity of Reid's first principles of morals follows from the second-person standpoint, and, in turn, answers the first half of the argument from strangeness by an analogy to mathematics, it follows all too directly. As we noted at the close of chapter two, there is nothing contradictory about saying that commands that must be followed apart from considerations of desire may only be given and received within a community that recognises such commands. Further, once we have supplied definitions of moral actions and moral agents, certain relations follow necessarily. But since we can construct abstract concepts at our convenience, nothing is proven thereby. All that these speculations demonstrate is that certain relations adhere among a given set of definitions, which is not the same as showing that there actually are reasons that are both objective and action-directing.[33]

A related objection may also be made against Reid's account of moral perception and motivation in an agent. For, as Mackie sees it, one of the chief problems with supposing that there are objective and action-directing reasons is that it necessitates the further postulation of a faculty that must both problematically 'see' the wrongness of an act and also provide an action-directing motive.[34] This is, of course, exactly what Reid proposes. Yet, for Mackie, the dual character of the moral sense is a suspicious muddle. 'How much simpler and more comprehensible the situation would be,' he writes in summary, 'if we could replace the moral quality with some sort of subjective response which could be causally related to the detection of the natural features on which the supposed quality is said to be consequential?'[35]

These two objections lead us to the core of Mackie's argument from strangeness. Although objectivists of Reid's type do not posit the existence of strange physical or metaphysical moral properties, they still require the postulation of something allegedly strange in their account of moral objectivity. Specifically, what they require is a type of reason which is both objective and action-directing, and a corresponding mental faculty which is both rational and motivating – in short, practical reason. The contrast is this: for Reid there is a kind of reason that immediately motivates the will, but for Mackie reason can only move the will indirectly, by presenting a desirable object to the passions. In Reid's terminology, this means that Mackie only believes that there are active powers and intellectual powers, but no simultaneously active and intellectual powers. Or, to make the same point more comfortably in the language of Hume, Mackie assumes that reason is inert.

Practical Reason: For and Against

The importance of this point cannot be overstated in the subjectivist/rationalist debate.[36] The entire argument from strangeness, as applied to Reid, hinges upon it. To put the matter succinctly: if Mackie is correct, and reason is inert, then moral rationalism must indeed posit something strange. Yet if Reid is right, and our moral sense is a faculty of practical reason – that is, if it is both an active and an intellectual power which can perceive objective and prescriptive relationships – then there is nothing strange about moral objectivism at all. Who, then, should we believe?

For Reid, his account is to be preferred for Baconian reasons: because his moral objectivism better describes actual moral language, practice and experience. We have already seen three arguments of this type in chapters three and four. The first was the argument regarding siege and shipwreck, where, as even Hume acknowledged, human beings are prone to treat moral imperatives as though their obligations adhere even when there is no possibility of obtaining the goods of peace and prosperity. As we noted in this regard, Reid in fact misreads Hume in this instance, but makes the same relevant point regarding Hume's assertion that there would be nothing unjust about enslaving a species that was, like human beings, rational, but also helplessly weak. Second, Reid also observed that the semantic difference between expressions of moral disapproval and personal dislike denotes just the type of difference between objective and subjective imperatives that moral subjectivism denies. Finally, he observed that even children appear to understand the idea of a promise as a binding agreement that adheres independently of either party's desires.

Surprisingly, Mackie agrees with Reid's observations, granting that our moral language and moral practice appear to treat moral imperatives differently than subjective desires. But given this, Mackie defends moral subjectivism by claiming that the form of our moral language and practice – and, by extension, our introspective experience of morality – is simply wrong.[37] Thus, to account for what Reid sees as good evidence for practical reason, Mackie proposes an error theory according to which we externalise – for various reasons – our desires such that we treat the ends of our desires as if they are in themselves desirable, instead of correctly seeing that they are desirable because we desire them.[38]

We have already encountered two error theories much like Mackie's. The first was Hume's argument that the tendency to treat justice as objective in siege and shipwreck is merely an irrational habit. The second was Cuneo's objection, advanced on behalf of Hume, that even if our moral language reflects our belief that moral properties are objective, neither the objective use, nor even the belief that such use is proper, gives us sufficient grounds for concluding that they are.[39] Beyond linking these two complaints, Mackie's error theory differs but little. In every version, the point of the error theory is the same: where our moral practice and language run counter to moral subjectivism and/or the belief that reason is inert, they must be wrong, and therefore ought not to count as good reasons for moral objectivism.

Reid's response to Mackie would therefore be the same as his response to Hume. Of course, it is true that if moral subjectivism is accurate, then our moral language, practice and introspective experience in the instances described above are in error. But why should we consider it more likely that it is our moral language and practice, and not moral subjectivism, that is mistaken? Reid, in other words, responds to the argument from strangeness with the Baconian claim that we should prefer the new organon to the old: that we should never purchase theoretical simplicity at the cost of dismissing relevant evidence. It is true that the world is more complicated if there are practical, objective relations among free agents and actions, and that human beings have the capacity to perceive and be motivated by them. But, then, the world is complicated. Physics would be much simpler without friction, and biology without epigenetics. Yet these are features of the world for which our theories must account. Thus, whatever the complications introduced and metaphysical questions left unanswered by moral objectivism, Reid argues that it is to be preferred to any account of morals which requires an error theory of such expansive scope that it subverts the best evidence we have of human moral experience.

Absent further evidence that the vast majority of moral language and practice is misleading, we therefore have little reason to believe that Reid's account contains anything strange enough to damage it. Yes, Reid thinks that moral relations are objective like mathematical axioms and prescriptive like hypothetical imperatives. Yes, Reid believes that the moral sense is a faculty of practical reason. And yes, that means that, for Reid, moral properties are importantly different from anything else. But this does not make them strange. To be strange, they must be not merely unique but unusual. And there are few things more common to human experience across all history, languages and cultures than the idea that some actions are right or wrong independent of our desires.

Notes

1. Reid, *Essays on the Intellectual Powers*, p. 111.
2. In this chapter and the next I am indebted to, but take a different line than Gallie, *Thomas Reid: Ethics, Aesthetics, and the Anatomy of the Self*, pp. 93–99.

3. Mackie, *Ethics: Inventing Right and Wrong*, p. 16.

4. Mackie, *Ethics: Inventing Right and Wrong*, p. 16.

5. Hume, *Enquiry Concerning the Principles of Morals*, pp. 312–323.

6. Mackie, *Ethics: Inventing Right and Wrong*, pp. 27–30.

7. Mackie calls the latter argument 'the argument from queerness', but I will call it 'the argument from strangeness' because, in current parlance, 'queerness' typically denotes issues relating to human sexuality, which Mackie did not intend to imply.

8. Mackie, *Ethics: Inventing Right and Wrong*, p. 37.

9. Mackie, *Ethics: Inventing Right and Wrong*, p. 44.

10. Mackie, *Ethics: Inventing Right and Wrong*, pp. 20, 35.

11. Mackie, *Ethics: Inventing Right and Wrong*, p. 38.

12. Hume, Treatise of Human Nature, p. 468. Partially quoted in Mackie, *Ethics: Inventing Right and Wrong*, p. 20.

13. See Mackie, *Ethics: Inventing Right and Wrong*, p. 39.

14. Mackie, *Ethics: Inventing Right and Wrong*, pp. 40–42.

15. Mackie, *Ethics: Inventing Right and Wrong*, pp. 25–26.

16. Mackie, *Ethics: Inventing Right and Wrong*, p. 29.

17. Mackie, *Ethics: Inventing Right and Wrong*, p. 38.

18. Mackie, *Ethics: Inventing Right and Wrong*, p. 38.

19. Martha K. Zebrowski, 'Richard Price, British Platonist of the Eighteenth Century', p. 31.

20. Reid, *Essays on the Active Powers*, p. 156.

21. Reid, *Essays on the Intellectual Powers*, p. 393.

22. Reid, *Essays on the Intellectual Powers*, p. 393.

23. Mackie, *Ethics: Inventing Right and Wrong*, p. 15.

24. Reid, *Essays on the Active Powers*, p. 169.

25. Hume, *Treatise of Human Nature*, p. 478. Partially quoted in Reid, *Essays on the Active Powers*, p. 295.

26. Reid, *Essays on the Active Powers*, p. 297.

27. Reid, *Essays on the Active Powers*, p. 296.

28. See Broadie, 'Making Sense of Moral Sense', p. 102; Roeser, 'Introduction: Thomas Reid's Moral Philosophy', p. 12; Cuneo, 'Reid's Moral Philosophy', p. 245.

29. Graham, 'Was Reid a Moral Realist?'.

30. Reid, *Essays on the Intellectual Powers*, p. 393.

31. Reid, *Essays on the Active Powers*, pp. 359, 173.

32. Van Cleve, *Problems from Reid*, p. 444.

33. See Wolterstorff, 'Reid on Justice', p. 197.

34. Mackie, *Ethics: Inventing Right and Wrong*, p. 41.

35. Mackie, *Ethics: Inventing Right and Wrong*, p. 41.

36. See Anscombe, *Intention*, especially §32–34.
37. Mackie, *Ethics: Inventing Right and Wrong*, pp. 34–35.
38. Mackie, *Ethics: Inventing Right and Wrong*, pp. 42–46.
39. Cuneo, 'Reid's Moral Philosophy', p. 252. Note, however, that Mackie rejects noncognitivism. See Mackie, *Ethics: Inventing Right and Wrong*, p. 35.

8

The Argument from Relativity

Practical Reason and the Argument from Relativity

In the previous chapter we saw that Mackie's argument from strangeness challenges moral objectivism by claiming that its theoretical complexity – with its objective, normative reasons and faculty of practical reason – is unnecessary. Second-order subjectivism, according to Mackie, is both simpler and describes human moral experiences as well or better. In response to this claim, we also saw that Reid argues that it is precisely the description of human moral experience that subjectivism gets wrong. By his lights, the theoretical simplicity of moral subjectivism is not worth the cost of its consequent error theory regarding moral language and practice. Yet, in the argument from relativity, Mackie attempts to turn this appeal to moral experience back upon the moral objectivists.

Mackie presents the argument from relativity to show that theories like Reid's misdescribe moral practice. Specifically, he believes that moral objectivism can ill account for observed features of moral judgement and disagreement. In this chapter, therefore, we take up the argument from relativity in order to see if Reid's moral theory can withstand Mackie's criticisms.

The Argument from Relativity

The First Part of the Argument from Relativity

Like the argument from strangeness, the argument from relativity comes in two parts. In the first half of the argument from relativity, Mackie argues that 'radical differences between first order moral judgements make it difficult to treat those judgements as apprehensions of objective truths'.[1] Mackie is clear that it is not merely the fact of moral disagreement that undermines moral objectivism, for there are clearly disagreements in other fields, like history and science, which Mackie considers objective. Mackie is also not saying that it is the mere number of moral disagreements that makes

its objectivity suspect. Rather, Mackie claims it is the wide variation in moral beliefs across history and culture that testifies against
the theory of moral objectivity. According to Mackie, although
people of different times, cultures and classes often disagree about
'history or biology or cosmology', we can satisfactorily account
for the scope of disagreement in these areas by the thesis that they
are caused by incomplete knowledge and/or errors in reasoning.[2]
Cross-cultural disagreement about morals, however, is so radical
that it is better accounted for by the thesis that it reflects various
'ways of life'.[3]

Consider, for example, monogamy. Mackie thinks it is just the
kind of moral norm that causes trouble for moral objectivists.
Moral objectivists hold that people practise monogamy as a way
of life because they approve of monogamy itself. This means that,
assuming those who approve of monogamy over other forms of
marriage are correct, there are some moral agents who correctly
perceive the moral truth of the matter, and some who don't. Yet, as
Mackie sees it, non-monogamous cultures are so common – both
historically and presently – that this explanation seems unlikely. If
monogamy is an objectively better way to structure human sexual
relationships than polygamy or polyamory, then why isn't it more
generally approved? Or, conversely, if it is not morally superior to
other ways, then why is monogamy itself so common?

To explain the diversity of marriage customs within second-
order moral subjectivism, Mackie makes two moves. First, he
reverses the direction of the objectivist explanation. For the most
part, people approve of a given set of moral practices, he believes,
not because those practices are, in themselves, morally praiseworthy, but because they happen to participate in a culture that has
historically approved of them. Second, he makes an important
distinction between moral ends and means. Like Hume, Mackie
believes that there are certain ends that human beings naturally
find desirable, and that those ends, discounting personal preferences, are largely uniform across the species. Yet, at the same time,
he believes that the means by which those ends can be achieved
are myriad. Thus, despite the general uniformity of moral ends, we
find a great diversity of moral practice, because different societies
happen to choose different methods for attaining them.

To see an example of how this account works, return to the
example of moral norms regarding human sexual relationships.
From a second-order subjectivist standpoint, it seems plausible to

believe that marriage norms differ among cultures because different societies attempt to secure commonly held ends in different ways. In some Islamic societies, for example, we may find polygamous practices of marriage because those societies see marriage as an institution directed towards the two ends of known paternity and economic security for widows and orphans. In Western societies, by contrast, we find the institution of marriage to be understood as a monogamous relationship because in such societies it chiefly addresses only the first of these ends. Other institutions, such as full franchise and property rights, are directed at the latter. The diversity of these customs is thus easily explained on account of the different methods by which each society attempts to achieve common ends.

By pointing up the diversity of moral norms across history and culture, Mackie may appear to endorse moral relativism. It may seem that explaining the diversity of moral opinions through appeal to the way various means achieve the same end makes it difficult to hold that some moral practices are better than others. Mackie, however, does not think so. Rather, he believes we may avoid moral relativism within second-order subjectivism by noting that some moral practices are in fact more likely than others to lead to the ends that human beings generally desire. Thus, for example, even though second-order subjectivism predicts a wide diversity of marriage norms, it does not prevent one from viewing monogamy as morally superior to polygamy on account of the fact that monogamy seems less likely to contribute to the economic and political oppression of women than polygamy.[4]

In short, Mackie argues in the first part of the argument from relativity that, by making a distinction between commonly held moral ends and diverse moral means, second-order moral subjectivism laudably splits the difference between moral objectivism and moral relativism, taking the best parts from each. Like moral objectivism and unlike moral relativism, it can account for the belief that some practices are morally superior to others. At the same time, like moral relativism but unlike moral objectivism, it can also account for the observed extent of moral diversity. In response to this argument, Mackie believes that some objectivists will attempt to walk the same tightrope by reducing the number and specificity of objectively true propositions. Perhaps objectivity only adheres in

such principles as provide the foundations of what Sidgwick has called different methods of ethics: the principle of universalizability, perhaps, or the rule that one ought to conform to the specific rules of any way of life in which one takes part . . . or some utilitarian principle.[5]

With such general principles, a moral objectivist could explain the extent of moral diversity in much the same way as a second-order subjectivist. Here, as with second-order subjectivism, moral diversity arises when various means are used to achieve common ends, the difference being that, on the objectivist account, these ends are approved on account of the rational recognition of objectively true principles, and not because they are commonly desired.

The Second Part of the Argument from Relativity

It is here, in reply to this expected objectivist response, that Mackie introduces the second part of the argument from relativity. According to Mackie, even if limited and high-level moral objectivism can plausibly explain the prevalence of moral disagreement, it cannot plausibly explain its character. Moral disagreement, according to Mackie, is characterised by strident debate about the rightness or wrongness of particular moral judgements and practices *per se*, and not, as the moral objectivist position in view must hold, because they are better or worse applications of general, objective duties. Such limited moral objectivists therefore find their moral theory in opposition to observed moral phenomena.

Mackie recognises that not all accounts of moral objectivism will find this feature of our moral life difficult to explain. According to Mackie, the fact that moral judgements arouse 'certain responses immediately' makes theories of '"[m]oral sense" or "intuition" . . . [an] initially more plausible description of what supplies many of our basic moral judgements than reason'.[6] However, the plausibility of intuitionism's immediacy is purchased at a cost. For while intuitionism is able to account for the felt immediacy of moral judgement, it has a hard time coping with the first half of the argument from relativity. If our moral judgements are immediate and intuitive, why do moral codes differ so greatly across cultures?

Beyond attempting to skewer moral objectivism on the horns of a dilemma between explaining the immediacy of moral judgement and the allegedly radical differences found among various moral codes, the second part of the argument from relativity also holds that all versions of moral objectivity struggle to explain why moral judgements are accompanied by emotional responses. Second-order subjectivists can easily account for the emotive character of moral disagreement. It is passionate because morals are grounded in our passions. Mackie believes that moral objectivists, on the other hand, are under the burden of explaining why moral disagreement is typically accompanied by stronger emotional responses than disagreement about other objective matters.

Applying the Argument from Relativity to Reid

As indicated in the presentation in the previous section, the argument from relativity is not particularly targeted at Reid's distinctive version of moral objectivism. The questions it presents to Reid's theory of rational moral sense, though, are clear. They are three in number. First, if the objects of moral judgements are objective relationships, then why is cross-cultural moral disagreement more severe than cross-cultural disagreement about objective fields like history and science? Second, if moral judgements are founded on first principles, then how can Reid explain their felt immediacy? Finally, if moral judgements are rational, then why are they often characterised by strong emotional responses? By Mackie's lights, to make his account of moral judgement as a faculty of practical reason plausible, Reid owes us an answer to each of these questions.

Reid's Replies to the Argument from Relativity

Against the Supposedly Especial Severity of Moral Disagreement

To recall the first part of the argument from relativity, according to Mackie, 'the well-known variation in moral codes from one society to another and from one period to another, and also the differences in moral beliefs between different groups and classes' provides indirect support for the subjectivity of moral norms since 'radical differences between first order moral judgements make it difficult to treat those judgements as apprehensions of objective truths'.[7] Two parts of this statement cannot be denied. In the first place, appeals to the cross-cultural variation of moral codes are common in subjectivist ethics. Second, if disagreements about first-order moral judgements are startlingly different from disagreements about other objective first-order judgements, then it would be difficult to treat moral judgements as apprehensions of objective truth. This syllogism, though, does not bother Reid in the least. For, being well acquainted with arguments of precisely this kind, Reid has his answer prepared. It is, simply, to deny Mackie's premise. To wit:

> The variety of opinions among men in points of morality, is not greater, but, as I apprehend, much less than in speculative points; and this variety is as easily accounted for, from the common causes of error, in one case as in the other.[8]

At first glance, this rejoinder may seem very weak since it merely denies what Mackie asserts. On the basis of what evidence, we might ask, could Reid 'apprehend' that moral disagreement is less severe than other kinds?

Once again, we return to the empirical argument Reid makes against moral subjectivism: that the recognition of a class of actions that are good and bad in themselves – and not on account of their tendency to increase utility and public honour, or to satisfy desires – is common across culture and history, as evidenced by the testimony of language and practice. For a specific example of this general cultural phenomena, Reid proposes that 'in all promises and in all contracts there is necessarily implied a moral obligation on one party and a trust in the other grounded upon this obliga-tion'.[9] Additionally, according to Reid, most cultures recognise the category of *honestum* – the idea that certain actions, such as wilful murder, theft and adultery, are not just unpleasant and harmful but *per se* wrong. His point is not that all cultures have the same moral norms and recognise the same moral principles. It is that it is typical of human beings to recognise the category of distinctively moral obligation.

In response to this argument, we may anticipate several sub-jectivist replies. First, it may seem that by pointing up the recog-nition of *honestum*, Reid has laid a trap for himself. For, if such agreement in morals is, as Reid claims, the result of self-evident judgement, then it seems that there ought not simply be less dis-agreement in morals than in history or the sciences, but virtually none. Reid, however, does not think that this consequence follows. As he writes in the *Active Powers*, we 'may, to the end of life, be ignorant of self-evident truths' because judgement 'even in things self-evident, requires a clear, distinct and steady conception of the things about which we judge'.[10]

Note that, in making this argument, Reid is taking a different route than the one Mackie suggests for moral objectivists. He is not saying that there are a few fundamental principles which everyone recognises, but whose application is difficult. To make that argument would contradict his assertion that most of our moral judgements are immediate and intuitive. Rather, as we saw in chapter one, it is simply not the case for Reid that first principles are always easy to recognise.

Second, it may also seem that by pointing to the recognition of *honestum* and the widespread practice of promise and contract, Reid is merely begging the question. After all, the existence of *honestum* and the nature of promise and contract is exactly what subjectivists and objectivists already disagree about. How then could appealing to one contested subject lead to agreement on another? If we had not already spent considerable time establishing Reid's arguments for both *honestum* and a rational foundation for promise and contract, this would be a fair question. If we were correct in chapter four that Reid's arguments in those cases appear to be sound, however, we ought not to consider this repetition detrimental to Reid's reply to the first part of the argument from relativity. If anything, the plausibility of Reid's account of *honestum* and promises ought to add to the strength of his argument here.

That said, there is a final obvious objection to this appeal: by saying that there is less variability in opinions about morals than other objective matters, Reid has overshot the mark. Even if one were to accept, for the sake of argument, that there are objectively true moral propositions, why should we disagree about them less than we disagree about Mackie's trio of history, biology and cosmology? Shouldn't all objectively true propositions be agreed upon in roughly the same proportion?

For Reid, the answer depends both on the nature of the inquiries and on the frequency with which they are undertaken. For one thing, while all speculative questions, such as those in history, biology and cosmology, are grounded upon first principles, they also require extensive reasoning. It takes, for example, quite a bit of mental labour to get from our casual observation of falling bodies to Newton's inverse square law. Moral judgement, as we have seen, is not like that. Most of our beliefs regarding morals are immediate judgements, and only rarely are we required to employ our reason to see whether an act is required, prohibited or morally indifferent. For another, most people, according to Reid, go through their life without any training in the speculative sciences or instruction in history. Not so with morals. So long as we live in society with other human beings, it is nearly impossible not to have some occasion to reflect on our beliefs.[11] According to Reid, this incidental training of the moral sense is not, as we will see, sufficient for most people. We would all be far better judges of our duties if we received formal schooling in them. Yet the incidental moral training we receive from living in society is still more extensive than the training most people receive concerning questions of history or science; and these more-frequent occasions for reflection generate greater clarity of conception and accuracy of judgement. Thus, because people have more opportunities to consider their judgements about morals than they do about other objective matters, there is more agreement about the former than the latter.

Like his replies to the previous two objections, Reid's response to this final objection is, I believe, *prima facie* plausible, and as such makes his counter-assertion that it is not in speculative but in moral matters that we find the greatest extent of cross-cultural agreement similarly plausible. Yet it is still a real question as to whether these replies are sufficient to show that there is, as Reid claims, greater agreement concerning moral matters than speculative ones. There are several reasons for this uncertainty. The first is that there are various ways to conceptualise what counts as an 'agreement' or 'disagreement' in moral and speculative matters. From what we have seen, it seems fair to say that Reid draws the comparison such that the realm of the 'moral' – about which he believes there to be general agreement – is rather circumscribed, while Mackie draws his borders expansively. Because of this difference, they are led to describe similar circumstances in opposite terms. For example, where Mackie sees the variety of marriage customs as a compelling example of disagreement, Reid considers the existence of promises and contracts, generally, as evidence of a fundamental agreement.[12]

Further, even if the relevant boundaries are drawn so as to prevent gerrymandering, neither Reid's nor Mackie's arguments can provide anything more than circumstantial evidence, because the question at issue is empirical, not philosophical. Once we have established what constitutes moral and speculative matters, the question 'Is there greater agreement about one or the other across history and culture?' becomes a matter not of philosophy, but of social science.

Unfortunately, even noting this distinction does not get us any closer to adjudicating this dispute. For there is, so far as I know, no definitive answer from either sociology or anthropology. No doubt, no small part of the reason for this lack is that, even with our categories in place, conducting an accurate assessment across history and culture presents practical problems due to the sheer number of judgements to be counted. In absence of a reliable comparison, therefore, let us withhold judgement as to whether Reid or Mackie is correct in this matter. Neither can muster enough theoretical evidence to decide what must ultimately be an empirical question. Nor, it seems, can the social sciences provide a reliable answer to a question so broadly phrased.

Yet, despite the fact that we cannot say whether there is actually more or less cross-cultural disagreement about morals than history or science, this acknowledgement does more damage to Mackie's position than to Reid's. Reid's assertion that there is more agreement in moral than scientific matters may be just as unprovable as Mackie's, but it is both more modest and less important to his moral theory. For Reid, the chief point is that the subjectivists are wrong to claim that there is obviously more disagreement about morals than about history or science. If it turns out that Reid is wrong such that there is only slightly more disagreement about history and science than morals, or an equal amount, or even slightly more disagreement about morals than history and science, it does little damage to his overall position. Reid, as we will see next chapter, has the resources to account for the existence of strong moral disagreement.

The same is not true, however, for Mackie. The first part of the argument from relativity stands or falls on the claim that disagreements about morals are so radical across culture and time that they are implausibly understood as disagreements about facts. For myself, Mackie's claim here is unconvincing because it minimises both the extent to which people of various times and cultures disagree about history and science and the durability of these disagreements. Yet, even if I am wrong about this and Mackie is correct, the matter is not nearly so clear that it may be asserted without a great deal of evidence. Mackie, however, only provides a few sparse examples, and does not seriously consider how dissimilar cultures may be in their understandings of the universe, physics or even mathematics. From Reid's Baconian perspective, therefore, the argument from relativity cannot currently be sustained, because it rests upon an unsupported hypothesis.

Reid's Account of Immediacy and Emotionality in Moral Judgement

If this characterisation is sound, the first part of the argument from relativity fails because, absent hard evidence, judgements about the extent of disagreement in various fields are little more than guesses. Happily for Mackie, the same difficulty does not occur in the other half of the argument from relativity. According to this part of the argument, the problem with objectivism is that it cannot account for two felt characteristics of moral judgements: that they seem immediate and are often accompanied by emotion. To see if Reid has a reply to these objections, let us take each in turn.

Regarding Mackie's observation that moral perceptions seem to be immediate, and not derived from high-level principles, Reid would undoubtedly agree. As we saw in chapter five, Reid believes the vast majority of our moral perceptions involve judgements of first principles, meaning that they are immediately apprehended, and are not extrapolated from a few foundational principles. This is true, as we saw, both with respect to particular moral judgements (the action I am considering right now is in line with my duty) and general moral judgements (in every case we ought to act that part towards another, which we would judge to be right in him to act towards us, if we were in his circumstances and he in ours). Thus, Mackie's objection regarding immediacy does not conflict with anything in Reid's account.

On the contrary, the apparent immediacy of moral judgement is more difficult for Mackie to account for than Reid. According to Mackie's – and Hume's – second-order subjectivism, when we consider certain actions to be moral, we often do so on the basis of a virtuously obfuscating habit which makes us think we are choosing between things which are good and bad in themselves, but which are ultimately approved by a limited set of natural desires. To be sure, Mackie and Hume posit a fairly large and diverse set of common desires, and therefore also a close connection between moral practices and the source of their praise- or blameworthiness. Yet however close the connection between desire and objectified moral proposition, it is not immediate. It is true that, on their subjectivist account, the connection may seem or become immediate by means of habituation. But this is a more complicated account than Reid's, which holds that moral judgements seem immediate because they are.

So much for immediacy. What of the emotional nature of moral judgement? According to Mackie, moral rationalists like Reid hold that moral judgements are both objective in the way of mathematical judgements and practical in that they motivate the will directly, without first exciting motivating passions. Yet this description, Mackie believes, flies in the face of our experience of moral approbation and disapprobation. According to Mackie, our moral judgements, as a rule, are more deeply felt than our judgements about mathematics or logic.[13] Yet here the moral objectivists seem to be saying that our moral responses are fundamentally based on objective judgements. What, then, accounts for the difference?

Like the argument regarding the immediacy of moral judgement, this argument does not cause trouble for Reid. As we saw in chapter six, Reid believes that there is both a natural and a normative connection between rational moral judgement and coinciding affective responses. Reid therefore agrees with Mackie that moral judgement is emotionally laden in a way that judgements about mathematical or scientific truths typically are not. But he disagrees that this is evidence that moral perception is exclusively affective. For him, it is both rational and, by dint of our constitution, affective.

Regarding both this assertion of naturally excited moral emotions and Reid's account of moral first principles, a subjectivist like Mackie may wish to reply that all this is special pleading. Surely, if we say that most moral judgements are immediate judgements, and also that supposedly objective moral judgements – unlike all other objective judgements – naturally excite emotions due to the 'constitution of our nature', then we can account for the immediacy and emotionality of moral judgement.[14] Does it not seem, though, that these explanations are all too easy? From the perspective of second-order subjectivism, both the assertion that most of our moral judgements are intuitive and the identification of moral judgement as just the kind of judgement that raises an emotional response seem to be nothing more than *ad hoc* additions to Reid's moral rationalism.

This concern is not one which Reid explicitly addresses. Yet, to this challenge, Reid would, I think, reply that to consider the apparently *ad hoc* nature of these two reflections problematic demonstrates a misunderstanding of proper philosophical method. As we saw in chapter one, Reid places great importance on the role of induction from evidence in what we now call philosophy. Therefore, when attempting to account for the widespread phenomena of immediate and emotional moral judgement,

Reid can do nothing but propose a moral theory that accounts for all of the features of moral language, practice and experience. Naturally, this theory should be neither absurd, nor contradictory, nor unnecessarily complicated. Yet, to consider it incredible because it is not deduced from a few simple principles, or suspect because it attributes additional capacities to the human mind than second-order subjectivism does, is simply to abandon Baconianism. The task of philosophy, for Reid, is to account for the observed regularities of nature. Explanations must therefore be as simple as possible to accomplish this task, but no simpler. And he is unwilling to give up either the apparent objectivity of our moral language and practice or the affectivity of our moral responses, simply for the sake of theoretical elegance.

Reid and the Arguments from Strangeness and Relativity

Having now applied both the argument from strangeness and the argument from relativity to Reid, it is helpful to take stock of the combined result. According to the argument from strangeness, moral objectivism proposes the existence of two strange entities: motivating reasons and a faculty which perceives them. Reid replies to these arguments by appeal to the active and rational power of the moral sense, which both perceives objective relationships among second-personal agents and actions and rationally motivates action in accordance with that perception. In other words, Reid claims that there is nothing strange about moral obligation because there is nothing particularly strange about either the perception of necessary relations among things in the world or the motive force of practical reason. In order to make trouble for this assertion, Mackie also supplies the argument from relativity, which argues that second-order subjectivism better describes the variation we find in moral codes across history and culture and the immediate, affective nature of our moral judgements. Yet the first half of this argument fails because it rests upon an unsupported hypothesis, while the features described in the second half are easily accounted for by Reid's description of the moral sense.

Despite these failures, however, Mackie's challenges give voice to the general sense that there is something troublesome about the nature of moral disagreement for moral objectivism, and especially for objectivist accounts like Reid's, which hold that our moral judgements are largely intuitive. Specifically, intuitionists like Reid seem to owe us an account not only of cross-cultural moral disagreement, but of the persistence of moral disagreement among people of the same culture and class. In the final chapter we take up this objection, which I call the problem of interminability.

Notes

1. Mackie, *Ethics: Inventing Right and Wrong*, p. 36.
2. Mackie, *Ethics: Inventing Right and Wrong*, p. 36.
3. Mackie, *Ethics: Inventing Right and Wrong*, p. 36.
4. Mackie, *Ethics: Inventing Right and Wrong*, p. 36. For a similar argument by Reid, see *Essays on the Active Powers*, pp. 177–178. See also Reid, 'Lectures and Papers on Practical Ethics', in *Thomas Reid on Practical Ethics*, p. 129. For an enlightening discussion of approaches to polygamy among seventeenth- and eighteenth-century moral theorists, see Heydt, *Moral Philosophy in Eighteenth-Century Britain*, pp. 203–227.
5. Mackie, *Ethics: Inventing Right and Wrong*, p. 37
6. Mackie, *Ethics: Inventing Right and Wrong*, p. 38.
7. Mackie, *Ethics: Inventing Right and Wrong*, p. 36.
8. Reid, *Essays on the Active Powers*, p. 171.
9. Reid, *Essays on the Active Powers*, p. 171.
10. Reid, *Essays on the Active Powers*, pp. 278–279.
11. Reid, *Essays on the Active Powers*, pp. 279–280.
12. Reid, 'Lectures and Papers on Practical Ethics', in *Thomas Reid on Practical Ethics*, pp. 69–70.
13. Like the extent of disagreement between moral and scientific matters, this assertion is debatable. However, because Reid also believes that our moral judgements arouse our passions more than other objective judgements, I will not address this counter-argument.
14. Reid, *Essays on the Active Powers*, p. 181.

9

The Argument from Interminability

Last chapter we looked at Reidian responses to both parts of the problem of relativity. The first part of this problem proposed that opinions about moral norms are so cross-culturally diverse that moral objectivism is implausible. As we saw, however, this turns out to be an unsupported hypothesis. The second part of the problem of relativity proposed that the immediate and emotional nature of moral beliefs comports better with a subjectivist account than an objectivist one. To this charge, we saw that neither the immediacy nor the emotionality of moral judgement causes any special problems for Reid. His account of moral judgement and his belief in a natural and normative connection between rational moral judgements and emotive responses in human beings describes the phenomena of moral belief in exactly the way Mackie endorses.

In this chapter we look at a related problem, which proposes that it is not just intercultural disagreement which makes Reid's moral theory implausible, but intracultural disagreement. This line of argument is amenable to subjectivist moral theories, but it is not an exclusively subjectivist view. For example, the moral objectivist Alasdair MacIntyre holds that Reid's moral theory cannot account for the apparent interminability of moral disagreement within a given cultural milieu. As we will see, the problem with Reid's moral theory, for MacIntyre and those who agree with him, is not that Reid has an objectivist view of duty, but that his specific objectivist account is implausible. Although MacIntyre does not give it this name, I will call this challenge to Reid's moral theory 'the argument from interminability'. And in this chapter, I will attempt to construct a Reidian response. As I see it, proponents of the argument from interminability make two mistakes. First, and fundamentally, they exaggerate the actual state of moral disagreement. Second, they seriously misread Reid's moral theory such that they present an oversimplified version of his moral sense. In contrast, I believe that although Reid is indeed comparatively optimistic about the reliability of the moral sense, and would further

argue that our intracultural moral disagreements are not theoretically irresolvable, he acknowledges that human beings face serious
challenges when attempting to discern the truth concerning duty,
and that, given our circumstances, these challenges may lead to
practically irresolvable moral disagreements.

MacIntyre's Argument from Interminability

MacIntyre on the History of Ethics

According to MacIntyre, '[t]he most striking feature of contemporary moral discourse is that so much of it is used to express disagreements; and the most striking feature of the debates in which
these disagreements are expressed is their interminable character'.[1]
This means that, for MacIntyre, any moral theory worth considering must be able to account for the intractability of modern moral
debate. MacIntyre's own explanation, as the well-known opening
of *After Virtue* proposes, is that our understanding of what constitutes 'the moral' experienced a catastrophe during the Enlightenment, while much of our moral language remained the same.
Whereas morality had once been understood within a holistic conception of human flourishing, it began to be understood as a set of
practical injunctions derived from non-teleological conceptions of
human nature.[2]

According to MacIntyre, once this shift was made, subsequent
disagreement concerning the character of human nature led to the
creation of several rival factions. In MacIntyre's telling, these factions are legion: emotivists, rationalists, intuitionists, utilitarians,
rights-theorists, etc. Furthermore, the method of moral delibera-
tion in each of these positions is, on account of their incompatible conceptions of human nature, incommensurable with all the
others. Yet every position also shares at least two things in common. First, each finds itself along a continuum roughly defined
by Hume and Kant. That is, each views the relevant facts about
human nature that give moral norms their authority to be our
desires, our reason or some combination of the two. And second,
on account of their simultaneous pre-Enlightenment terminology
and post-Enlightenment understanding of morals, all are defective
in some way.

Since Reid was both a product of the Scottish Enlightenment
and distinguishes the strictly moral from a wholistic concept of

human flourishing – for him, 'good on the whole' – he is certainly indicted in this. His moral theory, by MacIntyre's logic, must therefore be unsound. Although Reid largely goes undiscussed in *After Virtue*, MacIntyre makes Reid's alleged defect explicit in its sequel, *Whose Justice? Which Rationality?*. Here, MacIntyre claims that Reid cannot account for the intractability of moral disagreement within 'one and the same cultural order'.[3] This charge, though similar and closely related, is different from Mackie's charge that moral objectivists cannot account for the prevalence of moral disagreement between cultures. For Mackie it is intercultural differences that tell against Reid's version of moral objectivism, while for MacIntyre it is intracultural differences. That said, according to MacIntyre, both flow from the same source: an over-optimistic confidence in the natural practical judgement of humankind.[4]

As MacIntyre sees it, the result of such overconfidence in Reid was to make tradition and education superfluous to the development of moral judgement. Indeed, according to MacIntrye, tradition and education could only be for Reid hindrances to the moral sense, which is naturally reliable. By rights, MacIntyre claims, this excessively optimistic theory of human moral judgement should have seemed ridiculous by virtue of radical moral disagreement between cultures. Something like the widespread practice of polygamy, as noted in the argument from relativity, should have done it in. For whatever reason, though, MacIntyre thinks that the absurdity of Reid's moral optimism was not fully apparent until radical moral disagreement arose within its culture of origin. According to MacIntyre, it was

> the inability . . . either to explain the disagreement between those holding proslavery views and those holding antislavery views or to provide grounds drawn from the alleged fundamental moral principles to vindicate one side rather than the other which was a major factor in discrediting the moral philosophy of Reid.[5]

Thus, according to MacIntyre, Reid's philosophy encountered a double failure. It could neither explain why the disagreement over slavery persisted, nor provide any grounds for resolving the dispute.

This charge of insufficiency in the face of intracultural moral intractability has been repeated in a stronger form by William C. Davis. According to Davis, Reid himself 'would probably have been surprised to hear that deep, rationally interminable moral disagreement could be widespread among honest, mature people'.[6] That this accusation comes from Davis is particularly interesting because he is the author of an intriguing book on the connection between Reid's understanding of self-evidence and Scottish legal tradition.[7] He is, therefore, by no means unfamiliar with Reid's understanding of judgement. Yet, despite this familiarity, he believes the common occurrences of deep moral disagreement among members of the same cultural *milieu* provide clear heterogenous instances to Reid's moral theory.

Reid's Accounts of Moral Error and Development

If MacIntyre and Davis are right about Reid's moral theory, then Reid would indeed be unable to respond to the argument from interminability. They are, however, not. To see that this is the case we need to examine two further facets of Reid's moral theory: his accounts of the causes of moral error and the development of the moral sense. These accounts can largely be found in two places within Reid's corpus: first, in his discussion of moral prejudice, and second, in his prescriptions for moral education.

Reid's Account of Moral Error

MacIntyre and Davis are surely correct that, according to Reid, a properly functioning moral sense accurately perceives duties and motivates accordingly; for error, according to Reid, is not the 'natural issue' of judgement.[8] However, just because our faculties of judgement are naturally oriented to truth does not mean they are infallible. Factors within and without can cause them to fail. For Reid, therefore, there is an analogy between disease in the body and error in judgement.

Yet the fact that things can go wrong with the moral sense does not preclude us from describing its proper functioning. After all, we describe the normal function of lungs even though pneumonia exists. Rather, the existence of moral error means that, in addition to a description of the moral sense's typical function, we also need to describe the ways in which it can err, and the factors that lead it astray.

In chapter one we looked at some of the ways our judgement is led astray, in a different light. There we surveyed Reid's account of common errors of judgement under the categories of analogical reasoning, misleading terminology and unsupported hypothesis. This taxonomy was convenient at the time because in chapter one we were primarily interested in the types of errors Reid ascribes to philosophers. As we then noted, however, Reid himself borrows the more fanciful taxonomy of Francis Bacon, who categorises our errors according to their cause rather than their type. Because we are now interested not only in the types of errors the moral sense makes but also their cause, let us therefore do the same.

According to Reid's appropriation of the Baconian taxonomy, there are four types of errors in judgement. These, which Reid terms 'prejudices', are *idola tribus*, *idola specus*, *idola fori* and *idola theatri*.[9] The first type of prejudice – idols of the tribe, i.e. of humanity – is caused by principles of the human constitution which are 'highly useful and necessary in our present state; but, by their excess or defect, or wrong direction, may lead us into error'.[10] Reid gives five examples of natural mental tendencies of this kind. They are:

1. To overestimate the authority of our own opinions.
2. To measure lesser-known matters by greater-known matters.
3. To overvalue simplicity.
4. To apply our faculties of judgement to purposes for which it is incompetent.
5. To avoid one extreme by taking the other.[11]

It is hard to see from this list exactly how these tendencies could be, as Reid says, of any use. But it is likely he means that there are certain mental shortcuts, practical limitations and methods of approximation – like trusting what we know to help us learn what we don't know, and using Occam's razor – which human beings frequently, and often successfully, use on account of our limited mental ability, but which can easily lead us astray. In any case, this list is not intended by Reid to be a comprehensive catalogue. There are, as we will see, other natural human tendencies which are generally useful to human beings but can cause errors in judgement.

The second class of prejudice identified by Reid is Bacon's *idola specus*. The name comes from Bacon's comparison of the mind to a cave, in the sense that, as different caves receive light in different manners, so are human minds differently illuminated. These prejudices, according to Reid, are caused by a misuse of training – usually the inappropriate application of habit in one area of inquiry to another.[12] As examples of this kind of prejudice, Reid provides, among others, accounts of a musician who thought that there could only be three parts to harmony because there are only three persons in the Trinity, and of persons who are either too fond of the opinion of their sect or faction, or overly impressed by apparent paradox, to clearly judge about matters at hand.[13] As with the *idola tribus*, the tendencies behind this prejudice can be useful to human life when properly applied. Sometimes our knowledge of, or sensitivity to, the features of one area of investigation genuinely enlighten us when applied to another. But these tendencies can also be misleading in improper proportion. Unlike the former, however, they are the result not of nature, but rather of training.

The third class of prejudice – *idola fori*, or 'idols of the marketplace' – 'are fallacies arising from the imperfections and abuse of language'.[14] As discussed, Reid believes language is the product of both our natural constitution and the acquisition of habit. We are, he thinks, all born with the capacity to learn languages, and a disposition to structure language in a certain way – with, for example, various classes of nouns and verbs. Yet we only gain the full use of language through practice. Once we gain the use of a language, it becomes the medium of our thought, or, in Reid's terms, the inseparable sign of the thing signified. We cannot think without thinking in a language. Usually, according to Reid, this reciprocal dependence does not cause any errors. For we invent words and phrases to be useful, and then put them to their intended use.[15] Sometimes, however, we become so familiar with the form of our language that we fail to notice that we are applying it in a situation for which it is ill-equipped. This mistake, according to Reid, most often happens in philosophy since philosophy is not the use for which most of our language was made. Yet this error can affect any area of human judgement.

Finally, the last class of prejudice is *idola theatri*. These idols 'of the theatre' are prejudices of education that arise on account of 'systems or sects, in which we have been trained, or which we have adopted'.[16] They are therefore like *idola specus* in that they are caused by training. But *idola theatri* are more systematic – they present a wholistic picture of the world through which all other observations are viewed – and also inculcate the sense of belonging to a group. These groups can, of course, be political, but they can also be philosophical. For example, in his explanation of this prejudice, Reid gives the examples of Platonists, Peripatetics and Epicureans, who approach the same problems with different and incompatible presuppositions and defend their doctrines against all others.

It is worth noting that, when Reid describes these classes of prejudice in the *Intellectual Powers*, his examples largely regard speculative – that is, non-practical – judgements. Yet Reid's focus on speculative errors in the *Intellectual Powers* ought not to mislead us, as he also makes clear that prejudices can affect our practical judgements too. Indeed, in the *Active Powers*, Reid writes that we are more prone to error in practical judgement than in speculative judgement. The reason for this is that, although both practical and speculative judgements 'are liable to be misled by prejudices of education, or by wrong instruction', in matters of conduct 'we are also very liable to have our judgement warped by our appetites and passions, by fashion and by the cogitation of evil example'.[17] Thus, '[e]xperience shews' that while we are commonly led astray by prejudice 'in matters that are indifferent . . . [m]uch more may it happen in matters where interest, passion, prejudice and fashion are so apt to pervert the judgement'.[18]

It therefore appears that Reid believes that the moral sense is even more vulnerable to the corrupting effects of prejudice than our faculties of speculative judgement. Not only can our practical judgements be led astray by the same intellectual shortcuts and tendencies which prejudice our speculative judgements, they are also occasionally opposed by the inordinate influence of animal motives. According to Reid, these non-rational principles of action confound our moral sense in two ways. First, they skew our moral judgements by prejudicially distracting our attention. And second, they oppose the motivational force of our conscience, even when we overcome prejudice and judge correctly.[19]

Reid's Account of Moral Development

If the above is correct, then Reid's account of the moral sense is much less optimistic than MacIntyre and Davis would have us expect. Yet Reid may still be counted as something of a moral optimist on account of his belief that the moral sense is improvable. Like his account of moral error, Reid's account of moral development begins with his understanding of the moral sense as both an intellectual and an active power. To function properly, it must judge correctly, and effectively motivate action. For, whether we obey the deliverance of a faulty moral judgement or, conversely, reliably perceive our duty but fail to act accordingly, the result is moral error. Consequently, the development of the moral sense must have both an intellective and a practical component.

According to Reid, both the intellectual and active powers of the moral sense improve in three ways: through biological development, social development and intentional moral training. With respect to the first of these, the moral sense progresses, like all our faculties, from infancy to maturity. Thus, the conscience of an adult will almost always be more developed and less prone to error than that of a young child. Biological development alone, though, is scanty. For, as Reid sees it, without exercise, the moral sense 'is not so strong and vigorous by nature, as to secure us from very gross mistakes with regard to our duty'.[20] Reid makes clear just how weak he believes the purely biological development of our conscience is, writing that 'I am very apt to think, that, if a man could be reared from infancy, without any society of his fellow creatures, he would hardly ever show any sign, either of moral judgment, or of the power of reasoning'.[21] Biological development is therefore a necessary but not sufficient step in the acquisition of a reliable moral sense.

The statement that biological maturity alone does not enable reliable moral judgement is contrary to the way both MacIntrye and Davis describe Reid. But, as we have seen, this understanding is exactly in line with Reid's belief that we may live our entire lives without recognising self-evident truths. This is because, according to Reid:

> The most obvious truths are not perceived without some ripeness of judgment . . . [and o]ur judgment of things is ripened not by time only, but chiefly by being exercised about things of the same or similar kind.
>
> Judgment, even in things self-evident, requires a clear, distinct, and steady conception of the things about which we judge. Our conceptions are at first obscure and wavering. The habit of attending to them is necessary to make them distinct and steady; and this habit requires an exertion of mind to which many of our animal principles are unfriendly.[22]

Happily, we find occasion to exercise our moral sense by participation in a society of other second-personal agents. This is the second stage of moral development, and what it provides is both the opportunity and the impetus for perceiving and regulating ourselves in accordance with duty.[23] This is not to say that living in society gives the moral sense a continuous, or even thorough, training. Oftentimes, even behaviour in compliance with duty will be performed non-rationally, as happens when we unreflectively follow the example of others, or act after the manner of moral obligation for a non-moral reason, like the avoidance of pain. Yet sometimes, 'by attending coolly to the conduct of others, and observing what moves our approbation, what our indignation', we come to form more-distinct moral conceptions and judgements and pay better attention to the rational and non-rational motivations they produce.[24] Furthermore, as Copenhaver points out, socialisation is also the way Reid believes we develop our judgements about the moral quality of other agents. Whereas our original, instinctive moral judgements are chiefly about the morality of particular actions, '[i]n mature . . . moral experiences, the mind is directed to the *significance* of human behavior. It is directed by the derived moral value of *behaviour* to the original moral value of *agents*'.[25] Thus, by the mere accident of living in community with other second-personal agents, well-functioning human beings find their moral sense partially ripened, and add acquired moral perceptions to their original moral perceptions.

Such accidental and occasional training alone, however, if unaided by a more formal education, does not usually make the moral sense reliable in cases where it is affected by strong feelings of interest or the unnoticed influence of prejudice. As Reid puts it:

> The bulk of mankind have but little [directed moral education] in the proper season; and what they have is often unskilfully applied; by which means bad habits gather strength, and false notions of pleasure, of honour, and of interest, occupy the mind. They give little attention to what is right and honest.[26]

In this passage it is important to notice what Reid is not saying. Unlike his discussion of a person reared outside society, Reid is not saying that the incidental training of society is so weak that it prevents the moral sense from arriving at the rational principles of moral action. Rather, he is saying that, although the person reared in society can know his or her duties when they are clearly presented and unopposed by passion, without formal training such persons usually give so 'little attention' to their duties that they are prone to forget or ignore them whenever they are confounded by strong non-rational principles. To progress in moral maturity, therefore, we need to further train our moral sense such that it both judges correctly and motivates effectively, even under duress. And this, according to Reid, is why the third type of moral development is required: formal moral education.

Moral Systems

On account of the connection between the first principles of mathematics and the first principles of morals, we might expect Reid's account of formal moral education to proceed in much the same way as a mathematical education, by starting with fundamental first principles and building towards more complex operations and applications. But this assumption ignores two relevant disanalogies between mathematics and morals, which we have already noted. First, moral judgements, unlike mathematical judgements, are normative, in two senses. They are both rationally motivating and naturally excite complementary passions. Second, moral truths, unlike mathematical truths, are typically self-evident. While the practice of mathematics involves extensive reasoning from a few self-evident axioms and definitions, judgements about duty chiefly concern self-evident truths, and involve little reasoning.

For Reid, therefore, practical training in ethics most profitably proceeds through the teaching of a what he calls a 'system of morals'. Such a system

> is not like a system of geometry, where the subsequent parts derive their evidence from the preceding, and one chain of reasoning is carried on from the beginning; so that, if the arrangement is changed, the chain is broken, and the evidence is lost. It resembles more a system of botany, or mineralogy, where subsequent parts depend not for their evidence upon the preceding, and the arrangement is made to facilitate apprehension and memory, and not to give evidence.[27]

A system of morals is, consequentially, quite different than what Reid calls a 'theory of morals'. The former entails a clear explication of our duties, along with examples to facilitate recall. The latter, on the other hand, regards 'a just account of the structure of our moral powers'.[28] Moral theory, which constitutes the vast majority of philosophical ethics (including this book), is, according to Reid, largely superfluous to excellent moral practice. Insofar as it is useful, it is so mostly for the narrow task of combatting moral scepticism – a problem that, according to Reid, rarely occurs without the malign effects of a philosophical education.

The same cannot be said for moral systems. Unlike moral theories, moral systems are useful as tools for perfecting moral practice. In the *Active Powers*, Reid tells us that these systems, which deal chiefly with our duties to others and have been in fashion since the time of Greek antiquity, typically consist of systematically arranged reminders of our duties.[29] Additionally, in his own 'Lectures and Papers on Practical Ethics', we can find an example of a moral system assembled by Reid himself.

According to Haakonssen's reconstructed ordering of Reid's manuscripts, the 'Lectures' begin with one introductory lecture on ethical theory and then proceed in three unequal parts, according to the ancient tripartite division of duties to God, self and others. Duties to others, which is by far the longest of the three divisions, is then further divided according to the character of the 'others', with sections relating to duties among private persons, duties among family members, duties entailed by political connections and duties among states. Reid's stated purpose in surveying each of these categories and subcategories of duty is to give an account as detailed and comprehensive as possible. For, as he says in the *Active Powers*, just

> as the beauty of the laws of motion is displayed in the most striking manner, when we trace them through all the variety of their effects; so the divine beauty and sanctity of the principles of morals, appear most august, when we take a comprehensive view of their application to every condition and relation, and to every transaction of human life.[30]

As for the explication of each of these duties themselves, we can get a good sense of the style of Reid's lectures by considering the following section of a lecture regarding the immorality of revenge taking:

> The Symbol which our Scotch Kings were wont to put upon their Coins of a Thistle with this Motto *Nemo me impune lacessit* [No one harms me with impunity], suits well enough the Notions of a barbarous age.

And this is the best apology we can make for it. A Canadian chief at the head of his tribe might think himself honoured by such a motto. And our Kings were probably little better than Indian Chiefs when this Symbol was invented. If we consider the state of a Mind enflamed by resentment and meditating upon Revenge: It is surely of all states the most undesireable and unlovely. A fever or Ague cannot be more opposite to the sound health of the body than this State is to the health and happiness of the Mind. From these considerations I think it appears that that gentle forbearing and forgiving disposition of mind which was so amiably exemplified and so strongly inculcated by the divine Author of our Religion is so far from being contrary to reason, & good morals, that it appears even to Reason and to the Judgment of our moral faculty to be a magnanimous and heroical Virtue.[31]

This passage, and the long quotation from Juvenal that follows it, is typical of the 'Lectures'. As the analogy between practical ethics and botany suggests, there is little in the way of philosophical argument. Instead, the emphasis – as suggested by the literary, religious, historical and political allusions – is on eloquence and clear organisation. As such, it may seem at first glance that Reid's 'Lectures' are of little philosophical interest or practical use to us today.

Certainly, a similar judgement can be found in Hume's interpretation of one of the chief influences on the method and style of Reid's 'Lectures': Cicero's *De Officiis*. According to a letter he wrote to Francis Hutcheson, Hume seems to have understood Cicero's *De Officiis* to be an attempt at a complete catalogue of duties, for the reader to memorise and then follow like an instruction manual.[32] Although he found Cicero's catalogue of duties preferable to the moral systems of his day – like the seventeenth-century guidebook, *The Whole Duty of Man* – Hume thought any such attempt at comprehensiveness to be impossible. The variety of human life is simply too expansive to be catalogued. Furthermore, the method of memorisation and strict adherence was also, for Hume, a sub-optimal way of facilitating moral progress. For Hume, moral education consists of perfecting our sympathy and training our sentiments by coolly reflecting upon them and the situations that inflame them.[33] Therefore, while ethical guidebooks like *De Officiis* may inadvertently arouse moral feelings and offer occasion for such reflection, thereby accidentally promoting moral improvement, their intended emphasis on rule-following can only be misguided.

In other words, Hume's doubts concerning the effectiveness of the supposedly rote methodology of ethical guidebooks like Cicero's *De Officiis*, and courses like the ones outlined in Reid's 'Lectures and Papers on Practical Ethics', are motivated by his sentimentalism. Yet, one need not accept Hume's ethical theory to share his reservations. Understood in rulebook fashion, Reid's intricate catalogue of duties and emphasis on eloquence over argument makes the 'Lectures' appear both hopelessly dogmatic and parochial, more interested in indoctrination than education. Such a reading, though, seriously misunderstands Reid's purpose.

Reid on Moral Education

This much is true: Reid proceeds as he does in the 'Lectures' because he wanted to give his students an appreciation for the great variety of our duties, and also make specific examples of duty memorable. But he does this not because he believes an encyclopaedic account is possible, or that memorisation is itself worthwhile. Rather, Reid proceeds as he does because he believes that, through an appreciation of the wide variety of our duties and the consideration of specific remarkable examples, we may strengthen our moral sense such that we pay better attention to, and are more resolutely motivated to perform, our duties. Seen in this light, Reid's 'Lectures and Papers on Practical Ethics' are best understood as a series of drills. In one way, they are not unlike those that athletes use to improve in-game performance. No basketball player ever takes one hundred free-throws in a row during a game. And no golfer ever tries the same putt fifty times in a tournament. Yet these activities are still useful in training because they inculcate habits needed during competition. Similarly, we may never find ourselves faced with the chance of giving a hemlock-draught to our accuser, yet still improve our 'game-time' moral choices, by imagining ourselves in the place of 'the old man who dwelt near sweet Hymettus'.[34]

In making this comparison, however, we ought not to press this analogy so far as to believe that the purpose of moral training, for Reid, is mere habit-formation. If it were, that would undermine the rationality of the moral faculty and the freedom of the moral agent. Rather, as Buras points out,

> Reid's epistemology is developmental. We begin with instinctive beliefs. By the original principles of our nature various inputs trigger

specific beliefs as outputs. These beliefs enjoy a degree of immediate justification necessary for knowledge. But this knowledge is instinctive ... As reason develops, and experience accrues, we are sometimes able to confirm some of our natural beliefs by reasoning and reflecting from other beliefs. As we do, the epistemic status of natural beliefs is upgraded. Instinctive knowledge becomes reflective. A critical component in mental maturity, for Reid, is the development of reflective attitudes.[35]

A person who has undergone practical moral education, therefore, is not only more likely to have correct moral judgements simply because they have been habituated into making certain judgements and resisting or going along with certain emotive responses in appropriate circumstances. They are also likely to be better judges of the moral worth of actions and persons because they have gained the ability to reflect on, reason about and, hopefully, perfect their moral judgements.

Practically, then, Reid's understanding of moral education is not so different from Hume's. Both believe that our moral life is so variable that it cannot be exhaustively catalogued, and that our moral sense profits little from the mere memorisation of specific moral rules. Both also believe that it profits greatly through exercise. Given the stark differences in their moral theories, this may seem strange. After all, for Hume moral education is a matter of training our sentiments, while for Reid it is chiefly a matter of training a faculty of practical judgement. Yet once we recall that sentiment in Hume's moral theory plays largely the same role that practical judgement plays in Reid's, and that Reid further agrees with Hume that our passions play some role in moral motivation, the reasons for this overlap become clear. For both Reid and Hume, whatever it is that moves us to moral action should be the object of moral education.

Responding to the Argument from Interminability

Having canvassed Reid's views on moral prejudice and education, we may now return to the argument from interminability. To review: according to MacIntyre and Davis, Reid's philosophy can neither account for radical moral disagreement within one and the same social order nor establish a ground for rationally vindicating any given side in an intractable moral disagreement, because it is hopelessly optimistic about the accuracy of our practical moral judgements. If Reid were correct, they argue, then all moral disagreements ought to be rationally resolvable, whatever the cultural *milieu* in which they arise, by the mere application of natural practical reason. Unfortunately, as the example of disagreement over slavery in the eighteenth and nineteenth century shows, our moral faculties are not so strong or accurate as to overcome the biases of cultural conditioning, even when they lead to horrific moral errors.

Immediately, given our discussion above, we may say with confidence that the exact charge MacIntyre and Davis level at Reid – that he overlooks the influence of culture on moral belief – itself overlooks Reid's accounts of moral error and education. Indeed, far from dismissing the influence of culture, Reid believes that both incidental and formal training have a dramatic effect on our moral sense. It is, on his account, hard to see how someone raised in a corrupt society wouldn't have a corrupt moral sense.

That said, at least a portion of this criticism may be rescued by amending it such that Reid's mistake is not that he ignores the influence of moral education, but that he is overly sanguine about the reliability of the moral sense, even in the face of countervailing forces. By adapting MacIntyre's and Davis' criticism in this way, we may retain the charge that Reid's moral philosophy is incapable of answering the argument from interminability, as shown by Reid's inability to explain the protracted nature of the slavery debate in the eighteenth and nineteenth centuries, or provide a framework for its rational resolution.

This amended criticism may be made in two ways: one strong and one weak. According to the strong version, which is similar to the line advanced by Davis, it was not just Reid's philosophy but Reid the man who could neither foresee nor make sense of radical disagreement over slavery. As a matter of historical record, this charge cannot withstand any more scrutiny than the charge that Reid has a culturally independent conception of moral formation. Reid was not only alive but also a public figure during the 1772 Somerset case and the 1778 Knight case, which, taken together, effectively ended slavery in England and Scotland, though not the slave trade. Furthermore, Reid specifically condemns chattel slavery in his 'Lectures and Papers on Practical Ethics' as an abrogation of justice.[36] Unless, therefore, one wishes to also make the case that Reid was remarkably imperceptive or forgetful, it seems unlikely that he could have been unaware that both pro-slavery advocates and abolitionists believed there was a moral case to be made for or against the institution of slavery, respectively.

On the other hand, one could also, in the spirit of MacIntyre, make the weaker case that, even if Reid himself recognised the fact of radical moral disagreement concerning slavery, his moral theory cannot explain how such a disagreement could lead to violent conflict among the English-speaking elite of the eighteenth and nineteenth century. For, if Reid is correct that the grossest errors of moral judgement occur due to a lack of moral maturity, then the issue of slavery in the United States should have been resolved through rational argument grounded on shared moral principles. At least at the highest levels of government, debate over this issue occurred among people who had both the benefit of a civilised political culture and exactly the kind of practical moral education Reid recommended. Yet still, to quote Lincoln's second inaugural address, 'the war came'.[37]

This criticism, though, no less than the last, is at odds with Reid's explicit statements regarding the functioning of the moral sense and the effects of moral education. According to Reid:

> the history of past ages shows, that nations, highly civilized, and greatly enlightened in many arts and sciences may, for ages . . . hold the grossest absurdities with regard . . . to the duty we owe to our fellow-men, particularly to children, to servants, to strangers, to enemies, and to those who differ from us in religious opinions.[38]

MacIntyre and Davis are, therefore, once again guilty of ignoring Reid's actual position. For, although Reid does indeed believe that social development and formal education are critical to the maturation of the moral sense, he simply does not believe that either guarantee the avoidance of horrific mistakes in moral judgement. And he is especially aware of the way that our interests and attendant prejudices can lead us to misjudge our duties to those who are economically exploited and socially disadvantaged.

Prejudice, Slavery and Radical Disagreement

Given the above, we may confidently state that Reid is not as naïve as MacIntyre and Davis suppose. Yet even so, can Reid rise to the twin challenges of MacIntyre's charge, and provide both an explanation for how intractable moral disagreement occurs within one and the same culture, and a rational ground for resolving such disputes?

The answer, I believe, is a qualified yes, which we can see by comparing Reid's general account of moral error to actual moral disagreements. To do this, we may first ask, what are the features of moral disagreement which Reid's moral theory predicts? Isolating, for the sake of simplicity, just those effects not caused by immaturity, Reid's account of moral error leads us to expect at least three features of moral disagreement caused by prejudice. First, we ought to expect a general agreement concerning abstract principles of morals. These principles are, according to Reid, no more self-evident than particular moral judgements, but they are less likely to be affected by prejudice because, being abstract, they are less likely to intersect with our interests, and thereby arouse countervailing animal principles of action. Second, as a consequence of this abstract moral agreement, we ought also to expect a common and commonly understood moral vocabulary to be shared among the parties. Finally, we ought to expect the moral error that causes disagreement to be described by at least one type of prejudice.

How does this account fare when compared to actual moral disagreements? Clearly, we cannot test all moral errors to find if they bear these hallmarks, for the same reason that we could not tally moral and speculative cross-cultural and historical disagreements when we discussed the argument from relativity. Yet, given that both MacIntyre and Davis think the debate about slavery in the eighteenth and nineteenth centuries is particularly damning to Reid's account, it seems promising to look at several pro-slavery documents to see if we find errors of the type Reid would have us expect.

To try this proposed *experimentum crucis*, let us consider the following pro-slavery arguments found in the nineteenth-century declarations of secession, issued by the various Confederate states.[39] Typically, these documents accuse the northern states and the Republican party of the same three injustices. First, the seceding states assert that non-slave states and the Republican party have encouraged citizens not to return escaped slaves – a violation of the US Constitution, which enshrines the legality of slavery. For example, in the 'Declaration of the Immediate Causes which Induce and Justify the Secession of South Carolina' we are told that the section of the Constitution requiring free states to

return escaped slaves to slave states was 'so material to the compact, that without it that compact would not have been made'.[40]
Second, the northern states have not abided by the agreed-upon
method for determining whether new states are to be free or slave
states. Thus, the 'Declaration of the Immediate Causes which
Induce and Justify the Secession of the State of Mississippi from
the Federal Union' accuses the US federal government of refusing
'the admission of new slave States into the Union', a step which
will lead to the legal abolition of slavery by tipping the balance of
power in the US Congress to the Republican party.[41] Finally, the
southern states complain that the northern states have attempted
to use their political power to ruin the South by means of economic destruction – specifically, by undermining the institution
of slavery, 'the greatest material interest of the world'.[42] Several
seceding states also agree about the supposed error in judgement
that has led to these injustices. The northern states proceed from
the mistaken belief that the white and black races ought to be
treated equally under the law. Texas' declaration puts this most
explicitly, declaring that 'the servitude of the African to the white
race . . . [is] a relation that had existed from the first settlement of
[the American] wilderness by the white race, and which . . . should
exist in all future time'.[43]

All three of our expected features of moral error caused by
prejudice – general agreement concerning the abstract principles
of morals, a common and commonly understood moral vocabulary, and the applicability of one or more of Reid's categories of
prejudice to the error or errors made when applying shared moral
principles and vocabulary to the contested issue – are, it seems,
present. There is nothing strange about the apparent meaning or
general use of the word 'justice' in these accusations. If we grant,
for one terrible moment, the proposition that people of African
descent are so inferior to those of European descent that they are
property and not part of the moral community, then the injustice
of the North's actions follow as a matter of course. Both breach of
contract and attempts at economic oppression by political means
are, context removed, exactly what these documents declare them
to be: acts of injustice. The mistake in these documents, therefore, seems not to lie in their authors' abstract moral beliefs about
promise breaking or theft. Rather, the mistake appears to be a failure to correctly perceive that the property they accuse the North
of stealing – human beings – is not actually property but rather

fellow second-personal agents, and that any promises the North previously made to treat human beings as slaves are therefore invalid. Thus, although today we may find it difficult to comprehend the terrible mistake of those who defended slavery, we may easily explain the cause of their error within Reid's moral theory. The moral sense of the pro-slavery secessionists – which ought to have recognised slaves as second-personal agents to whom duties incompatible with slavery are due – was jaundiced by prejudice.

As for what class or classes of prejudice caused this error, we may have our pick. *Idola tribus* seems an especially likely candidate given the strong economic interest of these states in maintaining the system of chattel slavery. Additionally, we may detect the influence of *idola fori* in the language of racial difference, which inaccurately treated 'white' and 'black' as biological, as opposed to socially constructed, categories. We may also justly suppose there to be a fair bit of *idola specus* and *theatri*, caused by the extensive intellectual apparatus dedicated to explaining the innate superiority of the so-called 'white race' which thrived in the American South at the time these documents were written, and the social pressures of party politics. Whatever the particulars, though, the upshot remains. Despite its magnitude and persistence, there appears to be nothing unexplainable about the depth of moral disagreement regarding slavery in eighteenth- and nineteenth-century America, within Reid's account. It was, as it is so often described, a conflict between the accurate moral judgements of the abolitionists, and the viciously prejudicial judgements of those who supported slavery.

Are Our Moral Disagreements Interminable?

To this reply, a proponent of the argument from interminability may respond that, however plausible Reid's account of moral disagreement is when applied to the eighteenth- and nineteenth-century debate about slavery, it still does not address the central point, which is that current moral debates – like those concerning capital punishment, abortion and euthanasia – go 'on and on' and can 'apparently find no terminus'.[44] That is, perhaps Reid can explain the existence of radical disagreement in debates which have been resolved, but other, unresolvable debates still cause trouble for his moral theory. To this further challenge, a Reidian may respond by questioning the assumption that such debates will go on and on without terminus. Certainly, debates about these issues are going on, and have gone on for a long time. But the same could once have been said for slavery. No doubt, to many abolitionists and slave owners, that debate also felt interminable during the eighteenth and nineteenth centuries. Yet it did end, and not simply because the North won the American Civil War. Whatever party politics and use of force were required to legally abolish slavery in the United States, and whatever hideous remnants of its legacy remain, the pro-slavery position of the eighteenth- and nineteenth-century South is – I venture to say – intellectually exhausted on account of its counterfactual assertion that a person's moral status is dependent upon their skin tone or ancestry.

Does this mean then that Reid's moral theory precludes the possibility of interminable moral debate? And if so, can it respond to the second half of the argument from interminability and supply a rational basis for resolving all moral disagreement? Reid's answers to these questions are decidedly mixed. On the one hand, there is nothing in Reid's moral theory which indicates that moral disagreement is ever, in principle, irresolvable. As we have seen, Reid believes – all going well – our moral sense reliably perceives the objective relation of duty through rational, self-evident judgement. All moral disagreements are therefore theoretically resolvable by training our moral sense and/or putting it in such a position that it may clearly discern what is and is not our duty. Further, Reid writes in the *Active Powers*, 'it is the nature of human society to be progressive . . . there is a natural progress from rudeness to civilization, from ignorance to knowledge'.[45] This statement seems to indicate that, barring catastrophe, succeeding generations will have more refined moral senses than those that came before them, and resolve previously intractable debates through rational agreement.

Yet, in a late paper, 'Some Thoughts on the Utopian System', delivered before the Glasgow Literary Society in 1794, Reid also gives a gloomier prognosis. Having been recently disappointed by the violent turn in the French Revolution, which he initially supported, Reid writes that it seems 'to be the design of Providence' that we will always live 'among Men surrounded by Temptations, and whose Interests interfere & cross [one] another in innumerable instances'.[46] Thus, according to Reid, so far as we can tell, our moral sense will always be vulnerable to prejudices caused by animal principles of action which, though 'highly useful and necessary in our present state', are also prone to corrupt the judgements of our moral sense and to oppose its motives.[47] Therefore, while we have no reason to suppose that any given moral disagreement is in principle unresolvable, Reid's moral theory cannot say whether it will be in practice, for the simple reason that it cannot predict how much moral improvement is possible, or what events may aid or hinder our moral sense in times to come. Reid, in other words, does not try to predict the theoretical extent of moral perfection, because to do so would run ahead of evidence. Rather, like a good Baconian, he chiefly attempts to describe what can now be observed, that is, to be an interpreter of nature.

Notes

1. MacIntyre, *After Virtue*, p. 6.
2. MacIntyre, *After Virtue*, pp. 52–53. See also Anscombe, 'Modern Moral Philosophy'.
3. MacIntyre, *Whose Justice? Which Rationality?*, p. 332.
4. MacIntrye, *Whose Justice? Which Rationality?*, p. 329.
5. MacIntyre, *Whose Justice? Which Rationality?*, p. 332.
6. Davis, 'Reid on Moral Disagreement', p. 74.
7. Davis, *Thomas Reid's Ethics: Moral Epistemology on Legal Foundations*.
8. Reid, *Essays on the Intellectual Powers*, p. 527.
9. Reid, *Essays on the Intellectual Powers*, p. 527. See Bacon, *The New Organon*, pp. 41–46.
10. Reid, *Essays on the Intellectual Powers*, p. 528.
11. Reid, *Essays on the Intellectual Powers*, pp. 528–536.
12. Reid, *Essays on the Intellectual Powers*, p. 536.
13. Reid, *Essays on the Intellectual Powers*, p. 536.
14. Reid, *Essays on the Intellectual Powers*, p. 538.
15. Reid, *Essays on the Intellectual Powers*, p. 389.
16. Reid, *Essays on the Intellectual Powers*, p. 540.
17. Reid, *Essays on the Active Powers*, p. 188.
18. Reid, *Essays on the Active Powers*, p. 278.
19. Reid, *Essays on the Active Powers*, p. 193.
20. Reid, *Essays on the Active Powers*, p. 187.
21. Reid, *Essays on the Active Powers*, p. 279.
22. Reid, *Essays on the Active Powers*, pp. 278–279.
23. Reid, *Essays on the Active Powers*, p. 104.
24. Reid, *Essays on the Active Powers*, p. 279.
25. Copenhaver, 'Reid on the Moral Sense', p. 97
26. Reid, *Essays on the Active Powers*, p. 280.

27. Reid, *Essays on the Active Powers*, p. 281.
28. Reid, *Essays on the Active Powers*, p. 282.
29. Reid, *Essays on the Active Powers*, pp. 282–283.
30. Reid, *Essays on the Active Powers*, p. 281.
31. Reid, 'Lectures and Papers on Practical Ethics', in *Thomas Reid on Practical Ethics*, p. 67.
32. Hume, '13. To Francis Hutcheson', in *The Letters of David Hume*, vol. 1, pp. 34–35.
33. Hume, *Enquiry Concerning the Principles of Morals*, p. 294.
34. i.e. Socrates. See Juvenal, 'Satire XIII', in *Juvenal and Persius*, §180–187 & 189–192; quoted in Reid, 'Lectures and Papers on Practical Ethics', in *Thomas Reid on Practical Ethics*, pp. 67–68.
35. Buras, 'Revisiting Reid on Religion', p. 269.
36. Reid, 'Lectures and Papers on Practical Ethics', in *Thomas Reid on Practical Ethics*, p. 46.
37. Lincoln, *Lincoln's Greatest Speech*, p. 18.
38. Reid, *Essays on the Active Powers*, p. 280.
39. A collection of these documents may be found at https://en.wikisource.org/wiki/Portal:Confederate_States_of_America.
40. 'Declaration of the Immediate Causes which Induce and Justify the Secession of South Carolina'.
41. 'Declaration of the Immediate Causes which Induce and Justify the Secession of the State of Mississippi from the Federal Union'.
42. 'Declaration of the Immediate Causes which Induce and Justify the Secession of the State of Mississippi from the Federal Union'.
43. 'A Declaration of the Causes which Impel the State of Texas to Secede from the Federal Union'.
44. MacIntyre, *After Virtue*, p. 6.
45. Reid, *Essays on the Active Powers*, p. 339.
46. Reid, 'Some Thoughts on the Utopian System', in *Thomas Reid on Politics and Society*, p. 153. Punctuation and syntax original.
47. Reid, *Essays on the Intellectual Powers*, p. 528.

Conclusion: The Practical Implications of Reid's Defence of Duty

Suppose for a moment that Reid's moral theory is correct or, if not exactly 'correct', close enough to merit serious consideration. What should we do and cease from doing if there are objective, normative relationships among second-personal agents which we may immediately perceive through our fallible but improvable moral sense? Undoubtedly there would be personal ramifications. But these, like particular duties themselves, are so varied and dependent on circumstance that it is more useful to ask this question at a more general level. Therefore, in closing, let us return to the topic with which we began in the preface, and ask what it would mean to take Reid seriously in the field of education.

As I see it, if Reid is correct, then my students' attitude towards the standard ethics class I offer is perfectly understandable. They are frustrated and dissatisfied for two reasons. First, their intuitive moral judgements have not received the type of practical training that Reid recommends. Their moral faculty, therefore, is still unrefined and somewhat unreflective. Second, inchoate though they may be, these students' intuitive moral judgements clash with the wide variety of moral theories offered to them by the typical pantheon of philosophers, not simply because they think the philosophers are wrong or unconvincing – though they often do – but because philosophical ethics typically demands that moral practice be justified by something approaching a complete moral theory. In other words, the apparent fact that human beings recognise moral duties which swing free of pleasure or utility – *honestum* – is held in suspicion until it can be justified by a philosophical theory.

Of course, as a Baconian, Reid would find this procedure to be exactly backwards. For him, the primary task of philosophy is to recognise and categorise the regularities of nature for the sake of improving human lives. Moral theory, as we have seen, is therefore not the justificatory foundation to moral practice, but a second-ary task, useful but not strictly necessary for perfecting our moral judgement and dispersing confusion. If this is correct, then the next question to ask is what we should do about it.

As I see it, if Reid is correct, then there are three important implications for the task of moral education. The first is that we should immediately cease the standard practice of present-ing several moral theories in introductory philosophy and ethics courses, and then leaving it to the students to pick from among them. Though dramatic, this change is a clear implication of Reid's defence of duty. If Reid is right, then by presenting various moral theories as if they are all equally plausible, and then asking stu-dents with no particular expertise and only incidental training to judge their merits, we do no more good – and perhaps more harm – than if we presented rival theories of physics or biology to students in introductory science courses. 'Teach the controversy!' would be as ridiculous a slogan coming from those who favour the current pedagogy in moral philosophy as it is from contemporary proponents of intelligent design.

Second, just as we ought to reduce the importance of moral theory in the college classroom, we ought to increase the pres-ence of practical ethics at every grade level. If Reid is correct that even the best moral theory has limited pedagogical use, and that our moral sense is best improved through the exercise of obser-vation and attention, then we ought to revitalise the teaching of practical ethics. This suggestion may seem doubly difficult, on account of the lack of contemporary academic consensus concern-ing moral theory, and the political and cultural fragmentation that MacIntyre observed in the 1980s, which has arguably worsened in the interim. Yet Reid's account of morals suggests two ways in which we may assemble a curriculum for practical ethics even in these unpromising circumstances.

With respect to a lack of consensus about moral theory, Reid tells us that, for the most part, we don't need it. For him, the theory of morals 'has little connection with the knowledge of our duty; and those who differ most in the theory of our moral powers, agree in the practical rules of morals which they dictate'.[1] Further, what we do need, we already have. As Gordon Graham observes, the 'crucial question' for those who might wish to take up the project of Reidian practical ethics is not whether we agree on the philosophi-cal justification for our values, but to what extent we agree about what they are.[2] And here we do find some measure of academic and popular consensus in the language of rights and the resistance of arbitrary power.

This is not to say that assembling a system of practical ethics acceptable to the majority of citizens in any given polity would be easy. As Reid acknowledges, there are some moral theories which are so contrary, or even hostile, to the notion of duty that their practical implications are vicious. And, certainly, even among those with overlapping views of practical morality, there will be many disagreements. Yet we do not need to solve every disagreement before proceeding. Rather, our first step is simply to take note of existing agreements about practical ethics and build outward from there.

Thus, in assembling a course of practical ethics we need not start from scratch. While we will largely not find the shared resources necessary to begin a project of practical moral pedagogy in our contemporary philosophy classrooms, we can find them in other places. Some promising places to begin are in the literature and history classes, in the novels and history books, which – select courses in professional ethics aside – provide the only, and unintentional, practical moral training most young people receive inside schools today. Additionally, we may find them in political documents like the UN's 'Universal Declaration on Human Rights', which, though lacking any explicit moral theory to justify its assertions, expresses areas of overlapping consensus.

Certainly, the task of assembling a curriculum to teach practical ethics from these resources would be contentious, as the present debate over the appropriateness of honouring the accomplishments of former slaveholders and slave traders shows. Yet, we need not worry overmuch about sorting the characters of history and literature according to a clear division of heroes and villains. On the one hand, this too has already been partially done for us in the form of national myth and popular history. Few today would boo Martin Luther King, Jr, or cheer Adolf Hitler, and for good reason. And, on the other, the moral complexity of examples like Thomas Jefferson and Winston Churchill provide exactly the opportunities for exercising the kind of moral attention Reid recommends.

Finally, to take up the Reidian project of practical ethics, we ought to supplement the common, contemporary language of 'rights' with a language of 'duty'. The reason for this shift of focus is, once again, not theory but practice. According to Reid, the concepts of 'right' and 'duty' are theoretically reciprocal, having 'the same relation which credit has to debt'.[3] Every right implies a duty, and vice versa. Yet, it seems to me, discussions of practical morality in modern society overly focus on rights (what is owed to us) to the near exclusion of duty (what we owe to others and ourselves). To correct this imbalance, a practical ethics should therefore teach students not only to stand up for their rights, but to pay attention to and perform their duties.

Reid would not, of course, want moral theory to entirely disappear, either from the college classroom or *tout court*. He himself was a moral theorist and taught moral theory to his students. Yet Reid's understanding and defence of duty leads to two radical and, to me at least, deeply disquieting conclusions: first, that the kind of ethical pedagogy we find in the modern college classroom is not only incomplete but potentially harmful; and second, that to rectify this situation would require a substantial rethinking of both the task of philosophy and the place of morals in education. However, for all that, and whatever the difficulties of such reform, Reid would believe it to be of primary importance. For, as he writes in his late essay on Utopia,

> To teach Men to read & write, the use of Numbers, & the various Exercises that contribute to the health strength & agility of the Body, and even to teach Latin Greek Mathematicks and the various branches of Philosophy, & to instruct them in the principles of any particular Science or Art usefull in Society; all this, however skillfully performed, is but the Body of right Education. These Attainments are all of an ambiguous Nature, and may be used either to the Good or to the Hurt of Society, according to the Character of him who possesses them. And therefore, to form the Character of good Habits and good Dispositions, & to check those that are vicious; this is the Soul and Spirit of right Education.[4]

Notes

1. Reid, *Essays on the Active Powers*, pp. 282–283.
2. Graham, 'The Significance of Reid's Practical Ethics', pp. 236–237.
3. Reid, *Essays on the Active Powers*, p. 284. See also Garrett and Heydt, 'Moral Philosophy: Practical and Speculative', pp. 100–124.
4. Reid, 'Some Thoughts on the Utopian System', in *Thomas Reid on Society and Politics*, p. 145. Punctuation and syntax original.

Works Cited

'A Declaration of the Causes Which Impel the State of Texas to Secede from the Federal Union', 1861. https://en.wikisource.org/wiki/A_Declaration_of_the_causes_which_impel_the_State_of_Texas_to_secede_from_the_Federal_Union.

'A Declaration of the Immediate Causes Which Induce and Justify the Secession of the State of Mississippi from the Federal Union', 1861. https://en.wikisource.org/wiki/A_Declaration_of_the_Immediate_Causes_which_Induce_and_Justify_the_Secession_of_the_State_of_Mississippi_from_the_Federal_Union.

Allestree, Richard. *The Whole Duty of Man, Laid down In a Plain and Familiar Way for the Use of All, but Especially the Meanest Reader.* London: W. Norton for E. and R. Pawlet, 1704.

Andreotta, Adam, and Michael Levine. 'Revisionism Gone Awry: Since When Hasn't Hume Been a Sceptic?' *Journal of Scottish Philosophy* 18, no. 2 (2020): 133–155.

Anscombe, G. E. M. *Intention*. Second. Cambridge, MA and London: Harvard University Press, 2000.

———. 'Modern Moral Philosophy'. *Journal of the Royal Institute of Philosophy* 33, no. 124 (1958): 1–19.

Aristotle. "Categories." In *The Complete Works of Aristotle*, edited and translated by Jonathan Barnes, 1:3–24. Bollingen Series, LXXI. Princeton: Princeton University Press, 1984.

———. "De Interpretatione." In *The Complete Works of Aristotle*, edited and translated by Jonathan Barnes, 1:25–38. Bollingen Series, LXXI. Princeton: Princeton University Press, 1984.

———. "Posterior Analytics." In *The Complete Works of Aristotle*, edited and translated by Jonathan Barnes, 1:39–113. Bollingen Series, LXXI. Princeton: Princeton University Press, 1984.

———. "Prior Analytics." In *The Complete Works of Aristotle*, edited and translated by Jonathan Barnes, 1:39–113. Bollingen Series, LXXI. Princeton: Princeton University Press, 1984.

———. "Sophistical Refutations." In *The Complete Works of Aristotle*, edited and translated by Jonathan Barnes, 1:278–314. Bollingen Series, LXXI. Princeton: Princeton University Press, 1984.

———. "Topics." In *The Complete Works of Aristotle*, edited and translated by Jonathan Barnes, 1:167–277. Bollingen Series, LXXI. Princeton: Princeton University Press, 1984.

Bacon, Francis. *The New Organon*. Edited by Lisa Jardine and Michael Silverthorne. Cambridge Texts in the History of Philosophy. Cambridge: Cambridge University Press, 2002.

Baird, George. 'Notes from the Lectures of Thomas Reid'. Glasgow, 1780. Mitchell Library.

Barnes, Jonathan. *The Toils of Scepticism*. New York: Cambridge University Press, 1990.

Berkeley, George. 'A Treatise Concerning the Principles of Human Knowledge'. In *Philosophical Writings*, edited by Desmond M. Clarke, 67–150. Cambridge Texts in the History of Philosophy. Cambridge: Cambridge University Press, 2008.

Bowlin, John. 'Sieges, Shipwrecks, and Sensible Knaves: Justice and Utility in Butler and Hume'. *Journal of Religious Ethics* 28, no. 3 (1999): 253–280.

Broadie, Alexander. 'Making Sense of the Moral Sense'. In *Reid on Ethics*, edited by Sabine Roeser. Philosophers in Depth. London: Palgrave Macmillan, 2010.

Buras, Todd. 2021. 'Revisiting Reid on Religion'. *Journal of Scottish Philosophy* 19, no. 3 (2021): 261–274.

Burnyeat, Myles. 'Can the Sceptic Live His Scepticism?' In *The Original Sceptics: A Controversy*, edited by Myles Burnyeat and Michael Frede, 25–57. Indianapolis and Cambridge: Hackett, 1997.

Cicero, Marcus Tullius. *De Finibus [On Ends]*. Edited by Jeffrey Henderson. Translated by H. Rackham. Second. Loeb Classical Library 40. Cambridge, MA and London: Harvard University Press, 1931.

———. *On Academic Scepticism*. Hackett Classics. Indianapolis: Hackett, 2006.

———. *On Duties*. Edited by M. T. Griffin and E. M. Atkins. Cambridge Texts in the History of Philosophy. Cambridge: Cambridge University Press, 1991.

Clarke, Samuel. *Demonstration of the Being and Attributes of God and Other Writings*. Edited by Ezio Vailati. Cambridge Texts in the History of Philosophy. Cambridge: Cambridge University Press, 1998.

Cohon, Rachel. *Hume's Morality: Feeling and Fabrication*. Oxford: Oxford University Press, 2010.

Cohon, Rachel. 'Hume's Moral Philosophy'. In *The Stanford Encyclopedia of Philosophy*, edited by Edward N. Zalta. Metaphysics Research Lab, Stanford University, 2018. https://plato.stanford.edu/archives/fall2018/entries/hume-moral/.

Conrad, Joseph. *Lord Jim: A Tale*. Edited by J. H. Stape. Reprint. New York: Penguin, 2007.

Copenhaver, Rebecca. 'Reid on the Moral Sense'. *Canadian Journal of Philosophy* 41, no. S1: New Essays on Reid (2011): 80–101.

Copenhaver, Rebecca, and Todd Buras, eds. *Thomas Reid on Mind, Knowledge, and Value*. Mind Association Occasional Series. Oxford: Oxford University Press, 2015.

Cuneo, Terence. 'Does Reid Have Anything to Say to (the New) Hume?' In *Thomas Reid on Mind, Knowledge, and Value*. Mind Association Occasional Series. Oxford: Oxford University Press, 2015.

———. 'Reid on the First Principles of Morals'. *Canadian Journal of Philosophy* 41, no. S1: New Essays on Reid (2011): 102–121.

———. 'Reid's Ethics'. In *The Stanford Encyclopedia of Philosophy*, edited by Edward N. Zalta. Metaphysics Research Lab, Stanford University, Winter Edition 2016. https://plato.stanford.edu/archives/win2016/entries/reid-ethics.

———. 'Reid's Moral Philosophy'. In *The Cambridge Companion to Thomas Reid*, edited by Terence Cuneo and René van Woudenberg, 243–266. Cambridge Companions to Philosophy. Cambridge: Cambridge University Press, 2004.

———. *Thomas Reid on the Ethical Life*. Cambridge Elements in Ethics. Cambridge: Cambridge University Press, 2020.

Darwall, Stephen. *The Second-Person Standpoint: Morality, Respect, and Accountability*. Cambridge, MA and London: Harvard University Press, 2006.

Davenport, Alan Wade. 'Reid's Indebtedness to Bacon'. *The Monist* 70, no. 4 (1987): 496–507.

Davis, William C. 'Reid on Moral Disagreement'. In *Reid on Ethics*, edited by Sabine Roeser, 67–87. Philosophers in Depth. London: Palgrave Macmillan, 2010.

———. *Thomas Reid's Ethics: Moral Epistemology on Legal Foundations*. Continuum Studies in British Philosophy. London and New York: Continuum, 2006.

'Declaration of the Immediate Causes Which Induce and Justify the Secession of South Carolina from the Federal Union and the Order of Secessions'. Evans & Cogswell, 1860. https://en.wikisource.org/wiki/Declaration_of_the_Immediate_Causes_Which_Induce_and_Justify_the_Secession_of_South_Carolina_from_the_Federal_Union.

Demeter, Támas. *David Hume and the Culture of Scottish Newtonianism: Methodology and Ideology in Enlightenment Inquiry*. Brill's Studies in Intellectual History 259. Brill, 2016.

Ficthe, Johan Gottleib. *Foundations of Natural Right*. Edited by F. Neu-houser. Translated by M. Bauer. Cambridge Texts in the History of Philosophy. Cambridge: Cambridge University Press, 2000.

Foster, James. 'Reid's Response to Hume on Double Vision'. *Journal of Scottish Philosophy* 6, no. 2 (2008): 189–194.

———. *Thomas Reid on Religion*. Library of Scottish Philosophy. Exeter: Imprint Academic, 2017.

Gallie, Robert D. *Thomas Reid: Ethics, Aesthetics and the Anatomy of the Self*. Philosophical Studies Series 78. Dordrecht: Kluwer Academic Publishers, 1998.

Garrett, Aaron, and Colin Heydt. 'Moral Philosophy: Practical and Specula-tive'. In *Scottish Philosophy in the Eighteenth Century*, edited by Aaron Garrett and James A. Harris, 1: Morals, Politics, Art, Religion, 77–130. A History of Scottish Philosophy. Oxford: Oxford University Press, 2015.

Graham, Gordon. 'The Significance of Reid's Practical Ethics'. In *Reid on Ethics*, edited by Sabine Roeser. Philosophers in Depth. London: Palgrave Macmillan, 2010.

———. 'Was Reid a Moral Realist?' In *Common Sense in the Scottish Enlightenment*, edited by Charles Bradford Bow, 37–56. Mind Asso-ciation Occasional Series. Oxford: Oxford University Press, 2018.

Greco, John. 'Common Sense in Thomas Reid'. *Canadian Journal of Philosophy* 41, no. S1: New Essays on Reid (2011): 142–155.

Hankinson, R. J. 'Stoic Epistemology'. In *The Cambridge Companion to the Stoics*, 59–84. Cambridge Companions to Philosophy. Cambridge: Cambridge University Press, 2003.

Harris, James A. *Of Liberty and Necessity: The Free Will Debate in Eighteenth-Century British Philosophy*. Oxford Philosophical Mono-graphs. Oxford: Clarendon Press, 2005.

———. 'Reid on Hume on Justice'. In *Reid on Ethics*, edited by Sabine Roeser, 204–222. Philosophers in Depth. London: Palgrave Macmillan, 2010.

Heydt, Colin. *Moral Philosophy in Eighteenth-Century Britain: God, Self, and Others*. Cambridge: Cambridge University Press, 2018.

Hume, David. *A Treatise of Human Nature*. Edited by L. A. Selby-Bigge and P. H. Nidditch. 2nd ed. Oxford: Clarendon Press, 1978.

———. *Enquiries Concerning Human Understanding and Concerning the Principles of Morals*. Edited by L. A. Selby-Bigge and P. H. Nid-ditch. Third. Oxford: Clarendon Press, 1997.

——. *The Letters of David Hume*. Edited by J. Y. T. Greig. Vol. 1. 2 vols. Oxford: Oxford University Press, 2011.

——. 'Of National Characters'. In *Essays Moral, Political, and Literary*, edited by Eugene F. Miller, T. H. Green, and T. H. Grose, Revised, 197–215. Indianapolis: Liberty Fund, 1994.

——. 'Of Polygamy and Divorces'. In *Essays Moral, Political, and Literary*, edited by Eugene F. Miller, T. H. Green, and T. H. Grose, Revised, 181–190. Indianapolis: Liberty Fund, 1994.

——. 'Of the Study of History'. In *Essays Moral, Political, and Literary*, edited by Eugene F. Miller, T. H. Green, and T. H. Grose, Revised, 563–568. Indianapolis: Liberty Fund, 1994.

Hutcheson, Francis. *An Inquiry into the Original of Our Ideas of Beauty and Virtue in Two Treatises*. Edited by Wolfgang Leidhold. Revised. Natural Law and Enlightenment Classics. Indianapolis: Liberty Fund, 2004.

Johnson, Samuel. *A Dictionary of the English Language*. Edited by Beth Rapp Young, Jack Lynch, Dorner William, Amy Larner Giroux, Carmen Faye Mathes, and Abagail Moreshead, 1755. https://johnsonsdictionaryonline.com.

Kroeker, Esther. 'A Common Sense Response to Hume's Moral Atheism: Reid on Morality and Theism'. In *Common Sense in the Scottish Enlightenment*, edited by Charles Bradford Bow, 107–124. Mind Association Occasional Series. Oxford: Oxford University Press, 2018.

——. 'Reid on Natural Signs, Taste and Moral Perception'. In *Reid on Ethics*, edited by Sabine Roeser, 46–66. Philosophers in Depth. London: Palgrave Macmillan, 2010.

——. 'Reid's Moral Psychology: Animal Motives as Guides to Virtue'. *Canadian Journal of Philosophy* 41, no. S1: New Essays on Reid (2011): 122–141.

Lehrer, Keith. 'Chisholm, Reid and the Problem of the Epistemic Surd'. *Philosophical Studies: An International Journal for Philosophy in the Analytic Tradition* 60, no. 1/2: Papers from the 1990 Pacific Division Meeting of the American Philosophical Association (1990): 39–45.

Lincoln, Abraham. 'Printed Text'. In *Lincoln's Greatest Speech: The Second Inaugural*, edited by Ronald C. White Jr. New York: Simon & Schuster Paperbacks, 2002.

Locke, John. *An Essay Concerning Human Understanding*. Edited by P. H. Nidditch. Revised. Oxford: Clarendon Press, 1979.

Lohne, J. A. 'Experimentum Crucis'. *Notes and Records of the Royal Society of London* 23, no. 3 (1968): 169–199.

MacIntyre, Alasdair. *After Virtue: A Study in Moral Theory*. Second. Notre Dame: University of Notre Dame Press, 1984.

————. *Whose Justice? Which Rationality?* Notre Dame: University of Notre Dame Press, 1988.

Mackie, J. L. *Ethics: Inventing Right and Wrong.* New York: Penguin Books, 1977.

Mackintosh, James. 'Dissertation on the Progress of History'. In *The Miscellaneous Works of the Right Honorable Sir James Mackintosh: Three Volumes Complete in One*, edited by R. J. Mackintosh, 94–197. Philadelphia: Carey & Hart, 1846.

Mandeville, Bernard. *The Fable of the Bees: Or Private Vices, Publick Benefits.* Edited by F. B. Kaye. 2 vols. Indianapolis: Liberty Fund, 1988.

Miles, Jonathan. *The Wreck of the Medusa: The Most Famous Sea Disaster of the Nineteenth Century.* Illustrated. New York: Grove Press, 2008.

Newton, Isaac. *Opticks: Or, a Treatise of the Reflections, Refractions, Inflections and Colours of Light.* Fourth. London: William Innys at the West-End of St Paul's, 1730.

————. *The Principia: The Authoritative Translation and Guide: Mathematical Principles of Natural Philosophy.* Translated by I. Bernard Cohen, Anne Whitman, and Julia Budenz. Berkeley: University of California Press, 2016.

Nwigwe, Lillian. 'Embryonic Stem Cell Research: An Ethical Dilemma'. *Voices in Bioethics* 5 (2019). https://doi.org/10.7916/vib.v5i.6135.

Penelhum, Terence. *Themes in Hume: The Self, the Will, Religion.* Oxford: Clarendon Press, 2000.

Plato. *Theaetetus.* In *Plato: Complete Works*, edited by John M. Cooper and D. S. Hutchinson, translated by M. J. Levett and Myles Burnyeat, 157–234. Indianapolis and Cambridge, 1997.

Priestley, Joseph. *An Examination of Dr. Reid's Inquiry into the Human Mind on the Principles of Common Sense, Dr. Beattie's Essay on the Nature and Immutability of Truth, and Dr. Oswald's Appeal to Common Sense in Behalf of Religion.* Second. London: J. Johnson, 1775. https://archive.org/embed/anexaminationdroopriegoog.

Rees, Graham. 'On Francis Bacon's Originality'. *Intellectual News* 14, no. 1 (2004): 69–74.

Reid, Thomas. *An Inquiry into the Human Mind on the Principles of Common Sense.* Edited by Derek R. Brookes. The Edinburgh Edition of Thomas Reid 2. Edinburgh: Edinburgh University Press, 2000.

————. *Essays on the Active Powers of Man.* Edited by Knud Haakonssen and James A. Harris. The Edinburgh Edition of Thomas Reid 7. Edinburgh: Edinburgh University Press, 2010.

————. *Essays on the Intellectual Powers of Man*. Edited by Derek R. Brookes. The Edinburgh Edition of Thomas Reid 3. Edinburgh: Edinburgh University Press, 2002.

————. *The Correspondence of Thomas Reid*. Edited by Paul B. Wood. The Edinburgh Edition of Thomas Reid 4. Edinburgh: Edinburgh University Press, 2002.

————. *The Philosophical Orations of Thomas Reid*. Edited by D. D. Todd. Translated by Shirley Darcus Sullivan. Journal of the History of Philosophy Monograph Series. Carbondale: Southern Illinois University Press, 1989.

————. *Thomas Reid and the University*. Edited by Paul B. Wood. The Edinburgh Edition of Thomas Reid 10. Edinburgh: Edinburgh University Press, 2021.

————. *Thomas Reid on Animate Creation*. Edited by Paul B. Wood. The Edinburgh Edition of Thomas Reid 1. Edinburgh: Edinburgh University Press, 1995

————. *Thomas Reid on Logic, Rhetoric and Fine Arts*. Edited by Alexander Broadie. The Edinburgh Edition of Thomas Reid 5. Edinburgh: Edinburgh University Press, 2004.

————. *Thomas Reid on Mathematics and Natural Philosophy*. Edited by Paul Wood. Edinburgh Edition of Thomas Reid 9. Edinburgh: Edinburgh University Press, 2018.

————. *Thomas Reid on Practical Ethics*. Edited by Knud Haakonssen. The Edinburgh Edition of Thomas Reid 6. Edinburgh: Edinburgh University Press, 2007.

————. *Thomas Reid on Society and Politics*. Edited by Knud Haakonssen and Paul B. Wood. The Edinburgh Edition of Thomas Reid 8. Edinburgh: Edinburgh University Press, 2015.

Roeser, Sabine. 'Introduction: Thomas Reid's Moral Philosophy'. In *Reid on Ethics*, edited by Sabine Roeser, 1–22. Philosophers in Depth. London: Palgrave Macmillan, 2010.

Rowe, William L. *Thomas Reid on Freedom and Morality*. Ithaca and London: Cornell University Press, 1991.

Rysiew, Patrick. 'Reid and Epistemic Naturalism'. *The Philosophical Quarterly (1950–)* 52, no. 209 (2002): 437–456.

Sextus Empiricus. *Outlines of Scepticism*. Translated by Julia Annas and Jonathan Barnes. Cambridge Texts in the History of Philosophy. Cambridge: Cambridge University Press, 2000.

Shrock, Christopher A. *Thomas Reid and the Problem of Secondary Qualities*. Edinburgh Studies in Scottish Philosophy. Edinburgh: Edinburgh University Press, 2017.

Solnit, Rebecca. *A Paradise Built in Hell: The Extraordinary Communities That Arise in Disaster*. New York: Penguin Books, 2010.

UN General Assembly. 'Universal Declaration of Human Rights', 1948. https://www.un.org/en/about-us/universal-declaration-of-human-rights.

Van Cleve, James. 'Double Appearances Are Double Trouble: Reply to Foster'. *Journal of Scottish Philosophy* 6, no. 2 (2008): 195–196.

———. *Problems from Reid*. New York: Oxford University Press, 2015.

———. 'Reid on Single and Double Vision: Mechanics and Morals'. *Journal of Scottish Philosophy* 6, no. 1 (2008): 1–20.

Winkler, Kenneth P. 'The New Hume'. *The Philosophical Review* 100, no. 4 (1991): 541–579.

Wittgenstein, Ludwig. *Philosophical Investigations*. Edited by P. M. S. Hacker and Joachim Schulte. Translated by G. E. M. Anscombe, P. M. S. Hacker, and Joachim Schulte. Revised 4th. Chichester: Wiley-Blackwell, 2009.

Wolterstorff, Nicholas. 'Reason and Trust in Reid'. *Canadian Journal of Philosophy* 41, no. S1. New Essays on Reid (2014): 183–196.

———. 'Reid on Common Sense'. In *The Cambridge Companion to Thomas Reid*, edited by Terence Cuneo and René van Woudenberg, 77–100. Cambridge Companions to Philosophy. Cambridge: Cambridge University Press, 2004.

———. 'Reid on Justice'. In *Reid on Ethics*, edited by Sabine Roeser, 187–203. Philosophers in Depth. London: Palgrave Macmillan, 2010.

———. *Thomas Reid and the Story of Epistemology*. Modern European Philosophy. Cambridge: Cambridge University Press, 2001.

Wood, Paul. 'A Virtuoso Reader: Thomas Reid and the Practices of Reading in Eighteenth-Century Scotland'. *Journal of Scottish Thought* 4 (2011): 33–74.

Yaffe, Gideon. *Manifest Activity: Thomas Reid's Theory of Action*. Oxford: Clarendon Press, 2007.

———. 'Reid on the Perception of Visible Figure'. *Journal of Scottish Philosophy* 1, no. 2 (2003): 103–115.

Zebrowski, Martha K. 'Richard Price: British Platonist of the Eighteenth Century'. *Journal of the History of Ideas* 55, no. 1 (1994): 17–35.

Index